Negotiating Migrations

DEBATES IN ARCHAEOLOGY
Series editor: Richard Hodges

Islamization and Archaeology: Religion, Culture and New Materialism,
José C. Carvajal López
Loot, Legitimacy and Ownership, Colin Renfrew
Lost Civilization, James L. Boone
Museums and the Construction of Disciplines, Christopher Whitehead
The Origins of the Civilization of Angkor, Charles F. W. Higham
The Origins of the English, Catherine Hills
Pagan and Christian, David Petts
The Remembered Land, Jim Leary
Rethinking Wetland Archaeology, Robert Van de Noort and
Aidan O'Sullivan
The Roman Countryside, Stephen L. Dyson
Roman Reflections, Klavs Randsborg
Shaky Ground, Elizabeth Marlowe
Shipwreck Archaeology of the Holy Land, Sean A. Kingsley
Social Evolution, Mark Pluciennik
State Formation in Early China, Li Liu and Xingcan Chen
The State in Ancient Egypt: Power, Challenges and Dynamics,
Juan Carlos Moreno Garcia
Towns and Trade in the Age of Charlemagne, Richard Hodges
Tradition and Transformation in Anglo-Saxon England, Susan Oosthuizen
Vessels of Influence, Nicole Coolidge Rousmaniere
Villa to Village, Riccardo Francovich and Richard Hodges

Negotiating Migrations

The Archaeology and Politics of Mobility

Daniela Hofmann, Catherine J. Frieman,
Martin Furholt, Stefan Burmeister and
Niels Nørkjær Johannsen

BLOOMSBURY ACADEMIC

LONDON • NEW YORK • OXFORD • NEW DELHI • SYDNEY

BLOOMSBURY ACADEMIC
Bloomsbury Publishing Plc, 50 Bedford Square, London, WC1B 3DP, UK
Bloomsbury Publishing Inc, 1359 Broadway, 12th Floor, New York, NY 10018, USA
Bloomsbury Publishing Ireland, 29 Earlsfort Terrace, Dublin 2, D02 AY28, Ireland

BLOOMSBURY, BLOOMSBURY ACADEMIC and the Diana logo are trademarks
of Bloomsbury Publishing Plc

First published in Great Britain 2024
Paperback edition published 2026

Cover design: Terry Woodley
Cover image: Human footprints set in gypsum mud that hardened to rock
c. 23,000–21,000 years ago in White Sands National Park, New Mexico, USA
© National Park Service/NPS/Alamy Live News

A catalogue record for this book is available from the British Library.

Library of Congress Cataloging-in-Publication Data
Names: Hofmann, Daniela, author. | Frieman, Catherine, 1982- author. |
Furholt, Martin, author. | Burmeister, Stefan, author. | Johannsen, Niels, author.
Title: Negotiating migrations : the archaeology and politics of mobility / Daniela Hofmann,
Catherine J. Frieman, Martin Furholt, Stefan Burmeister and Niels N. Johannsen.
Description: London ; New York, NY : Bloomsbury Academic, 2024. | Series: Debates in archaeology |
Includes bibliographical references. Identifiers: LCCN 2023059699 (print) | LCCN 2023059700 (ebook) |
ISBN 9781350427662 (hardback) | ISBN 9781350427709 (paperback) |
ISBN 9781350427679 (pdf) | ISBN 9781350427686 (ebook)
Subjects: LCSH: Human beings–Migrations–Case studies. | Archaeology–Political
aspects–Case studies. | Emigration and immigration–Political aspects–Case studies.
Classification: LCC GN370.H6424 2024 (print) | LCC GN370 (ebook) |
DDC 304.8–dc23/eng/20240418
LC record available at https://lccn.loc.gov/2023059699
LC ebook record available at https://lccn.loc.gov/2023059700

ISBN: HB: 978-1-3504-2766-2
PB: 978-1-3504-2770-9
ePDF: 978-1-3504-2767-9
eBook: 978-1-3504-2768-6

Series: Debates in Archaeology

Typeset by RefineCatch Ltd, Bungay, Suffolk

For product safety related questions contact productsafety@bloomsbury.com

To find out more about our authors and books, visit www.bloomsbury.com and
sign up for our newsletters.

Contents

Figures

Tables

Author Biographies

Stefan Burmeister is Director of the Varusschlacht Museum und Park Kalkriese in Germany. His research interests span the Iron Age, Roman and Migration Period archaeology of Europe. He has published extensively on the possibilities of identifying migration archaeologically, as well as on archaeological approaches to ethnicity.

Catherine J. Frieman is Associate Professor of European Archaeology at the Australian National University. She is a material culture and technology studies specialist, and has conducted research in western Europe, the UK, south-east Asia and Australia. Her research interests include the nature of archaeological enquiry, patterns of innovation and resistance, the role of aDNA for modelling past societies, social theory, skeuomorphism and Neolithic and Bronze Age flint daggers.

Martin Furholt is Professor of Prehistoric and Social Archaeology at Kiel University. His research focuses on social and political organization of Neolithic Europe, with a special interest in mobility and social change as well as the impact of aDNA analyses on the field. In 2021–2, he co-headed a Centre for Advanced Study project on migration narratives at the Academy of Sciences in Oslo.

Daniela Hofmann is Professor of Stone Age Archaeology at Bergen University, who has worked in the UK, Germany and Norway. Her research focuses on integrating archaeology and the natural sciences to address, amongst others, migration, kinship and social relations in Neolithic Europe. In 2021–2, she co-headed a Centre for Advanced Study project on migration narratives at the Academy of Sciences in Oslo.

Niels Nørkjær Johannsen is Associate Professor of Neolithic Archaeology at Aarhus University. His main research focus is on the

Neolithic of northern and central Europe. Present and recent projects include empirical and theoretical efforts to promote the integration of aDNA data with archaeological, palaeoenvironmental and other lines of evidence, cognitive approaches to material culture, and the development and impact of wheeled-vehicle technology in prehistoric Europe.

Acknowledgements

This book could not have been written without the generous assistance of the Centre for Advanced Study (CAS) in Oslo, which funded a one-year project entitled 'Exploring the Archaeological Migration Narrative: The Introduction of Farming and Animal Husbandry in Southern Norway', led jointly by Martin Furholt and Daniela Hofmann in 2021–2. It was this project that allowed us to bring together the authors involved in this book, as well as many other stellar researchers, to talk about all things related to migration and archaeology. We would like to thank all of our project members for supporting us so energetically and for all the discussions and help they have provided. Many of us have been or are migrants, some have relocated multiple times, and it was good to share part of the way with you.

The leadership and administrative staff at CAS have also been stalwart supporters, providing an inspiring working environment, help in all things organizational and financial and not least a relaxed atmosphere and plenty of food. So a big thank you to Camilla, Elmar, Kristin, Maria and Rune – we hope we have behaved ourselves.

Heartfelt thanks are also due to James Flexner (University of Sydney) for his swift, thoughtful and constructive comments on parts of Chapter 3. An anonymous peer reviewer also gave generously of their time to help improve the manuscript, for which we are very grateful. As always, these individuals are not to be blamed for any shortcomings in the final outcome.

Finally, many colleagues have assisted with sourcing images, holding inspiring guest seminars and providing much-needed moral support during the final stages of manuscript production. There are too many to thank individually here, but we will do it in person next time we meet!

1

Introduction

Archaeology and Migration

New technologies or the advancement of old ones – ancient DNA analyses, isotope analyses, GIS, archaeometry etc. – have brought with them an interest in large-scale questions and big-picture perspectives on the past. Among these, especially in the Anglophone literature, migrations loom large. Although migration never lost its explanatory significance in some archaeological traditions, notably in parts of central and eastern Europe, the topic was largely overlooked by American and British scholarship of the 1960s to 1990s and those researchers most strongly influenced by it (for a historical overview, see e.g. Anthony 1990; Chapman and Hamerow 1997; Daniels 2022: 4–9). Even where migration *was* accepted as an explanatory framework, it rarely formed the centre of attention; and, with few exceptions (e.g. Burmeister 2000; Prien 2005; Rouse 1986), it was not studied as a process in its own right or from a comparative angle until much more recently (e.g. Baker and Tsuda 2015; Burmeister 2017a; 2017b; Cabana and Clark 2011; Cameron 2013).

Scientific discourse does not take place in a vacuum. The archaeological perspective on past migrations has been biased by specific national attitudes, historical traditions, and contemporary politics (e.g. Härke 1997; 1998). On a supra-national level, IOM-Gallup attested in 2015 that 'in almost every region of the world people are more likely to be in favour of migration than against it. The one, notable exception to this is Europe' (IOM 2016: 4). As Liisa Malkii (1992) makes clear, our Western thinking is characterized by an ideology of sedentarism, which also makes its impact in contemporary politics. For instance, the Dutch right-wing politician Geert Wilders gave a much-publicized speech in March 2011 in which he argued that Germanic immigrants had brought down the Roman Empire. With this historical experience, he conjured up a bleak future for Europe in the face of alleged 'Islamization' by migrants.

In such arguments, people are bound to places, nations to territories. The common metaphor of cultural roots and rooted identities implies an unambiguous location. Since one can only be part of one tree, the metaphor evokes temporal continuity and territorial fixity (see also Clifford 1988: 338). More recently, Mimi Sheller and John Urry (2006) have proposed a shift towards a 'mobilities paradigm', which aims to disrupt assumptions that societies and individuals are primarily sedentary and movement exceptional. This has provoked scholars to shift their focus to a broad range of mobile behaviours in societies traditionally classed as sedentary. Yet we also recognize that the continuum between routine movements as part of daily existence on the one hand, and often traumatic and exceptional events of displacement on the other, must somehow be subdivided if we want to avoid flattening out the experience of migration.

Archaeologists have, in the main, been latecomers to these general theoretical developments. As a result, when new migration narratives offered in particular by paleogenomic studies began to appear in rapidly increasing numbers, it often proved challenging to integrate them successfully with archaeological results.[1] This difficulty also partly stemmed from the initial archaeogenetic focus on processes of considerable geographical and chronological extent – a scale at which most archaeologists are not comfortable working. Right now, then, the main challenge is no longer to recognize that migrations have taken place, but how to think about them (Anthony 2023; Daniels 2022).

For the Neolithic of Europe, the main focus of this volume, this resulted in renewed attention to the processes by which migrant populations introduced animal husbandry and agriculture, as well as to the arrival of 'steppe people' marking the transition to the Final Neolithic and Bronze Age (Corded Ware, Bell Beaker and related phenomena of the third millennium BCE) here. Initially, archaeogenetic papers took a relatively coarse approach to both transitions, compiling data from a limited number of samples over large temporal and spatial scales (e.g. Fu et al. 2012; Omrak et al. 2016), which were then often optimistically interpreted and linked to other large-scale transformations, such as linguistic change (for criticism, see e.g. Frieman and Hofmann 2019; Furholt 2018; 2019a; 2019b; Hakenbeck 2019; Ion 2017; 2019; E. Jones 2019; E. Jones and Bösl 2021; Veeramah 2018). Recently, more nuanced site- and region-based analyses have been produced which centre on individuals, kinship patterns and other social relationships (e.g. Fowler et al. 2022; Knipper et al. 2017; Le Roy et al. 2016; Mittnik et al. 2019; Rivollat et al. 2016; 2023; summary in Kristiansen 2022: 43–54). Moreover, it has been suggested that, with the genetic data and statistical tools now available, several migration histories involving different numbers of populations may be equally likely (Maier et al. 2023), inviting discussion of alternative scenarios and re-empowering other forms of evidence.

The relationship of archaeological data to linguistic evidence has also been discussed with renewed vigour, bolstered by the connections made between genetic turnover and linguistic change (e.g. Haak et al. 2015; Kristiansen et al. 2017) and the ease of comparing the tree-like diagrams created for both. However, criticism of this has been mounting: convergence and various contact phenomena have been systematically neglected in scholarship, although such possibilities have been raised periodically (e.g. Comrie 2008; Kroeber 1960; Mufwene 2001; Robb 1993; Zimmer 1990a; summary in Demoule 2023: 33–118). In the light of these critiques, alternative histories of Neolithic language change can be explored.

With this in mind, compared to discussions in other fields, other geographical areas and other time periods (e.g. the US Southwest or the Migration Period – see below), the kinds of questions tackled and the ways in which migration is discussed in the Neolithic of Europe remain relatively 'blocky'. The concept of migration is not yet fulfilling its potential for history-making, largely because discussions of key questions surrounding the process of migration and its relation to identities are only just beginning.

In this book, we develop a considered archaeology of migration and explore it through global case studies at different geographical and temporal scales. At one level, we focus on one set of connected cases from a relatively long and geographically wide-ranging phenomenon – the Neolithic of Europe. By bringing this into dialogue with other migration scenarios from different periods and across the globe, we offer new insights into the complexity of interactions involved in migration episodes and thereby write 'history' in the sense of drawing out the importance of local contingencies in how migration processes are initiated and develop. This is achieved by focussing on different social and geographical scales, from supra-community down to individual interactions and biographies – simplified here as large-, middle- and small-scale dynamics. In a sense, writing this volume itself has taken the structure of interconnected journeys. Borrowing a metaphor from Lewis Binford (1980), the Neolithic of Europe serves as our base camp, from which we sally forth into other regions and periods, returning with new models and ideas with which to enrich our interpretations.

The choice of destinations is, as always, subjective and determined by research questions – for our comparisons, we looked to those case studies that dealt with similar problems to the ones now being discussed in Neolithic Europe. We have chosen examples with rich histories of multidisciplinary investigation, a vibrant contemporary research community, and a history of interpretation that draws on different data and applies different models than commonly used by European Neolithic specialists. Thus, our sounding board for thinking about large-scale migrations is the archaeology of Remote Oceania, as one of the most evocative series of long-distance journeys. The European Middle Ages, in contrast, have seen some of the most contested debates on the nature of ethnicity. The Pueblo migrations were chosen because of the research focus there on household-level decisions to migrate, while the examples of early colonial entradas into the Americas were added because the issue of translators gave us the tools to discuss linguistic change in third-millennium BCE central Europe. In none of these cases do we wish to imply that these global case studies can function as shortcuts to understanding 'what the European Neolithic was like' (nor, vice versa, does the pattern of migration in various phases in Neolithic Europe 'explain' migrations in other parts of the world). The cultural and historical trajectories are too obviously different for that. Rather, we wanted to compare how similar kinds of questions have been tackled in the different scholarly traditions, and whether the narrative strands emergent from that research could usefully be interwoven with each other to frame a particular aspect of the migration process more clearly.

At another level, this juxtaposition allows us to make wider points about the role and organization of migration in small-scale societies and the complexity of social relations underlying it. We do this by centring the role of politics in migration events, here meaning interpersonal relations between individuals and groups negotiating power imbalances and potentially conflicting interests. This is an explicit counter-balance to the preoccupations with identifying single prime movers (such as climate or population pressure), instead stressing that both the historical trajectories in the past and our archaeological narratives in the present are inescapably situated in power relationships.

This book is an ideas book. We want to sharpen archaeological sensibilities for the diverse factors, often hard to quantify, that characterize migration processes and shape their outcomes. Therefore, we have not engaged statistically with the enormous quantities of genetic and isotopic data now being accumulated, or attempted any demographic modelling here. These are important tasks, but of a very different kind. Instead, we follow the intricate paths of specific archaeological detail to offer a broader range of scenarios and elements that should be more fully included in both qualitative and quantitative thinking on migration.

The structure of the text

In Chapter 2, we start with a discussion of the role of migration in archaeological reasoning, focussing on how migration entangles with narratives of power. As archaeologists are also social actors in the present, and given that archaeological material has already been used in political debates surrounding contemporary migration, we spend some time outlining the modern-day factors that have crept into some of our archaeological narratives, using the Linearbandkeramik and the European Migration Period as case studies. This is followed by a discussion of the political interactions in non-state societies, focusing on the power relationships and decision-making processes at the scale of actual human interactions in the past.

Using this foundation, the rest of the book sets out to apply our politics-centred perspective to trace further trajectories of mobility, social interaction and the formation of new social and community identities in each of our case studies. Our aim is to demonstrate that migration is a constant feature of Neolithic human society, and that as such there is no unitary model that can explain the motivations for or impacts of any one past migration event. This insight also applies to studies of past migrations generally.

Moreover, we take an expansive and cross-disciplinary approach to make the effects of migration and large-scale mobility visible at various social scales. As a consequence, we argue that there are many entry points to the archaeology of migration. The Big Data approach (e.g. Kristiansen 2022) has its place, as does the detailed specificity of close regional analysis and social interaction advocated here. Migration narratives have historically been driven by top-down modelling and supra-regional observation, and we do not reject the major insights of these studies. We do, however, think it is time to plant our feet firmly on the ground and treat migration as the complex, nuanced and differently-experienced social phenomenon it is and also was in the past.

Each chapter is built around contrasting case studies of archaeological migration narratives, one drawn from the European Neolithic and one from other times and places, to broaden our interpretative perspectives and illustrate the methods and materials from which we draw our insights. We first introduce a case study with a long scholarly tradition of discussing migrations and then contrast it with an aspect of the Neolithic European sequence, showing how the different research traditions can enrich each other. Each chapter also discusses a thorny theoretical concept that has been associated with these scales: ethnicity, community and agency.

Chapter 3 starts with one of the classic examples of 'migration to an empty land', the settling of Remote Oceania. Here, there has been much debate concerning both when specific island groups were first reached and the level of intentionality that was involved. It now seems clear that migration was intentional and often driven by the kinds of processes we here characterize as 'political' – the emergence of charismatic leaders and the decisions of others to follow them. Such migrations could in turn lead to the emergence of new group identities, which can be interpreted as dynamically and situationally created ethnic groups. The Pacific evidence is then contrasted to the first Neolithic settlement of Denmark, Britain and Ireland, which also required a maritime component (albeit over much, much shorter distances) and where the extent of continued interaction between the potential source areas and the newly settled regions is also debated. This shows how even archaeological phenomena that likely begin from a common root quickly diverge into different historical trajectories due to decisions and adjustments taken at smaller social scales.

Chapter 4 foregrounds smaller-scale social units, such as households and kin groups. In the pueblos of the US Southwest, our initial case study, migration and re-location are central to identities at this scale and are supported by elaborate strategies of community fissioning and fusion. Ritual and mythology play a large part in integrating new arrivals into established communities and in framing the social and spiritual importance of migration. After discussing the fluid nature of 'community' in these settings, we juxtapose them with the Alpine foreland Neolithic, where we can track levels of mobility that match those of the Puebloan case study, albeit generally covering short distances. In this area, we argue that shared economic tasks and a deliberate de-emphasis of behaviours that could lead to social inequality, rather than ritual action, played the strongest integrative role initially, but that this changed over time.

Chapter 5 turns to the individual scale. By exploring the experiences of historically attested female and child translators and narratives of child abduction mainly from the US Great Lakes area, we show the influence these individuals had on establishing hybrid forms of interaction, including linguistic change. We describe the challenges of multi-ethnic communities in colonial settings, for instance concerning gendered task divisions. After reflecting on whether individual agency can (or should) be traced archaeologically, we bring insights of this case study to bear on narratives of migration in third-millennium BCE Europe, when Indo-European languages are thought to have spread. Examples of mobile children from Neolithic central and western Europe, alongside the creative re-interpretation of key symbols (such as axes and pottery) in what are now the Netherlands, show how large-scale horizons of change can be written differently when we focus on the level of individual actors.

Chapter 6 draws together the insights from these three scales of analysis. While migration is a complex process wherever it occurs (Anthony 2023), adding the concept of the micro-scale of interpersonal politics is a good hook to anchor this complexity in the narratives we write. Our view of Neolithic Europe is fundamentally different when we do not see it from the vantage point of a sedentary paradigm; but equally, the European case studies have something to add to migration research generally. Writing about migration is a matter of scale, but focusing too much on the large-scale patterns is also a choice that obscures the diversity of actors, the mutability of identities and the variety of outcomes of their meetings. Speaking about these less linear and more braided stories is an important contribution archaeology can make to appreciating migration as a fundamental part of the human condition.

Paradoxically, migration has deep roots. In Chapter 7, we therefore promote new ways of telling (past) migrations in the present. Articulating these deep histories of migration alongside contemporary concerns makes archaeological research more relevant to the present. It also helps us navigate the thorny personal and political concerns of migrants and migrations with greater knowledge, perspective and empathy.

2

Why a Politics of Migration?

Why do we talk about migration the way we do?

The idea of migration that shines through – directly or indirectly – in many archaeological and archaeogenetic case studies is shaped by two rarely acknowledged analogies: the European colonial expansion; and the present experience of migration filtered through the news media (Burmeister 1998; 2000; Hofmann et al. 2021; van Dommelen 2012; cf. Wiedemann 2020; Wimmer and Schiller 2003). Beginning with the former, from the fifteenth century CE onwards, various European nations sponsored explorers to map lands unknown or barely known to them, and to identify and extract resources. The extent to which this was possible, and the form this took, depended on the relative military might and size of the European expeditions (e.g. Gidney 2021; J. Wills 1993). Yet in many cases, 'trade' soon turned into extraction by force, often based on disregard for the rights and perspectives of the people living in the lands in question, morally sanctioned with reference to the civilizing and/or Christianizing mission of Europeans (e.g. Adas 1989; Césaire 1955; D. Walter 2017). This process saw European outposts set up around the world and elements of European cultural life transplanted to new environments. At the same time, local and indigenous populations suffered from introduced diseases, had their land stolen and homes destroyed, found their ways of life threatened, were forced to convert to new religions and, in the most extreme situations, faced displacement, slavery and attempted genocide at the hands of the military or by settlers themselves (Wolfe 2006).

This form of migration, which reached its apex with European settler colonialism and is still ongoing (e.g. Mikaere 2005; I. Watson 2014), is violent, totalizing and extractive, driven by the power of centralized bureaucratic states, and in its later stages by more loosely organized entrepreneurs and religious groups. While many European migrants remained in their new homes (the 'settler' part of settler colonialism), others returned to their European countries of birth. Homi Bhabha (1994) enjoins us to understand the colonial–colonized relationship as complex and transformative, creating an interstitial, hybrid space between disparate cultures, practices and ways of life. Nevertheless, the power dynamics at play in settler-colonial migration are inescapable: in this context, these Europeans were a threat to the indigenous people, their land and cultural practices, all of whom were deemed barriers to the authority of one or more distant European states. The success of the settler-colonial venture was linked to a mixture of the belief in superior morals and superior technology, a schoolbook example for how allegedly more 'developed' societies would come to dominate the globe, based on crude forms of social Darwinism (Adas 1989), which are still widely popular in academic and semi-academic contexts (e.g. Diamond 1997; Fukuyama 2012; Pinker 2011; for a critical view, see Graeber and Wengrow 2021). The deeply transformative character of these events, and the ultimately vast numbers of people involved, even led some geographers (e.g. Zelinsky 1971) to suggest a 'mobility transition' in modern times, prior to which migrations would have been very much the exception.

The second often unacknowledged influence on migration thinking is the perception of a modern – alleged – 'migration crisis' of unprecedented proportions. This builds on decades of scare-mongering about migrants, much of it linked to eugenics movements and their efforts at limiting migration by particular disfavoured (typically non-white, but also disabled or ill) people (Bashford and Levine 2010; Hansen and King 2001; Okrent 2019; Shah 2020: 32–62, 94–127). In its current iteration, this 'crisis' is described as comprising large numbers of individuals from the global South who are attempting to resettle in countries of the global North, i.e. in Europe, North America and Australia/New Zealand. Undoubtedly, the reasons for many of these individual migrations have their origin in crisis situations, such as warfare or famine. Yet the extent to which this is perceived as a 'crisis' in the destination countries is driven by political interest and press coverage. In 2020, 281 million migrants living outside their home country were registered worldwide (Figure 2.1). So-called internal migration, i.e. movements that remain within national borders and account for the largest proportion of migrants in developing countries, is not even taken into account. So many people have never previously been on the move. The share of migrants in the total population remains

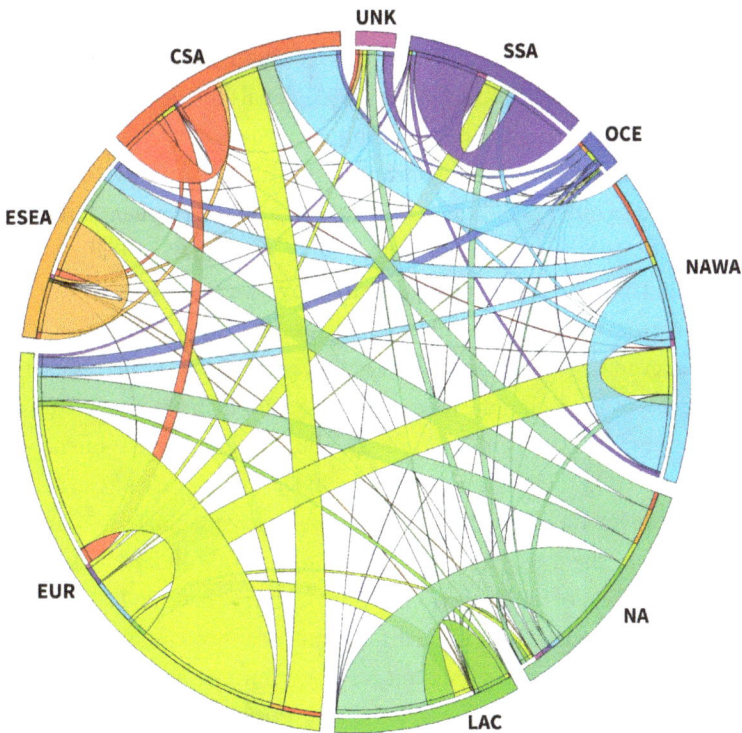

Figure 2.1 The main migration flows between different world regions in 2019, the last year before the Covid pandemic restricted the movement of people. SSA=Sub-Saharan Africa; OCE=Oceania; NAWA=North Africa and West Asia; NA=North America; LAC=Latin America and Caribbean; EUR=Europe; ESEA=East and South-East Asia; CSA=Central and South Asia; UNK=Unknown (United Nations 2019: back page).

small, having increased from 2.3 per cent in the 1970s to its current 3.6 per cent (IOM 2021: 23). Yet the predicted negative results concerning widespread social breakdown (as summarized in Shah 2020: 32–62) never materialized; indeed, the dependency crisis among Europe's elderly people would worsen considerably without net migration (United Nations 2016: 21–2).

Communications from official bodies like the US Department of Homeland Security (2019) and Europol (2022), or media outlets like the *Washington Post* (Taylor 2015), constantly characterize these migration levels as unprecedented. This not only heightens a general sense of threat, but also neglects the deep history of regional and supra-regional migration. For example, in his overview of European migration since the Middle Ages, Klaus Bade (2003) details the flows of seasonal migrations between different agricultural regions or by sailors and mercenaries, rural–urban relocations and displacements due to religious and other persecutions, as in the case of the Huguenots. Using nineteenth-century census records, mainly from France, Bade could show that over 300,000 persons were on the move as seasonal labour, or as workers settling for several years (for example in domestic service), across seven large international migration networks in western Europe (Bade 2003: 7). Including Russia would vastly increase those figures (Lucassen and Lucassen 2013: 54–5). These migrants were often not well received in their host societies; but, at least in the case of Germany, the narrative of a crisis scenario has been largely manufactured in the media from the 1970s and 1980s onwards, mostly independently of actual numbers of migrants reaching the country (Bade 2003: 218–87).

Perceiving migrations in terms of Early Modern colonial contexts and of the contemporary 'migrant crisis' is informed by a state logic of politics and power, creating 'a "reception crisis" in the global North' (Hamilakis 2018a: xiv). Migration is cast as both aggressive, involving the imposition of the will of one coherent group over another, and transgressive, threatening the basis of the state as orderly governance. Yet state monopoly over the control of movement is a very recent historical phenomenon (Isayev 2022: 134–6). By using this situation as an (unacknowledged) basis, archaeological narratives have come to artificially narrow the range of interpretative options they consider (Chapman 1997). At worst, they continue to legitimize 'statist' narratives of top-down control – and conflict when 'borders' are breached – as an inevitable part of human existence (Ince and Barrera de la Torre 2016). A crucial aim of this volume is to provide an alternative approach. However, as the term 'migration' can cover many different processes at various social scales, we will first sketch out a definition of migration as used in this book.

Defining migration in archaeology and beyond

As Stefan Burmeister (2000: 539) notes, all too often in archaeology '[m]igration itself is seen neither as being in need of explanation and thus as a research topic in its own right nor as a potential explanation for the manifestations of cultural change'. Even though some of the parameters of the old debates changed, in essence migrations are often still used as stock explanations, rather than being seen as complex anthropological, biological and technological events (Ion 2019). One cannot avoid thinking about migrations and mobility when faced with the need to explain 'out-of-placeness' in the archaeological record. But how to do this is open to exploration.

One key problem with defining migration is how (or indeed whether) to distinguish it from mobility. We share here Burmeister's (2017a: 58) view that there is no definite and clear dividing line between the two. For most archaeologists, migration is generally an issue of scale (e.g. Bellwood 2013: 2–3). For example, summarizing the discussion for the US Southwest, Barbara Mills (2011) notes that most definitions are based on either the distance covered, the number of people moving or the speed and duration of the event. In general, 'migration' is used to cover the processes at the larger end of the scale and/or relatively fast events. While these criteria can be traced archaeologically, at least in favourable circumstances, they are also relatively blunt instruments that need to be adapted situationally (when is a distance 'long'?) and which may change in the course of an ongoing migration process.

In addition, archaeologists have begun to ask more ambitious questions, leading to alternative ways of classifying mobility events in general, and characterizing migrations in particular. In their discussion of the uneasy interface between archaeology and ancient genetics, for instance, Niels Johannsen and colleagues (2017: 1119) list a number of questions to consider for past migrations: Who is migrating? How is a group's identity maintained throughout its journey? How is identity negotiated in the arrival region and through local contacts? Similarly, Mills (2011) has expanded the list of commonly used criteria to include the reasons for migration (environmental, economic, ideological, political, forced...), on what basis a destination was chosen (pre-existing exchange, kinship, ritual...), the ratio of immigrants to locals (low, medium, high) and the relations between them (hostility, co-residence, blending/assimilation), which may be partly based on the degree of perceived difference between groups (Clark et al. 2019). From a longer-term perspective, the consequences of migration for the destination area may vary (negligible, focused on some areas, pervasive) and there may be more or less conflict with already resident populations. Finally, we should not neglect the demographic impact of migrations on the source areas (negligible, significant decrease, depopulation).

Once all these factors are added into the mix, migrations appear as complex processes, in particular where several connected episodes of movement (rather than simple, wave-like scenarios) are involved, generating 'a complicated social map of migrant enclaves, zones of hybridity, and areas of local resistance' (Clark et al. 2019: 265). Similarly, social anthropologists have pointed out that migrations have complex spatial and time dynamics. For example Nancie Solien de Gonzalez (1961: 1265) classifies them as: 'seasonal', 'temporary nonseasonal', 'recurrent', 'continuous' and 'permanent'. How we deal with this complexity is a matter of disciplinary style, also depending on available sources and their epistemological limits. Caroline Brettell and James

Hollifield (2015: 5) compare the different ways in which historians, anthropologists, political scientists, demographers or economists frame this topic by giving weight to various dimensions of the phenomenon. For example, geographers are interested in spatial distributions, historians tend to focus on the relation between movement and time, while anthropologists prioritize how migration affects social relations and identity.

As a pragmatic definition for the present volume, we include as 'migrations' those situations in which at least one of the dimensions listed in Table 2.1 scores near the bottom of the table (and two dimensions where group size is involved). This is evidently not a watertight definition, which is in any case impossible, nor does it cover all potential aspects, but it has the added benefit to retain those categories which are open to empirical archaeological investigation. It also provides an initial, rough framework according to which our case studies can be compared. The most obvious cases are those in which large groups move large distances quickly and find the totally alien Other. But, depending on the combinations, many different processes can also qualify. In what follows, we are particularly interested in how smaller-scale decision making and social interaction come to shape migration events, even those which have so far been primarily discussed from the point of view of large-scale patterns.

Archaeological discussions of migration processes have emphasized very different aspects in different world regions. In the European Neolithic, there has been a tendency to concentrate on large-scale patterns and to find explanations which work at these large scales. David Anthony's (1990) approach of push and pull factors has been particularly popular and has informed narratives of migration as driven by large-scale demographic processes (e.g. Shennan 2018) or by climatic and ecological factors (e.g. Brandt 2017: 194–7). Here, we complement such perspectives by prioritizing how migration reconfigures the relationships between people, both within the migrating group and between it and those in the destination area. We therefore do not begin with large-scale outcomes needing corresponding large-scale reasons,

Table 2.1 Defining migration. Factors according to which mobility is often classified are shown as columns. In this volume, 'migrations' are those processes in which at least one of the factors scores near the bottom of the column (or two factors, if one of them is population size/composition). In each column, combinations of options are also possible in a given setting

Composition	Physical distance	Temporality	Cultural distance
Individual	Neighbouring region nominally within home territory	Regular mobility (e.g. seasonal)	New region well known; pre-existing relations with home
Family	Neighbouring region outside home territory	Frequent to-ing and fro-ing between new region and home (perhaps once every eighteen to twenty-four months)	New region known; some pre-existing relations with home
One or more cohorts (gender groups, age groups, professions, etc.)	Beyond the immediate vicinity of home	Occasional visits between new region and home (perhaps once every two to five years)	New region known; no relations exist between there and home
Extended family	Extensive journey between home and the new region	Rare visits between new region and home (more than five years between journeys)	New region poorly known, but some pre-existing relations with home (e.g. extended kin)
Several families	Totally foreign or unknown region	Single journey with no returns	New region poorly known; no relations between there and home
Whole community Several communities Ethnic group			New region totally unknown

but by recognizing that migration is a profoundly social phenomenon, driven by historically situated decisions.

Working from this bottom-up perspective necessitates an explanatory framework that can combine aspects of personal and group identity, which have a dynamic of their own, with environmental, economic and social processes that impact multiple scales. We argue that this can best be achieved by recognizing past decision-making as inherently political, even at small social scales.

Mobilities and mobile pasts

While much of our archaeological interest in mobile worlds and past migrations stems from disciplinary history and the emergence of new methods, such as palaeogenomics, the last two decades have seen investigations of mobility as social practice across the social sciences. The so-called mobilities turn within social geography asks us to consider mobility as a core feature of lived experience and to shift our focus away from a normalization of sedentism.

In an influential monograph, French anthropologist Marc Augé (1995) theorized roads, airports and other crossroad locales as 'non-places', places outside our normal relational spheres, where identity and history have no tether. Reacting against this long-established tradition of studying endpoints rather than interstitial journeys, a number of scholars in the early 2000s began to argue for a recentring of mobile practices and sites of mobility. Movement, they argue, is not outside the flow of daily life and personal experience, but intrinsic to it (e.g. Cresswell 2006; Cresswell and Merriman 2011; Ingold 2007; 2011; Lefebvre 1974; 1992; Urry 2007). Through transiting across space, we create meaningful places and shape our worlds (which in turn shape us) (Cresswell 2014; Palmberger and Tošić 2016). Moreover, a focus on mobility offers us insight into complex social phenomena and power relations, as mobility is differently governed and experienced based on one's gender, age, ethnicity, nationality or other aspects of identity (Glick Schiller and Salazar 2013; Sheller 2016; Uteng and Cresswell

2008). The levels of friction and freedom experienced in the course of mobility shape how one engages with the wider world and reflect power structures, value systems and histories of mobile practices (Cresswell 2010).

Over the last decade, many archaeologists have found inspiration in this body of research, drawing on it to reframe discussions of past movement (e.g. Aldred 2020; Bell 2020; Daniels 2022; Gibson et al. 2021; Leary 2014). Their work variously theorizes bodily engagement with the environment through the experience of movement; reinterprets well-known sites, reframing their development within traversed landscapes; and asks whether the traditional archaeological focus on stationary places masks a more complex and mobile past reality. However, Tim Cresswell's (2010) reminder that mobility has politics, that it is both governed by and itself impacts on power relations and, consequently, that constellations of mobility have social and political histories, has been less deeply explored by archaeologists (though see Frieman and Hofmann 2019; Frieman et al. 2019). Here, we seek to redress that balance through a focus on a highly politicized form of mobility: migration.

Why does the study of migration need politics?

Migration in contemporary political discourse

The archaeological discussion of migration is also always a public discourse (Bartels et al. 2023). To give one example, we turn to debates surrounding the end of the Roman Empire, a question that has been controversially discussed since the Middle Ages. Every era had its own views on this. Alongside growing evidence, beliefs, world views and political intentions decisively shaped narratives of the fall (Demandt 2014). Even modern historical scholarship is hardly objective in its approach. European history of the twentieth century, with its world wars, the beginnings of international understanding post-1945 and the

European unification process of recent decades, affects assessment of Rome's decline. In the 1990s, for example, a major EU project on the transition of Late Antiquity into the European Middle Ages explicitly avoided talk of the decline of the Roman Empire – a view that was in any case very much fixed on the West, since the Eastern Roman Empire continued to flourish until 1453 CE – and emphasized the transformative character of Late Antiquity (Wood 2006). This pacification of history has its justification, but is not always in line with the written records.

Historical studies since the 2000s have again stressed the violent aspects of Germanic immigration and connected these to the decline of Rome. The comprehensive studies by British historians Bryan Ward-Perkins (2005) and Peter Heather (2005), for example, trace the interplay of Rome's military and economic weakness and the (partial) successes of Germanic groups, many of which subsequently disappeared quietly from the historical stage. A conglomerate of the privatization of social wealth and the lack of tax revenues; the insufficient financing of the army, which increasingly depended on Germanic forces; and military failures pushed the Roman Empire into a downward spiral, leaving it unable to develop a sustained resistance to Germanic encroachments or integrate the immigrants. Even if the Roman Empire might not have fallen without Germanic migration, its decline cannot be attributed monocausally to immigration.

But even scholars who should know better can fall into the rhetoric of easy solutions. In a 2016 newspaper article in the *Frankfurter Allgemeine Zeitung*, one of Germany's leading daily newspapers, the eminent historian Alexander Demandt summarizes his view of the fall of Rome as follows: the Roman Empire was tolerant towards foreigners, but the flow of poor, child-rich and bearded immigrants – note the suggestive imagery here – overstretched the integrative power of Roman society and ultimately led to a shift in power structure and, thus, to Rome's downfall (Demandt 2016a). Demandt reduces a complex, 200-year-long process to a single fact with a monocausal explanation: the failure to defend against or naturalize Germanic peoples (also Demandt 2014: 595). In an interview accompanying the article,

Demandt (2016b) explicitly exhorts the then German Chancellor Angela Merkel to limit the influx of migrants – this is his lesson from Roman history, which, in this reading, had an inevitable outcome.

The argument has caught on. The German far-right party NPD put up a poster in the 2019 European election campaign with the slogan 'Stop the invasion: migration kills! Resistance – now'. The NPD was not alluding to the many migrants who lost their lives along the external borders of the EU and especially on the Mediterranean Sea, but to the alleged victims of violent acts by migrants in Germany. A subsequent lawsuit against the NPD for incitement to hatred was rejected by the court. The twenty-one-page justification for the decision is accompanied by an historical summary of the fall of the Roman Empire with reference to Demandt's newspaper article and to the extermination of the indigenous population of the Americas by European settlers. Ultimately, the accusation of incitement was rejected because the statement 'migration kills' was seen as a description of the facts, which are allegedly 'understandable to anyone who deals with the history of migrations' (Hessenrecht 2019).

This is a negligent simplification of historical migration research which, following Klaus Bade (1994: 7; translation S.B.) 'cannot . . . offer any perfect-fit answers from history to open questions of the present or even historically proven patent remedies. But it can provide basic orientations and empirical values. Without such historical perspectives, efforts to shape the future in the explosive social problem areas of migration, integration and minorities could turn into a disoriented blind flight'.

Discourse on migration is always also a form of politics of migration. The example above shows that even historical migration processes dating back some 1,500 years can have an influence on current debates, can be instrumentalized for political purposes and can affect the mindset of researchers. Greater complexity, we argue, can be attained only if we re-adjust the scale of the narratives we write and foreground the variable outcomes of messy political interaction in the past. This should be a key aspect of the pasts we write.

Past politics of migration

The important events that make big impacts on our narratives of (pre) history are those that happen at a scale that we today associate with 'political' action – i.e. the large scale. In societies of the kind we envisage for the Neolithic, however, the sort of political action most salient to people's lives would have operated almost entirely at smaller scales (our modern 'private'). Politics here means household politics, marriage politics and occasional and regular negotiations of power in terms of, for example, convincing your kin to breed more pigs for a feast, to build a house, start a raid or justify a journey. To understand migration from the bottom up, as a historically situated process, we need to link these smaller-scale dynamics to large-scale patterns.

As used here, the term politics refers to negotiating between different, possibly diverging, conflicting or mutually opposed interests, values and worldviews of individuals or groups, and to how decisions are made and executed. This definition consciously diverges from the current tendency to define politics in terms of its institutional context in modern society and its focus on top-down leadership and government structures (for recent critique, see Lund et al. 2022). This is most visible in the political economy approaches that have influenced European archaeology through the writings of, amongst others, Eric Wolf (1999), Brian Hayden (2001), Marshall Sahlins (1974) and especially Timothy Earle, whose delineation of a Bronze Age political economy has strongly shaped the way politics is perceived in archaeology. Earle's foundational book *How Chiefs Come to Power* (1997) encapsulates in its title the focus on elite action and the relative neglect of the political role and possibilities of the remainder of the population.

This focus on top-down politics is based upon a similarly skewed underlying concept of power. Most discussions of power draw heavily on Max Weber, who defines it as 'every possibility within a social relationship to impose one's will even against resistance, no matter on what this possibility rests'[1] (Weber 1976 [1920/1]: 38). Weber's definition is so influential because it reflects the modern concept of power, as expressed by Hobbes, Voltaire or Nietzsche (Lund et al. 2022).

It is decidedly individualistic and confrontational (Lund et al. 2022), stressing how power can be wielded *over* resources or people, rather than focusing on the more open power *to* achieve one's goals (e.g. Shanks and Tilley 1987: 71). And while Weber's definition includes all kinds of power, almost all of his discussion concerns top-down domination (the German *Herrschaft*), clearly at the heart of his thinking. This power concept is grounded in and geared towards describing nineteenth-century state societies with a monopoly on the use of force. From that perspective, power rests upon (male) individuals at the top of the (state-imposed) hierarchy and politics is about who gets to that top. Power is ultimately the ability to command and to be obeyed (see Lund et al. 2022).

Such a concept of power and politics is reductionist even when it comes to describing our current society, and it certainly does not represent the full range of power and politics in non-state contexts. The top-down focus overlooks horizontal and non-hierarchical social structures (Amborn 2019; Borck and Clark 2021) and neglects the small scale and the bottom-up part of politics, where leaders need to be accepted, but also can be resisted, ousted, killed, or their power evaded (e.g. Brück and Fontijn 2013; Fontijn 2021). There can be strong restrictions on, for example, how acceptable it is to flaunt wealth and influence (e.g. Rosenberg and Rocek 2019), while even in agricultural societies, there may be considerable freedom to 'vote with one's feet' and leave behind situations in which power imbalances are becoming too great (e.g. Beck 2006; Kopytoff 1987). Moreover, individuals and households integrated into wider 'public' political structures have their own politics which may articulate with the public sphere, but do not need to.

What is needed here is a concept of politics and power that is not skewed towards governments, chiefs or village councils, but takes into account the political nature of all social interaction and the capacity of people in all kinds of societies to consciously reflect on questions of social structure, power, leadership and so on (Graeber and Wengrow 2021; Lund et al. 2022; Stanish 2017). Such power concepts are available through the work of Michel Foucault (1982), but more fundamentally through Hannah Arendt's (1970) idea of power, which she defines as the possibility to collectively act, the force of collective consensus without which there is no society. Hence, we can reimagine power as grounded in collectively shared values and social norms that shape social relations and human behaviour in a given historical context. Politics then describes the ways in which individuals and groups relate their actions and decisions to such norms and values, which of them are being honoured, how to deal with conflicting views and with deviations. Arendt's concept is famous for setting power as the opposite of violence, seeing the latter rather as an instrumental force. Power and violence are also complementary, in the sense that, while they always appear in tandem, more of one means less of the other: 'Power and violence are opposites; where the one rules absolutely, the other is absent. Violence appears where power is in jeopardy, but left to its own course it ends in power's disappearance' (Arendt 1970: 55), and '[t]he extreme form of power is All against One, the extreme form of violence is One against All' (Arendt 1970: 42). Pierre Clastres (1989 [1974]; 1994 [1976]) casts this as the distinction between coercive and non-coercive power, or his socially embedded and socially unembedded power.

Feminist theory, especially as articulated by Black feminist thinkers, posits that power is exerted along a number of axes, i.e. that it is intersectional and structural (Crenshaw 1991; hooks 1982). Within this framework, feminism is rearticulated as a fight against structural forces of oppression that entangle gender, race, class, ethnicity etc. rather than exclusively the battle for (some) women to be able to access traditional masculine power (Biana 2020). Thus, the web of relations in which one is entangled and one's own identity shape how one experiences and engages with the complex, often fluid dynamics of interpersonal and institutional power. This is the mechanism that underlies the feminist aphorism that 'the personal is political'.

For our understanding of politics as a phenomenon permeating every social interaction, a concept of power rooted in the collective helps us recognize the political, i.e. power-related, nature of the social negotiations around all manner of questions, including whether or not to migrate, where to and with whom. Intersectional approaches force us to grapple with the complex lives and relations of past people and to attempt to understand how different individuals may have been differently impacted by or engaged in migration activities. The coercive, top-down variant of politics remains an important factor in social negotiations, but it necessitates a basis of collective consensus and must be understood in relation to socially embedded, collective power. This also restores dynamism to archaeological models (see Lund et al. 2022): where power is conceptualized as distributed across a network of actors and contexts, it can be appreciated as contestable, unstable and changeable, as a driving force for the transformations and events that we observe archaeologically. This broadly chimes with approaches based on heterarchical thinking in archaeology (Crumley 1995) and with anarchist positions (e.g. Borake 2019; Borck and Sanger 2017; Flexner and Gonzalez-Tennant 2018).

To sum up, our definition of politics should be applicable to prehistoric – usually small-scale, non-state – societies and should thus not focus on the modern institutional frames of politics, but upon political questions and political negotiations at all scales of social interaction, from close kin gathered around a single hearth to the wider community.

Migration, politics and the European Neolithic

The Neolithic of central and north-western Europe, which serves as our 'base camp' in this book, is often characterized as a foundational transformation of all aspects of past life. Initially defined based on the introduction of polished stone tools, across much of Europe agriculture and sedentism were soon identified as the more significant changes, as these would have caused substantial population increase (Childe 1936, more recently e.g. Bocquet-Appel 2008; 2011; Shennan 2018) and further social transformations. In addition, compared to hunting and gathering lifestyles, Neolithic societies produce vastly more material culture, including large quantities of often elaborately decorated pottery, as well as domestic and monumental architecture, which creates new kinds of ties between people and places. Finally, being bound up in evolutionary narratives of increasing mastery over the environment, the Neolithic was frequently also connected to new divinities concerned with fertility, or a new sense of time and the importance of ancestors, or at least a fundamental shift in human–animal relations (e.g. Bradley 1993: 1–21; Cauvin 2000; Ingold 2000; Watkins 2005), although this is increasingly cast as a negative development (e.g. Wells 2010; Wickham-Jones 2010).

Given these many and fundamental changes, it is little wonder that the Neolithic was initially seen as spread by migration (with ultimate roots in the Near East). Within the culture historical paradigm of the first half of the twentieth century, there was in any case a propensity for explaining material culture changes as the results of population movements and the subsequent imposition of new object styles characteristic of a given 'people' (for a summary, see e.g. Trigger 1989: 148–206). Partly, this was a view encouraged by the short chronologies available, which made transformations seem rapid and abrupt (Whittle 2018: 19–47). In the second half of the twentieth century, the increasing availability of ^{14}C dates revealed the much longer duration of most prehistoric cultures and provided an independent means for checking other elements of the culture concept, such as postulated directions of influence (Renfrew 1973). As a result, particularly in north-west European archaeological traditions, migration was largely rejected as an explanation for change, sometimes all too categorically (for criticism see e.g. Anthony 1990; Chapman and Hamerow 1997). While a pioneering attempt at combining modern genetic patterns and ^{14}C data reconstructed a demographic 'wave of advance' for the spread of the Neolithic (Ammerman and Cavalli-Sforza 1979), later scholars working from a broadly post-processualist perspective strongly critiqued these ideas, instead according a leading role to indigenous hunters and gatherers (e.g. Scharl 2004; Whittle 1996). Mobility (for example connected to herding) was acknowledged, but migration of larger numbers of people over longer distances was considered unlikely.

In central Europe, in contrast, both processualist and post-processualist paradigms enjoyed limited popularity. The basic premises of the culture concept, which related material traits to a closed social group, were critiqued repeatedly (e.g. Brather 2000; Eggert 1978; Veit 1989; Wahle 1941; Wotzka 2000; see also below on the Migration Period), but 'cultures' remained too convenient a shorthand to abandon. In spite of this, migration as a social process was rarely problematized within Neolithic archaeology (and if so, then by scholars outside the mainstream, e.g. Frirdich 2005; Sommer 2001). In both the Anglophone and the central European research traditions, scholarly attention largely turned to other topics – in the former case for example the importance of monuments and ritual in Neolithic life, in the latter domestic architecture, pottery-based chronology or economic questions. These were often tackled at a regional or local scale. Although long-distance exchange was recognized in the Neolithic, it was assumed that for most people, life would have played out within a relatively circumscribed territory.

Nevertheless, migration was seen as the likely start for the Linearbandkeramik (LBK), which spread across most of central Europe in two distinct waves. Eventually, around the turn to the fifth millennium, it fragmented into more regionally circumscribed successor groups, such as the Stroke Ornamented Pottery (SBK) culture or the Hinkelstein culture. This fragmentation was to an extent counteracted by the emergence of the spatially more expansive Michelsberg culture, which straddles the transition of the fifth and fourth millennia; in other areas regional groups such as Altheim persisted. At roughly this time, Neolithic things and practices also spread into new areas, such as the Alpine foreland, the north European plain, or Britain and Ireland. Again, there is subsequent regionalization of the initial large-scale entities (for example the Funnel Beaker/TRB culture), until an eventual, relatively homogeneous Final Neolithic horizon, comprising the Corded Ware and Bell Beaker cultures, becomes established (for general introductions, see e.g. Whittle 1996; contributions in Fowler et al. 2015; Milisauskas 2002) (Figures 2.2–2.4).

	Britain & Ireland	N Germany & S Scandinavia	E France	N Alpine Lakes	Central Germany	E Hungary, Slov., NW Bulg., SW Rom.
2500 BCE	Bell Beaker	Bell Beaker	Corded Ware	Corded Ware	Corded Ware	Vučedol
	Late Neolithic				Globular Amph.	
3000 BCE	Middle Neolithic	Later TRB	Seine-Oise-Marne	Horgen	Salzmünde	Baden
3500 BCE						(Proto)Boleràz
	Early Neolithic	Early TRB	Michelsberg	Pfyn, Cortaillod	Baalberge	Tiszapolgàr, Bodrogkeresztür
4000 BCE				e.g. Egolzwil, Cortaillod	Gatersleben	
4500 BCE			Cerny			
	Mesolithic	Mesolithic	various post-LBK		SBK, Rössen	Tisza & Vinča B-D
5000 BCE			LBK	Mesolithic	LBK	
						LBK & Vinča A
5500 BCE			Mesolithic		Mesolithic	

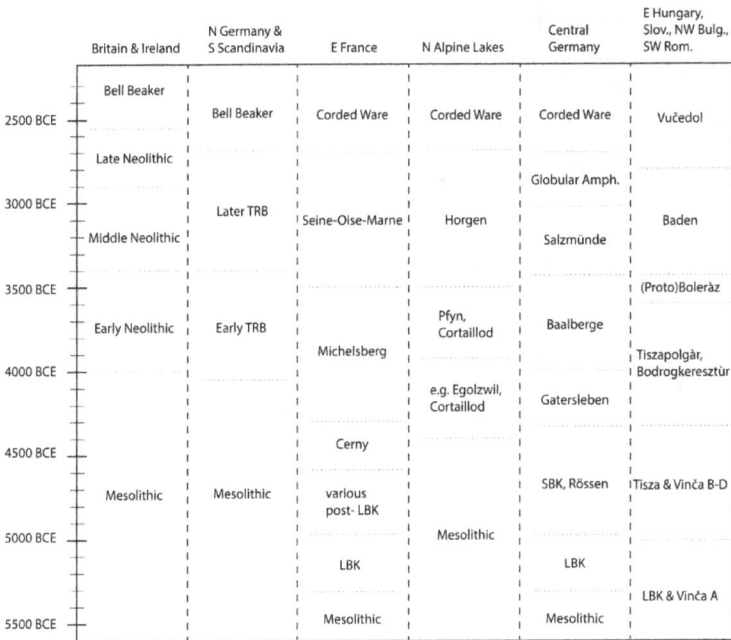

Figure 2.2 Chronology chart of the European Neolithic, with the main archaeological units of classification named in the text.

This very rough picture hides the regional and site-specific work that has been carried out over the last decades and which considerably nuances this picture – but this attention to regions also led to the relative minimization of continent-wide patterns as a useful scale of analysis. New biomolecular data, both isotopic and genetic, have fundamentally changed this trend, as they highlight considerable degrees of mobility and clear horizons of population turnover at the beginning of the Neolithic, as well as at the onset of the Final Neolithic (for early studies see e.g. Allentoft et al. 2015; Brandt et al. 2013; 2015; Haak et al. 2010; 2015; Mathieson et al. 2015; for archaeological critiques e.g. Frieman and Hofmann 2019; Furholt 2018; 2019a; 2019b; Hofmann 2015; Johannsen et al. 2017; Vander Linden 2016).

The resulting optimism in the explanatory potential of new scientific methods, allied with Big Data (e.g. Kristiansen 2014; 2022), is not

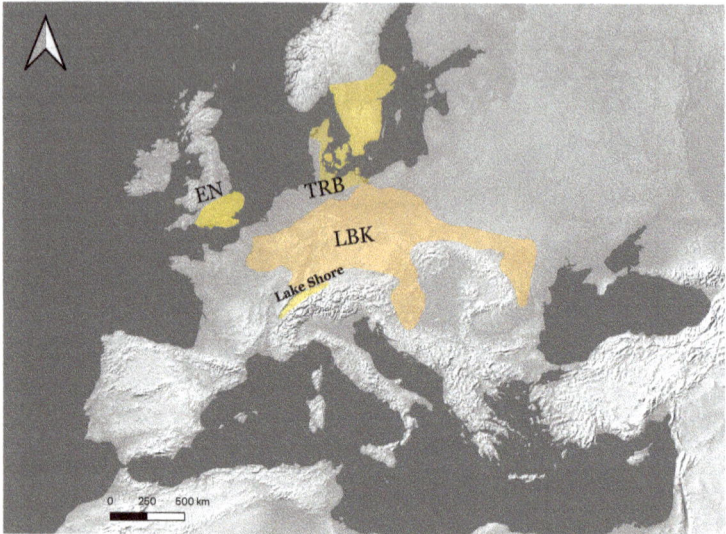

Figure 2.3 Simplified map showing the expansion of a Neolithic way of life across Europe, with the main archaeological units of classification referred to in the text (made with Natural Earth, free vector and raster map data @ naturalearthdata.com).

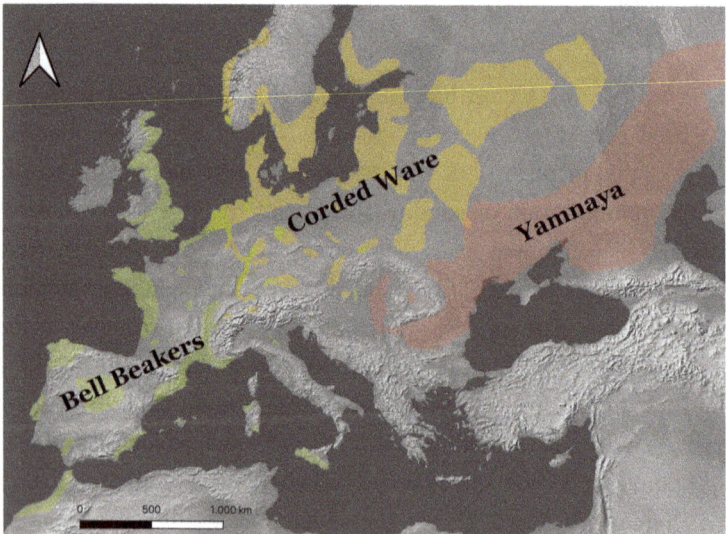

Figure 2.4 Simplified map showing the extent of the main archaeological units of classification during the third millennium BCE in Europe (made with Natural Earth, free vector and raster map data @ naturalearthdata.com).

entirely unopposed (Ribeiro 2019; T. Sørensen 2016; 2017), but has returned migration to the forefront of the archaeological agenda. As argued above, however, our understanding of the actual social processes has remained limited. There has, moreover, been a tendency to domesticate this new-found, un-settled Neolithic by restricting migration to specific, tightly defined time horizons and connecting them to hard push factors, such as demographic pressures or environmental instabilities (see e.g. Brandt 2017; Shennan 2018). However, even in between these watershed moments, Neolithic life hardly flowed at a sedate pace. Large-scale radiocarbon dating programmes at various sites across Europe (summarized in Whittle 2018) have shown the often episodic, boom-and-bust nature of Neolithic activities. Significant numbers of people congregated quickly, but dispersed just as fast, and this was not a rare or one-off phenomenon. These insights have far-reaching implications for how we think about 'sedentary' Neolithic societies more generally, in particular regarding the reasons and mechanisms behind both mobility and migration. It is here that a focus on politics can contribute, even in situations where a lot of data have already been amassed. To illustrate this, we first turn to the Early Neolithic LBK culture, which spread over large areas of central Europe through migration.

A migration event in search of politics – the LBK

The LBK has long formed a textbook case study for a Neolithic migration event. In spite of some critical voices, which noted diversity in material culture as indicating hunter-gatherer adoption (summarized in Scharl 2004: 57–84), most archaeologists subscribed to a migration-driven model comprising two main waves. In the first, the so-called earliest LBK began in western Hungary, eastern Austria and south-west Slovakia and moved from there into central Europe around 5500 BCE. In a chronologically separate horizon, a second, west- and eastward expansion was associated with more regional pottery styles, such as

Flomborn or Notenkopf (Cladders and Stäuble 2003). The two processes were also interpreted separately, but few scholars addressed head-on whether migration in these phases actually differed in character.

Christiane Frirdich (2005) and Ulrike Sommer (2001) are two notable exceptions to this trend. Both proposed models of earliest LBK expansion as a status-related behaviour, where groups showcased their economic prowess by sponsoring colonizing endeavours. Earliest LBK settlements are thin on the ground, so that it is hard to identify obvious demographic or environmental push factors. In addition, migration is risky and costly (see also Strien 2017a) – it needs a surplus of grain and domestic animals, especially if pioneer groups are moving long distances and will be far from support networks, perhaps crossing the territory of hostile groups. Being able to sponsor long-distance migration would thus be one way for a community to demonstrate economic and social clout. It was argued that this kind of socially sanctioned, prestige-driven migration was orchestrated by elders, who controlled the distribution of resources. However, once colonization met with resistance – in the form of determined hunter-gatherers, or because no further loess soils were available – the basis of the elders' authority was threatened. This led to profound social changes and new forms of expressing prestige, such as through particularly long houses (Figure 2.5) or lavish grave goods (Frirdich 2005; Sommer 2001).

These models were some of the first for Neolithic Europe to explicitly consider migration as a social strategy. Fridrich (2005) and Sommer (2001) charted a progression from long-distance migration by medium-sized groups (several households together) in the earliest LBK to a later situation with marked territorial boundaries. This would have entailed the kinds of processes we have termed 'political' and would have been rather messy and regionally diverse, opening up potential new avenues for research. Yet in this case, the addition of new kinds of data, like strontium isotopes and ancient DNA, while adding vastly to our understanding, has also resulted in closing down many of those potential avenues, presenting instead a 'big picture' kind of answer.

Figure 2.5 Exterior impression of a reconstructed LBK longhouse in Straubing Zoo, Bavaria. The house is *c.* 37 metres long (photo: D. Hofmann).

Given the large number of excavated sites and good state of research, the LBK has been a favourite test case for applying new bioarchaeological methods. For instance, an early study of strontium and sulphur isotopes at Vedrovice in Slovakia revealed a high number of non-local persons. In line with the site's early date, this was interpreted as showing significant influx by Neolithic colonists or acculturated foragers (Zvelebil and Pettitt 2008). Subsequent aDNA work (e.g. Brandt et al. 2013) has conclusively shown that local hunter-gatherer populations played at best a marginal role in the spread of the LBK into central Europe. Isolated cases of admixture apart (e.g. at Brunn in Austria, Nikitin et al. 2019), the low proportion of 'Western Hunter-Gatherer' DNA that can be detected is most likely down to admixture events early on in the expansion, rather than to continuous admixture (Childbayeva et al. 2022: 4). Hunter-gatherer signatures in central Europe only increase much later in the Neolithic, for example in the Michelsberg culture (e.g. Rivollat et al. 2020). As this genetic evidence clearly showed which biological populations introduced a Neolithic way of life to central Europe, few further questions were asked of the process itself.

For later phases of the LBK, strontium isotopes indicated high female mobility in particular, which was interpreted as the exchange of wives in a patrilocal system (summarized e.g. in Hedges et al. 2013: 367–8). In contrast, isotopically local males were identified as more likely to be buried with polished stone tools than the few non-local males, so the former were identified as the heads of successful patriclans (Bentley et al. 2012) – and the latter as of lower status. These isotopic patterns were connected into a powerful new model using evidence from the settlement of Vaihingen in Baden-Württemberg, where the existence of 'clans' or 'neighbourhoods' was suggested on the basis of material culture preferences and differential field management. Some 'clan' groupings eventually left the site, and this was interpreted as a result of their subordinate social position and inability to access good agricultural land nearby (Bogaard et al. 2011).

These models are more detailed than is possible for many less well documented prehistoric case studies and they include elements of politics in the sense sketched out above. However, the discussion was all too quickly closed down in favour of a new, somewhat predictable consensus. There was a tendency to see migration as connected to specific subgroups, often of a lower social status – either women who moved at the behest of men (using Sr isotopes), or disadvantaged social groups driven from their land (as argued archaeologically). Economically powerful male 'clan' heads became the linchpin of LBK social life, and migration had arguably become an undesirable and atypical behaviour at the group level, or was limited to people (women) who moved as resources for the patriclan. This focus on uniform patterns of social interaction over vast areas risks brushing over variability and historical situatedness to a degree that misrepresents past realities, and we return to how this has impacted the LBK in Chapter 6 (see the section on consequences for our understanding of migration). First, we take some inspiration from discourses around the more recent European Migration Period, where a greater variety of sources has resulted in problematizing many aspects of past migrations that Neolithic scholars often take for granted. What had been portrayed rather stereotypically as movements of clearly circumscribed, static peoples has turned out to be highly complex and dynamic movements of open and changing groups of political actors, whose ethnic identities were created and reshaped along the way.

Identifying migrants and migrant identities – the Migration Period

Like the Early Neolithic, the Migration Period is a time of considerable population shifts. If one believes Roman historiography, the entire known world was on the move. A multitude of peoples were in search of new perspectives and new areas of settlement. For our purposes, the Migration Period offers a rich source for tracing three interlinked lines of argument. First, a discussion of the terminology and interpretative tropes connected to 'the Migration Period' shows the impact our own (historically derived) ideological frames have on the interpretation of what happened. Second, a close reading of the available sources breaks through the identification of tribes as closed and pre-defined ethnic groups, which has repercussions for other places and times. Finally, this discussion highlights the problems connected with identifying migration archaeologically and the need for interdisciplinarity.

The ideological framework of 'the Migration Period'

Beginning with the ideological frame, ancient written sources provide a rich and long-dominant strand of evidence. They paint a complex history of events, with the names of individual historical persons, myriad named migrating peoples, dates and places creating a colourful picture of an eventful time, difficult to decipher with its many parallel events and intertwined causalities (Halsall 2008; Meier 2019; Pohl 2002a). The archaeological record is comparatively underdeveloped, but provides sufficient evidence that both material culture and cultural practices arrived at new places. It therefore seemed to self-evidently support the historically known facts. However, relying on historical sources comes with its own ideological background, and in this case this begins with basic definitions.

In German-speaking archaeology, the Migration Period is referred to as 'Völkerwanderungszeit' – the era of the migration of peoples. This term is anchored in both scientific and popular language and is defined on the basis of historical sources. The Migration Period began in 375 CE with the arrival of the Huns on the eastern border of the Roman Empire and the Goths crossing the Danube, and ended in 568 CE with the founding of the Lombard Empire in Italy. As historical cornerstones, they are largely arbitrary. The Migration Period thus outlined had no historical significance either for the groups migrating into the Roman Empire or for the Romans; rather, naming this period was a significant act for German historians. They saw the Migration Period as the downfall of Rome, and the Germanic peoples – as ideologically constructed German ancestors – as its heirs. The term thus embodies a national perspective that is rooted less in the historical events of the past than in the process of German nation-building in the eighteenth and nineteenth centuries (e.g. Schiller 1790: xxix).

In contrast, in southern Europe and the Mediterranean zone, the destination areas for early medieval Germanic migrations, one does not speak of 'migrations of peoples' but of 'barbarian invasions' ('les invasions barbares', 'le invasioni barbariche' or 'las invasiones bárbaras'). These are also modern terms. Whether it is the migration of peoples or the invasion of barbarians, the ideological subtext is undeniable.

Another example, that of the Anglo-Saxon migration to Britain, shows how even new, science-based studies can be influenced by received terminologies and assumptions. Interpretations of the Anglo-Saxon migration to England had long oscillated between the extreme positions of mass immigration with genocide of the resident population and small-scale immigration of elites (e.g. Arnold 1984; Dark 1994; Härke 2011; Higham 1992; Hodges 1989). Today, the picture is regionally diverse, highlighting the heterogeneity of migration processes (Hills

2003; 2011). Heinrich Härke (2011) had presented a model of Anglo-Saxon immigration to Britain in which the British population was not displaced or killed, but rather socially marginalized in a segregated society. It is this model that was picked up in a number of genetic studies, initially based on interpreting modern-day DNA signatures (Capelli et al. 2003; M. Thomas et al. 2006; Weale et al. 2002 – with dissent from Hills 2009; 2015).

The time of migration reconstructed from genomic data is determined by probability calculations based on specific demographic parameters. Therefore, how we envisage the demographic composition of the migrants, their number in relation to the indigenous population, the duration of migration, the socio-economic relationship between locals and newcomers, as well as their respective reproduction rate all influence the statistical outcome. In addition to Anglo-Saxon migration, there were other migrations to Britain in the centuries before and after, which also impacted today's genetic map. Using different parameters, John Pattison (2008), for example, came to a different assessment of the impact of Anglo-Saxon immigration (see M. Thomas et al. 2008 for an immediate critique). He saw the data as consistent with elite, rather than mass, immigration. A decision as to which of the underlying parameters best reflects the historical situation cannot be made from the data itself, so different solutions remain possible.

The geographical origin of the immigrants, as determined using modern-day genetic maps, should also be viewed critically. Y-chromosome haplotypes can be used to identify the common ancestry of different populations. However, if Michael Weale and colleagues (2002) find a strong genetic similarity between the present-day inhabitants of central England and Frisia, this does not mean that Frisia is the ancestral homeland of 'the English'. Today's Frisia has also experienced a series of demographic upheavals in its history (Abdellaoui et al. 2013; Altena et al. 2020; Lao et al. 2013), so that here, too, the genetic map is the result of various migration processes. It would be naïve to think that the regions that are not the focus of an immigration analysis have remained unchanged.

The postulate of an Anglo-Saxon segregated society, sometimes glossed as 'apartheid society', deserves special attention (M. Thomas et al. 2006). Based on their analysis of recent DNA, the authors conclude that there could not have been many instances of interbreeding between Anglo-Saxons and native Britons in the first two centuries. They suggest that specific social mechanisms, such as those found in apartheid societies, are needed to maintain such long-lasting segregation. This is based on the probability calculations of various models explaining recent DNA patterns, but it has also been formulated before using historical (Higham 1992: 193; Woolf 2007) and archaeological (Härke 2003) arguments. The interpretation of an 'apartheid society' is thus ultimately not rooted in DNA analysis, but based on general sociological considerations and the interpretation of seventh-century legal texts. Apartheid is a very specific legal system that cannot be reduced to closed marriage groups. Reproductive segregation along ethnic lines can also be justified by different social mechanisms, which do not carry the racial connotations 'apartheid' acquired through its use in a recent South African context. Even in today's western countries, there are more or less obvious social barriers between different groups that counteract intermixing even after generations of immigration.

Ethnicity in formation – a diversity of processes

If the Migration Period can no longer be characterized in terms of a grand meta-narrative of migrating 'peoples' (see Meier 2019), how are we to envisage the social groups involved? The texts written by ancient authors, on which this meta-narrative of a threat to the Roman Empire (and its critiques) largely rest, are not protocols of past events, but texts with a clear narrative intention, depending on the author's time and agenda. All are subject to an *interpretatio Romana*, which follows the stylistic devices of contemporary barbarian discourses or seeks to exemplify Christian world views. The knowledge of Roman authors, especially about newly emerging groups, was generally insufficient and there was usually no interest in differentiated presentation. At least in the early phases of contact, encounters often occurred on the battlefield and in diplomatic contexts. This meant that the Romans were usually aware of only a small section of the foreign groups involved, which had a lasting effect on their ethnic designation. Just the *origo gentes*, some of which were written much later, reflect the internal perspective of the barbarian groups and were long regarded as the actual history of the respective peoples, providing information about their migrations. In nineteenth- and early twentieth-century scholarship, the groups described by the Romans were understood as primordial peoples with origins in a dark, long-distant past.

The groundbreaking work by Reinhard Wenskus (1961) on the genesis of the early medieval *gentes* led to a change in perspective. He saw the *gentes* not as natural, self-contained communities of descent, but as an open, continuously changing group of political actors (Pohl 1998; Steinacher 2011; Wolfram 2008: 91–2). Herwig Wolfram (1988) has developed this new perspective for the Goths. Using the *Getica* by Jordanes, the Gothic *origo gentes*, he shows how the Goths constructed their ethnic identity and created a community of descent primarily through subjective convictions. The constructed common history, based on a long tradition of migration, created a stabilizing effect for this otherwise heterogeneous community. The founding text of the Goths does not offer an objective Gothic history, but a subjective tradition and thus provides insights into the process of Gothic ethnogenesis.

Tracing this process in more detail shows the complexity of how ethnic designations came to be established. In the middle of the third century CE, Goths settled in the northern Black Sea region and regularly raided Roman territory. Towards the end of the third century, the Tervings and Greutungi were differentiated and subsequently appear as independent actors in Roman records. During this period, the Tervings settled in Dacia, which had been abandoned by Rome, and provided military support and border security by treaty. In 376 CE, they could no longer withstand the pressure of Hun expansion and invaded Roman territory. The result was a forty-year period of constant mobility through the Roman Empire (Figure 2.6), across the Balkans and Italy to

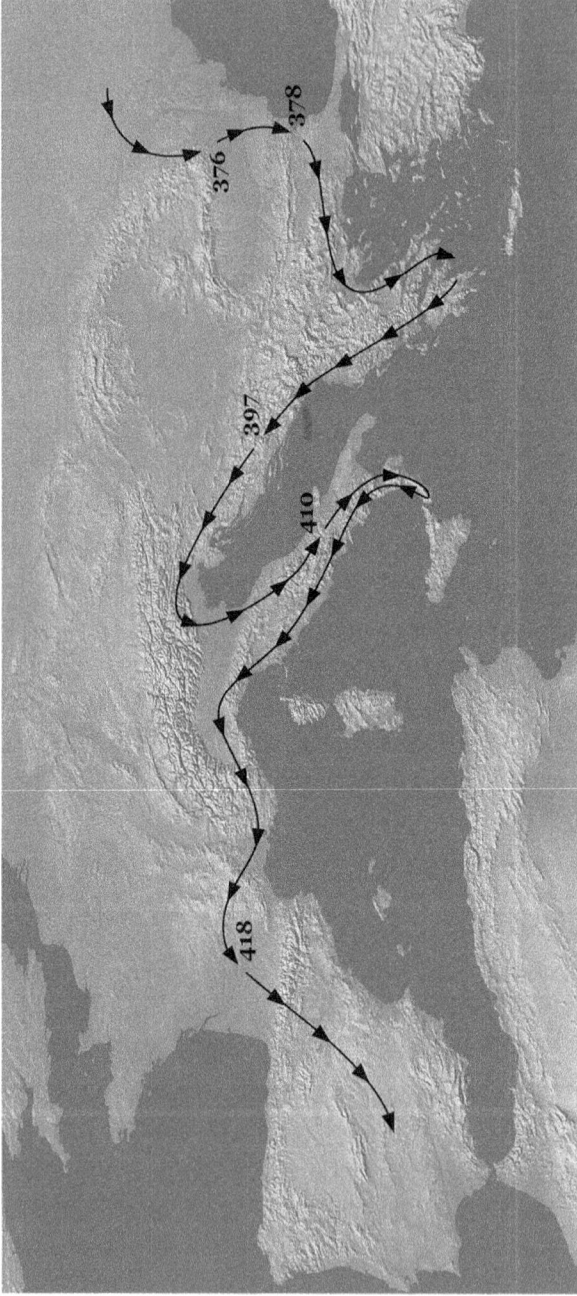

Figure 2.6 Map of the Terving/Visigoth migrations (made with Natural Earth, free vector and raster map data @ naturalearthdata.com).

southern France, during which these groups variously exploited the rivalry between western and eastern Rome, plundered entire regions (extracting money for 'peace'), but also repeatedly formed the backbone of the Roman armed forces. They were as much players in an ongoing struggle for political predominance as they were pawns of different powers. It was not until 418 CE that they were able to settle in southern Gaul and founded the Kingdom of Toulouse, which was bound to Rome by treaty and temporarily stretched from Spain to the Loire. Ultimately, the Goths could not withstand the expansive pressure of the Franks and moved to the Iberian Peninsula, where they held their kingdom until the Muslim conquest of Spain in the eighth century (Pohl 2002a: 40–69).

The Greutungi were an important power in the north Black Sea region until they were subjugated by the Huns and joined them in invading the Roman Empire; nevertheless, several Gothic groups also remained behind and continued to live in the Crimea until the sixteenth century. Only when Hunnic rule collapsed with the death of Attila in 453 CE did they become an independent player, ruling Italy and other parts of the western Roman Empire from the end of the fifth century. Due to internal rivalries over the throne and external pressure, they lost their power and were finally absorbed into the Franks and Lombards in 562 CE (Meier 2019: 805–25).

The example of the Goths (Heather 1998; Wolfram 1988) is typical for the time and other large Germanic groups, such as the Lombards (Jarnut 1982; Pohl and Erhart 2005) and Vandals (Steinacher 2016), have similar histories. The aim of these groups was not to destroy the Roman Empire or to weaken it, but rather to profit from it. Even if they sometimes fought against the Empire, at other times they guaranteed its military success. Not only did the Roman army consist largely of Germanic units from the fourth century onwards, but the military command structures were also firmly in Germanic hands; increasingly, they took on political leadership within Roman society, too. The respective groups could only establish themselves as a political power through their military strength, which is why a large, powerful army was a prerequisite for success within the Roman Empire. These were no longer the tribal units that may have existed many generations before migration, but polyethnic mixtures. Successful armies were joined by numerous groups, including freed or escaped slaves from the Roman provinces. These associations were a reservoir that, like a vacuum cleaner, sucked in other groups in the regions through which they passed, and where people without prospects might feel attracted to promises of a better life.

This raises the question of the identity of these migratory collectives. As we have shown, identities were not stable (Pohl 2002b: 237); after all, Gothic identity formed only in the Roman Empire (Heather 1998). For Wenskus (1961: 73–5, 138) these polyethnic groups harboured small tradition-bearing nuclei, mostly composed of the upper class and its retinues – but these sometimes did not exert any lasting influence on material culture, which is why we have to consider an uncoupling of material culture and ethnic self-awareness. It is to these cores, however, that Roman historiography looked for its ethnic designations. Michael Kulikowski (2002: 83) argues that Roman authors usually noticed mainly the militarily active parts of barbarian groups and also referred to them when they spoke of *gens*, which is another reason why we do not get a truly representative picture of the populations that were on the move.

Identifying 'migrant individuals'

Can archaeology contribute something genuinely new to this debate on the character of early medieval ethnicity? Archaeologically, the focus has long been on directly identifying migrants, using above all female jewellery and burial rites which appear to be foreign. Yet mostly, archaeology merely served to confirm the information gained from written sources. For instance, in the case of the Goths, a migration from the mythical homeland in Scandinavia cannot be identified archaeologically. The archaeological phenomena most associated with the Goths are the Chernyakhov culture in the western Black Sea region and the Sîntana-de-Mureş culture in Roman Dacia (Gomolka-Fuchs 1999; Magomedov 2004). Their appearance in these regions in the third and fourth centuries is explained by Gothic immigration. These cultures can be derived from the Wielbark culture in Poland, thus providing another stepping stone of the Goths' migration in the first half of the first millennium CE. The tribal history of the Goths is projected into the past and thus an ethnic continuity is constructed. While the later cultures show similarities to the Wielbark culture, however, they also exhibit diverse influences suggesting mobility, contact and cultural transfer. An ethnic identity of the respective groups cannot be inferred from this, and indeed ancient authors also show the mixture of peoples that were united under the collective name of the Goths (see also Steuer 2021: 105).

The further stages of the Gothic migrations are virtually untraceable archaeologically. Only with the Kingdom of Toulouse in the fifth century and the Kingdom of Toledo in the sixth century does an influx of 'Gothic'-inspired finds and new burial customs become archaeologically visible. Essentially, two contrasting approaches compete for the interpretation of the archaeological evidence, always with reference to historical records (see Eger 2005; 2020). In one view, Spanish grave goods reveal a specific costume that can be traced back to the Chernyachow-Sîntana-de-Mureş culture. The Goths would thus have preserved their 'tribal costume' for over two centuries, which, in conjunction with the written sources, would allow us to identify the Spanish graves with the Visigoths, who had formed from the Tervings. A second, opposing view is the *mode danubienne* proposed by Michel Kazanski (1989). For him, the so-called 'Gothic' costume is a general Danubian fashion, which developed from a combination of many different, but above all equestrian-nomadic, influences. The high social prestige that the Huns in particular enjoyed at that time led to this fashion being adopted by a cosmopolitan aristocracy, often of Germanic origin. Although the influence of the Danubian costume style in Spain suggests external cultural influences, it does not necessarily indicate a migration, and certainly not one that could be ethnically identified.

Barbara Sasse (1997) even argues that after decades of migration, the Visigoths no longer had an independent material culture that would allow us to distinguish them archaeologically from the Late Roman population.

The ethnic interpretation of archaeological evidence is a weak methodological tool to trace the identity of migrant groups. The social processes both within the migrant collectives and between the migrants and the host society usually also lead to a realignment of migrant identity. These are processes that run in several directions and which also took place in the Migration Period. With the growing social importance of barbarian groups in the Roman Empire and the increased social prestige of immigrants in Roman society, the cultural habitus of all those involved changed. As Emperor Theodoric is supposed to have said, a poor Roman imitates a Goth and a respected Goth imitates a Roman (quoted from Meier 2019: 89). Germanic finds and cultural practices on Roman territory are not directly identifiable with Germanic immigrants, but can also denote acculturated Romans or a new hybrid society (see e.g. Fehr 2010). Archaeological studies on the *habitus barbarus* point to Germanic forms of costume and jewellery as a distinguishing feature of a new elite in Roman society, which included both Romans and Germans (von Rummel 2007; 2010; critically Eger 2011).

The limitations of archaeology in the study of migration become clear when the results of aDNA and other biomolecular methods are taken into account, which indeed promise to hold the answers to many long-running debates. So far, there have only been a few genomic studies; their potential will be briefly illustrated using two case studies, the migration of the Lombards and the Anglo-Saxons. Although we can now identify mobile individuals directly, many questions also remain concerning, amongst others, the social impact of their arrival.

From the middle of the sixth century CE, a new burial custom appeared in Italy: the burial of the dead in a specific costume, alongside amulets and weapons, food and drink. Previously, graves had been largely unfurnished Christian burials associated with the autochthonous population. The new custom has direct predecessors in Lower Austria, southern Moravia and western Hungary. Based on written sources, it is identified with the Lombards and their invasion of Italy. In the seventh century, the Lombard habitus begins to dissolve: women are soon indistinguishable from Romance ones, and men also adopt Romance clothing accessories, although weaponry remains. This is seen as a process of Romanization of the immigrant Lombards (Bierbrauer 2004).

According to this argument, the burial custom is used as an ethnic marker, but while its appearance can be attributed to Lombard influence, there is no certainty that all such graves contain immigrant Lombards. The cultural practice that emerges here gives a good indication of cultural patterns that were common among the leading Lombard groups, but it does not manifest a Lombard identity (Pohl 2005: 561). Several questions remain unanswered: does the burial custom only reflect the social elite or was it practised by the entire population? How open is this custom to other groups, such as the resident Romance population?

First molecular biological analyses have revealed the genetic composition of Lombard communities (K.W. Alt et al. 2014; Amorim et al. 2018; Vai et al. 2019). The Pannonian cemetery of Szólád in present-day Hungary and that of Collegno in northern Italy (Amorim et al. 2018) have been almost completely analyzed. Both burial communities show similar cultural features that are otherwise foreign to the respective region. The dating of the cemeteries fits well with the known historical dates of the Lombard migration. Kurt Alt and colleagues (2014) had previously developed a three-phase occupation model of the Szólád cemetery comprising little more than twenty years. The genomic analyses for both Szólád and Collegno show that these burial communities were organized according to biological kinship groups. Likewise, in both cases the burial community consisted of groups of different ancestry: in each case individuals of northern European ancestry were more richly equipped than those with southern ancestry. Yet whether this expresses social hierarchies is an open question; it could also be a matter of different cultural practices with different social reference systems. Both groups remained separated from each other. In Collegno, Sr isotopes identified the groups with southern aDNA signatures as the local population, as also confirmed by mtDNA (Vai et al. 2019). The group with southern aDNA signatures in Szólád had also migrated, but from a different region than the group with northern ancestry. At least in Pannonia, the population was therefore composed of different migrant groups. On the one hand, bioarchaeological analyses confirm previous assumptions about the Lombard migration, but they also give us further insights into the inner structure of the migrant groups. The heterogeneous composition of the migrant group in Szólád had certainly not been seen before.

Returning to the thorny question of Anglo-Saxon migration, first aDNA studies are now available (Gretzinger et al. 2022; Schiffels et al. 2016; Töpf et al. 2006) and reach divergent results. According to Stephan Schiffels and colleagues (2016), 38 per cent of the modern population of eastern England can be traced back to Anglo-Saxon immigration. The Anglo-Saxon population, however, would have been strongly genetically mixed, showing close genetic relations to Britons as well as to diverse north-west European groups, with no evidence of greater segregation. Persons with British ancestry had been buried in a culturally Anglo-Saxon manner; in some cases they were more richly endowed than the immigrants in the same burial ground (Figure 2.7). The assumption of an Anglo-Saxon apartheid society would have to be rejected on this basis. The larger study by Joscha Gretzinger and colleagues (2022) shows a more differentiated picture with regional characteristics. There are cemeteries in which persons of British ancestry are buried in an Anglo-Saxon way and there were kinship relations between natives and immigrants. In contrast, in the burial ground at Apple Down, the two ancestry groups were differently endowed and there were no kinship relations between them for generations. It is obvious that the relationship between natives and immigrants varied from region to region.

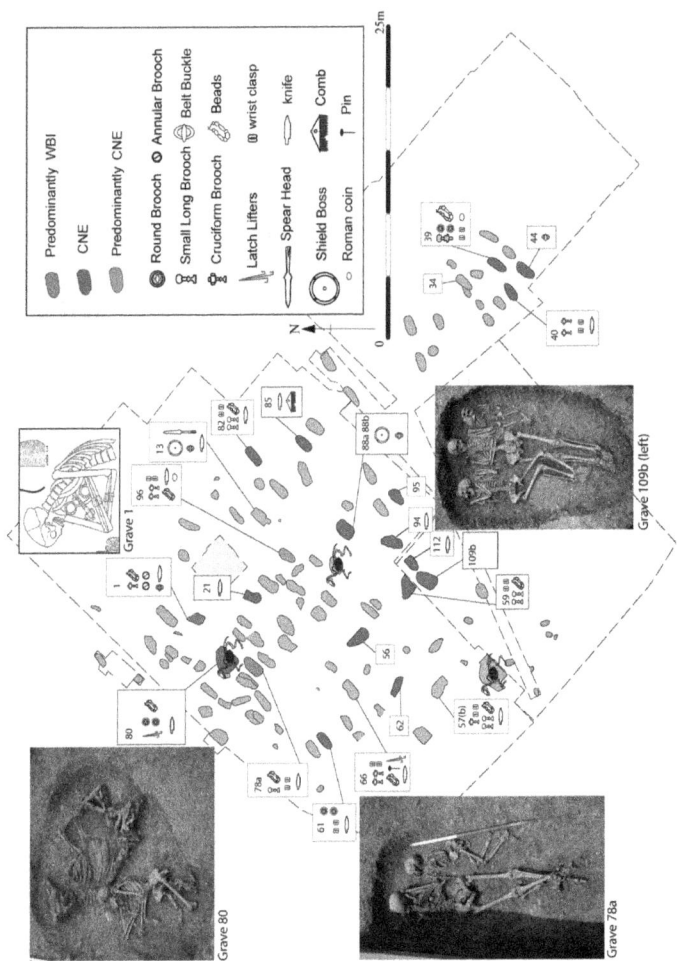

Figure 2.7 Anglo-Saxon burials from Oakington with predominantly WBI (Western British and Irish) ancestry; CNE: Continental Northern European ancestry (illustration: Duncan Sayer).

Conclusions

What our theoretical reflections and both the LBK and the Migration Period case studies show is that politics are integral to how we tell the past – both in the questions we do (not) ask and in the terms we use, but also for understanding the diversity of past social processes. Our data sets are also strongly interdependent – reading ancient texts impacts archaeological and DNA readings, for example. To bring these points across more clearly, we need the work of all the disciplines involved in past migration studies. In terms of the prehistoric case studies that follow, the Migration Period shows us that there are few straightforward answers about how migration worked, what happened afterwards or how people constructed their identities. Even for large-scale and long-term processes, identifying identity in terms of ethnicity is therefore complicated, although we hope to show that it can also be fruitful.

3

Migration at the Large Scale

Building on the discussions begun in Chapter 2, in this section we trace different processes of ethnogenesis, chosen from two different regions of the world. Beginning with Remote Oceania, where uninhabited islands were settled, we show that even in such a situation, people's ethnic identity was malleable and subject to change. This emerges even more clearly for the Neolithic of north-western Europe, where common roots nevertheless led to regionally divergent trajectories. While ethnicity thus remains a concept that is useful for thinking through emerging identities, it cannot be applied as a blanket term over the kinds of spatial and temporal scales that archaeologists have traditionally assumed.

Settling Remote Oceania

There have been several migrations into Oceania and Polynesia, with the largest islands and landmasses – which are also the western-most in the region, forming Near Oceania – already settled in the Pleistocene, roughly coeval with the European Upper Palaeolithic. However, most of the debate surrounding migration refers to the islands and archipelagos of Remote Oceania (Figure 3.1). Three horizons are generally defined: the Lapita and parallel phenomena, which introduced domesticates into Remote Oceania from c. 1500 BCE and reached as far as Fiji and Samoa (e.g. Fitzpatrick and Callaghan 2013); an expansion into central and eastern Micronesia in the last few centuries BCE; and, finally, the settlement of the most outlying islands of east and south Polynesia, including Aotearoa/New Zealand, Hawai'i and Rapa Nui (Easter Island), a long-term process which began c. 900 CE (e.g. Anderson 2009: 1503;

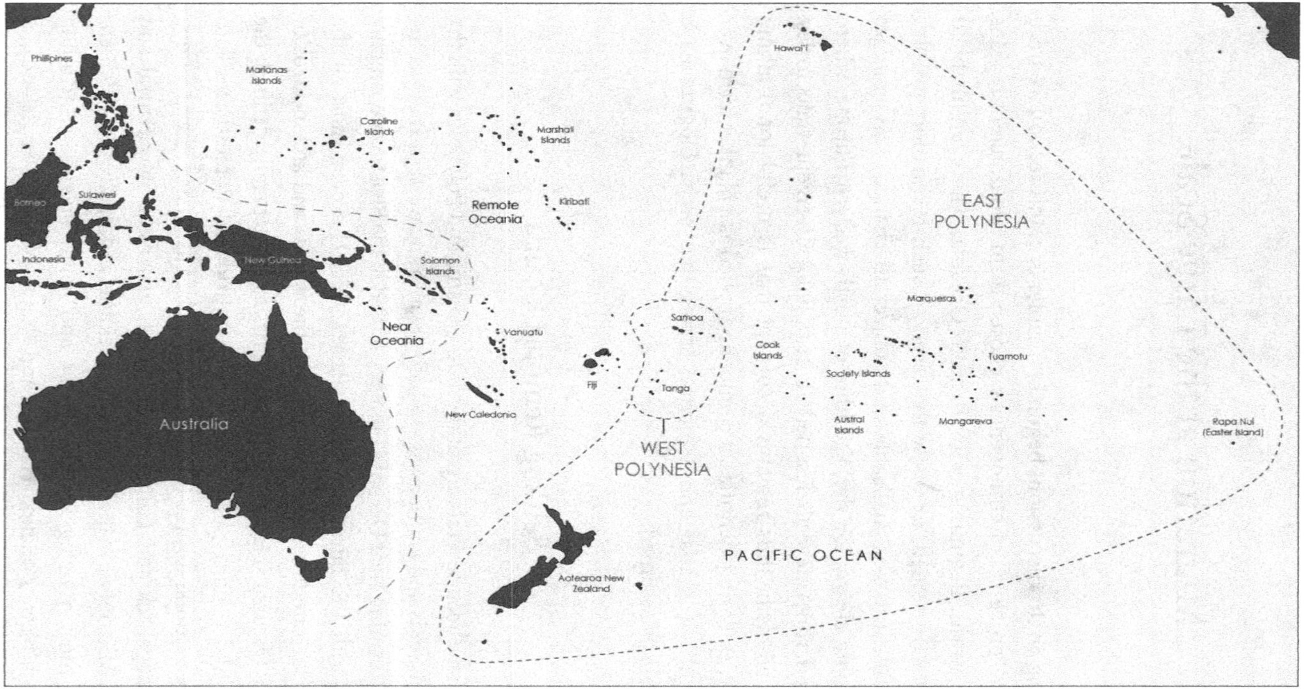

Figure 3.1 Simplified map showing the expansion of human settlement across Remote Oceania (adapted after a map by Guillaume Molle).

Irwin 1980: 325; Kirch 2010; 2017: 200). By about 1300 CE, all major islands were settled (McFadden et al. 2021: 48). This last horizon has captured the scholarly and popular imagination thanks to the vast distances covered and the risks of voyaging, as well as the rich ethnohistoric record. Hundreds of people could be on the move at any one time. Taken together, this lends itself to a narrative of technological prowess and a kind of frontier spirit inherent in settling previously uninhabited places, but also of ecological catastrophe.

Discussion of Polynesian settlement is hampered by the uncertainty that surrounds the interrelated factors of dating, sailing technology and reasons for expansion. The earliest sites have often been substantially impacted by erosion or shoreline displacement and there are few short-life radiocarbon samples without inbuilt off-sets. What counts as reliable evidence for settlement is also debated – artefacts from securely dated layers (i.e. a very strict approach to chronometric hygiene), or also environmental proxies for human presence (Horsburgh and McCoy 2017: 5–8; Kirch 2011; 2017: 198–200). Depending on the answer, short chronologies (e.g. settlement of Hawai'i as late as the thirteenth century; Wilmshurst et al. 2011) are contrasted with longer ones, favoured here, whereby central eastern Polynesia could have been settled in the tenth century, the Marquesas and Hawai'i from the early eleventh century and Aotearoa around 1250 CE (an estimate supported by both radiocarbon dating and oral tradition), with Rapa Nui potentially a couple of generations previously. Attempts to settle Norfolk Island and the sub-Antarctic islands are evidenced in the 1300s (e.g. M. Allen 2014; Anderson and White 2001; Horsburgh and McCoy 2017: 7; Kirch et al. 2010; I. Smith 2008; R. Walter et al. 2017: 354; Wilmshurst et al. 2011). In spite of this overall longer timeframe, available dates suggest a 'starburst' pattern, in which periods of short, intensive and fast forays covering long distances are separated by lulls with little or no voyaging to unknown destinations (Anderson 2017; Kirch 2011: 16).

Much energy has gone into establishing how this pattern emerged (e.g. T. Thomas 2008). One suggestion stresses opportunity: it takes time to develop the necessary nautical skills. While 'traditionalists' stress the sophistication of pre-contact sailing technology based largely on Māori myths, 'historicists' argue that key technological innovations such as triangular sails, lateen rigging (which makes sailing against the wind possible) and double-hulled or outrigger craft were not present throughout the sequence, making return voyages difficult or impossible at times (for a summary, see e.g. Anderson 2017; 2018; Finney 1991). At its most extreme, Andrew Sharp (1956) proposed that settlement proceeded entirely by chance episodes of undirected drift. This is unlikely even on its own terms, as accidentally marooned groups would rarely have been demographically viable while serendipitously carrying all the crops and domesticated animals that were introduced to newly settled islands (Suggs 1960: 82–5; N. Thomas 2021: 164). With more evidence accumulating, it has also become untenable. Most scholars now acknowledge the deep history of seafaring know-how in the region, and accept that migration voyaging was intentional and highly sophisticated, could involve several hundred people in substantial canoes and proceeded by dead reckoning and by using stars as fixed points (see e.g. Irwin 1992: 43–53; R. Walter et al. 2017). Yet this does not mean that all technological solutions were in place from the start (for criticism and discussion, see e.g. Anderson 2017; 2018: 473–9; Finney 1991; N. Thomas 2021: 69–71). Instead, this more dynamic view of sailing technology as constantly evolving could offer a possible explanation for the longer time lags between bursts of expansion.

Another set of explanations argues that migrations occurred at particular crisis points. Decreased agricultural yields occasioned by El Niño events (Kirch 2017: 46) or environmental degradation and demographic pressures (Pearce and Pearce 2010) are frequently mentioned, alongside more rapid catastrophes such as volcanic eruptions (e.g. Ballard 2020). Moving east across Polynesia, larger landmasses and archipelagos with plenty of arable land give way to volcanic high islands and eventually to low-lying coral islands with little topsoil, no standing freshwater sources and reduced biodiversity (Irwin 1980: 324; McFadden et al. 2021: 55). Once settlers introduced their integrated agricultural system (Figure 3.2) – sometimes termed

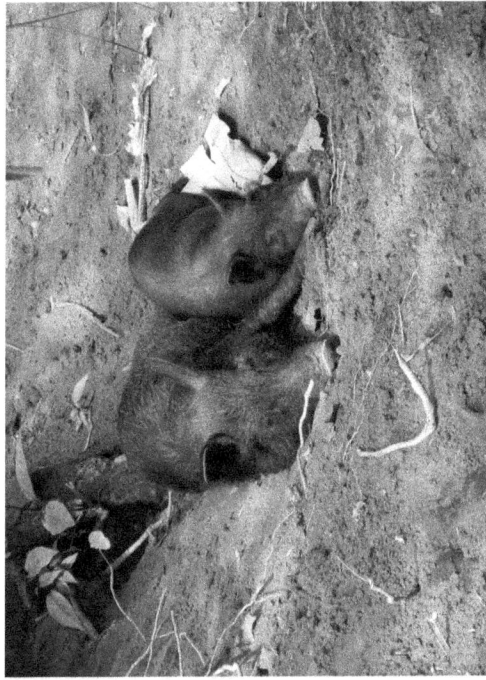

Figure 3.2 Elements of the 'transported landscape'. *Left*: Mixed planting of banana, papaya, taro and other crops outside of Dillon's Bay, Erromango Island, Vanuatu. *Right*: Pigs taking a well-earned rest at Waisisi, Tanna Island, Vanuatu (photos: James Flexner, taken during collaborative fieldwork with the Vanuatu Cultural Centre (VKS)).

the 'transported landscape' (Kirch 1982) or 'portable economy' (Irwin 1980: 324) and consisting of yam, taro, sweet potato, breadfruit and bananas, pigs, chickens, dogs and (possibly unintentionally) rats – these fragile ecosystems were quickly impoverished, causing the extinction of numerous bird and reptile species, or even the collapse of fish stocks (Anderson 2009). This self-inflicted ecological degradation then occasioned further out-migration (Anderson 2009: 1504).

In contrast, Clare McFadden and colleagues (2021) use the human skeletal record to suggest a repeated demographic trajectory for each island, beginning with rapid growth and then levelling off as carrying capacity is reached (McFadden et al. 2021: 55–66). Indeed, comparing sequences of the first appearance of domesticated resources reveals more flexibility than the idea of a 'transported landscape' suggests, with a greater focus on hunted and collected resources on some islands (Anderson and O'Connor 2008), or a staged introduction of only some domesticates in others. Particularly pig and dog, which require larger spaces and more varied resources, become rarer further east (Anderson 2009: 1511–15). It is unclear whether this diversity, increasingly also documented isotopically (e.g. Commendador et al. 2013; Fenner et al. 2021; Field et al. 2009; Herrscher et al. 2018; Swift et al. 2018), was planned by settlers in accordance with the affordances of each island, or was a re-adjustment after environments became depleted, but this variety documents an 'extraordinary reinvention of subsistence and life' (N. Thomas 2021: 126) by colonists.

Even for Rapa Nui, often cast as a textbook example of human-induced ecological collapse, the case appears to have been significantly overstated, and although species diversity on the island did reduce over time, the earliest European explorers reported on a well-adapted society with surplus food to trade (Boersema 2018; Ingersoll et al. 2018). While heavily impacted by humans, even the environments of small and outlying islands could be managed in sustainable ways over many centuries (e.g. Swift et al. 2021). Although unexpected factors, such as climatic downturns, could have devastating effects locally (Leppard

2016), this seems to particularly affect the smallest and most isolated islands, with the introduction of European diseases around 1500 CE likely a main culprit.[1] Survivors apparently resettled elsewhere (Leppard 2016: 24).

In many cases then, the rapid speed of expansion during the burst phases was driven by colonists who left long before any putative ecological or demographic collapses pushed them on (see also Irwin 1980: 325). This has brought a variety of social reasons back onto the agenda, such as fleeing from warfare, increasing hierarchies or the expansionist tendencies of neighbours (e.g. Anderson 2018: 481; Kahn et al. 2018: 353; Kennett and Winterhalder 2008), exile (Anderson 2006; Suggs 1960: 78) or the prestige that could be gained from a successful venture (Akerblom 1968: 92–3; Bellwood 2013: 197; Kirch 2017: 90; N. Thomas 2021: 115–18; for a wider Austronesian context, see also Fox and Sather 1996). These explanations make sense because migration is by no means a 'cheap' option. Excluding cases when people may have had to flee at short notice after a military defeat (and who may have travelled towards allies rather than into the unknown), migration and settlement required the stockpiling of crops, including various tree species, as well as viable herds of domesticated animals. Seaworthy canoes took specialist skills to build, alongside ritual and ceremonial investment (Irwin 1992: 220; Suggs 1960: 74–6; N. Thomas 2021: 153). It is unlikely that this was within easy reach of communities in the throes of ecological collapse. Finally, successful migration needed considerable navigational know-how, accumulated over time (Figure 3.3). Most plausibly, small scouting parties set off against the prevailing wind to search for new land, ensuring they could return once their provisions were nearly exhausted (Irwin 1992: 55–62).

Part of these apparently contradictory models – ecological decline, demographic pressure, violence or the search for renown – could be explained by different scales of analysis, or by combinations of factors. For instance, the impact of environmental challenges could have been exacerbated if social formations were more hierarchical and

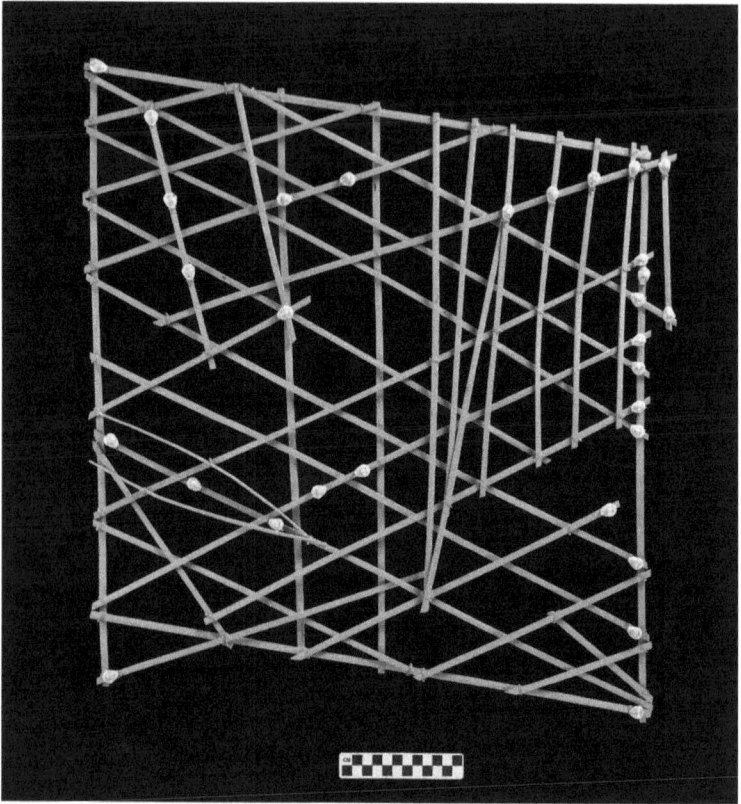

Figure 3.3 A so-called star chart used in Polynesian navigation. This example is from the Marshall Islands (photo: Richard M. Wicker; © Denver Museum of Nature & Science; catalogue number A926.1.D.P).

less flexible. In general, the question is why migration was seen as the desirable strategy to cope with various problems and pressures, whether environmental, demographic or social (Leppard 2014; 2021). It is here that ethnohistorical sources come in. Although recorded substantially after the events they recount, and thus unlikely to accurately inform on a specific journey or verifiable migration route, they provide insight into how Polynesians themselves experienced and made sense of voyaging and what they considered plausible (Finney 1991: 396; Richards 2008; N. Thomas 2021: 187).

In both Hawai'i and Aotearoa, where sources are richest, oral traditions recount the arrival of named ancestors in named canoes from the respective homelands Hawaiki and Kahiki. These form the basis of local genealogies and a group's social position. Alongside the hope of increasing personal status, disagreement or social pressure in the home community is mentioned as initiating migration, but this did not prevent return voyages. However, these were apparently rare and were considered significant navigational feats (Suggs 1960: 160). Sources also stress the ritual investment at each step of voyaging, from canoe building to establishing a new community, and the large economic outlay that was necessary. Drawing on Polynesian understandings of history as forming a guide to action in the present (see e.g. Kame'eleihiwa 1986: 28–9 as quoted in Finney 1991: 399; Sahlins 1985: 55), Colin Richards (2008: 216) describes how colonizers were inspired to set off in the expectation of encountering a new homeland, from which others would in turn journey on. Through voyaging, people and their canoes aligned themselves with the feats of their ancestors. In this sense, '[v]oyaging was not forced upon people as a last resort of escape or adventure; people simply embraced it as a way of life' (Richards 2008: 217). Therefore, long-distance voyaging was opted for even when settling closer to home could also have solved the problem (N. Thomas 2021: 118).

The addition of ancient DNA changes little with respect to these general points. One key issue is the relative contribution of 'Papuan' and 'First Remote Oceanian' (FRO; sometimes also called 'Austronesian') components of various populations and the ultimate geographical origin and date of spread of the latter. The Papuan component is traced back to the Palaeolithic settlement of island south-east Asia and Near Oceania (Gosling and Matisoo-Smith 2018), while FRO is generally associated with the Lapita expansion. Complex and regionally diverse histories of Papuan and FRO interaction were then played out across both Micronesia (Liu et al. 2022) and Remote Oceania (Matisoo-Smith 2015) and are archaeologically documented in areas like the east coast of Papua New Guinea (Shaw et al. 2022). Similarly, the DNA of commensal species shows the slow coming together of the 'transported landscape' from several roots – domestic pigs from peninsular south-east Asia (Horsburgh et al. 2022; Larson et al. 2007), chickens from the Philippines (Thomson et al. 2014) and rats from multiple sources (Matisoo-Smith 2015: 97). To this can be added one-off South American introductions like the sweet potato (Roullier et al. 2012), evidently associated with some limited admixture of human populations as well (Ioannidis et al. 2020).[2] Ancient DNA has also identified a second, far-reaching expansion into Remote Oceania in the late Lapita or immediately post-Lapita period, bringing a substantial component of Papuan DNA signatures to islands initially populated by people carrying FRO genomes (Lipson et al. 2018; 2020; Posth et al. 2018). Finally, a third phase involved the back-migration from eastern Polynesia of individuals with a greater FRO component; this phase in particular seems to have impacted different areas to greatly differing extents and likely involved multiple events of a 'braided stream' variety (Lipson et al. 2020).

Archaeologically, Taiwan was considered a likely source area of Lapita migration, but now seems less promising on genetic grounds (Choin et al. 2021). In addition, the post-Lapita expansion, albeit carried by people exhibiting different genetic signatures, continues Lapita patterns in terms of which islands likely provided the immediate starting points, which archipelagos were settled and which ones were leapfrogged over (Lipson et al. 2020). This implies the continuing social importance of voyaging, its associated institutions and know-how, across a genetic divide. The picture is further complicated by populations genetically similar (but not identical) to Lapita, but with different pottery traditions and economic choices, crossing 2,000 km of open ocean to settle the Marianas at approximately the same time (Pugach et al. 2021). The true extent and complexity of the migration phenomenon can thus be understood only if social trends over a wider area, cross-cutting traditional divisions such as island south-east Asia, Melanesia, Micronesia etc., are taken into account. The cultural, genetic and linguistic diversity of the region today has very deep roots indeed.

Pacific migrations and Neolithic Europe in dialogue

How migrations have been written about in Polynesian scholarship is in many ways similar to discourses on Neolithic Europe. There has been a tendency to romanticize the initial settlement of new lands, especially if this involved risk. Some of the blind spots are also rather similar for the two areas. Pacific migration events are sometimes narrated as if they proceeded once, from a single homeland and to a precise destination, with the most isolated islands taken as the most influential models (criticized e.g. by Irwin 1992: 77) and with a focus on demographic or ecological crises as the main drivers. Much less space is accorded to disentangling the composition of canoe crews (from one or several communities?) and to continued migration between already settled islands (Anderson 2018: 484), such as during voyages from east to west (Irwin 1980: 329–31). Part of the reason lies in disputes concerning the feasibility of return voyaging (e.g. Anderson 2017), alongside archaeological visibility (e.g. Irwin 1992: 78–9, 103). Yet only continuous interaction of this kind can explain the enormous diversity of the Melanesian and Polynesian cultural areas (Bedford and Spriggs 2008; Terrell 1988: 15–23, 149) and help to bridge the categorical division between the two. Contacts between islands may not always have encompassed extremely long-range voyages, but remained central to gaining personal renown; 'society was in this sense inherently extra-local' (N. Thomas 2021: 123).

The strong focus on foundation events should hence be complemented with interest in longer-term blending, continuing migration and local innovation (incidentally also indicated by studies on modern DNA, Karmin et al. 2022). Both the piecemeal introduction of the 'transported landscape' and the fact that communities in trouble felt they could move to other islands illustrate that 'migration was seldom a single movement, and much more often a phase of movements back and forth' (Anderson and O'Connor 2008: 7). This is also supported by the regular exchange of all sorts of objects – from stone axes and bark cloth to red feathers and whale teeth – which moved both eastwards and westwards at least until about 1450 CE, at which point elite competition and warfare may increasingly have soaked up available resources (M. Allen 2014; Kahn 2018).

There are also several points to take away from the Pacific discussion. One is how migration ventures were steeped in (mythical) history and required substantial ritual investment – a feature generally neglected for the European Neolithic. Also, neither environmental degradation, demographic pressures or warfare are strong enough to explain the entirety and scope of Polynesian settlement, nor why these challenges should be met with the relatively costly option of migration. Far from being a last resort, voyaging and settling perpetuated central aspects of Polynesian identity and cosmology. Almost immediate onward migration of parts of a settler population was considered the norm – again in contrast to Neolithic European narratives, where it is generally supposed that people moved in order to then permanently settle.

Perhaps the main difference between Pacific and European views on migration is the scale at which decision making is seen to lie. In the European case, regardless of the size of the social groups that supposedly migrated, the frame of reference explaining the migration is that of archaeological cultures. These are ultimately interpretative substitutes for ethnic groups, conceived in a relatively traditional manner. The Pacific case reminds us that the key decisions – the work that needed to go into hosting rituals, building and equipping canoes and so on, as well as the diplomatic manoeuvring necessary to assemble a large enough colonizing group – took place within individual lineage and kinship units and often proceeded from localized and personal factors, such as dissatisfaction with one's position. This, alongside the emergent aDNA evidence from Oceania (e.g. Flexner et al. 2019; Spriggs and Reich 2019; Spriggs et al. 2019), provides yet another challenge to the past existence of clearly definable ethnic groups, at least of the kind in which genetics, cultural expression and language are assumed to co-vary and which form the backbone of the European culture-historical paradigm.

Interpretative challenges: Re-negotiating 'ethnicity'

This juxtaposition of Oceanian and Neolithic European migration narratives highlights one common research problem we wish to take further here: the connection between migration and ethnicity. In so far as it is conceptualized as static and essentializing, ethnicity has been repeatedly challenged not just for the Migration Period (see Chapter 2), but also from within European prehistoric scholarship. Its relationship to archaeological cultures has been especially contested (e.g. Eggert 1978; Furholt 2019a; 2021; Hodder 1982; S. Jones 1997: 1–50; Olsen and Kobyliński 1991; Veit 1989; Wahle 1941; Wotzka 2000). Yet if we think of ethnicity as group-level identity making in practice, this opens more interesting questions of how ethnicity is maintained, negotiated and/or changed through time, potentially as part of migrations.

There have been three levels of criticism. First, ethnicity is a fraught concept well beyond archaeology and is deeply embedded in contemporary political discourses (e.g. Espiritu 2013; Hu 2013; Song 2013; Voss 2015: 657; Weik 2014: 296). As ethnic labels are often imposed on people from the outside in the course of unequal power relations (e.g. A. Smith 2008: 29–31; Stone 2003: 32–8; Voss 2008: 26–7) and also often remain analytically vague (S. Jones 1997: 56–70), perhaps it would be best to abandon them.

Second, there are issues of definition. Many differentiate between essentialized definitions, used to reinforce inequality, and interactional definitions, which accord substantial levels of agency to individuals and trace how ethnic identity is situationally defined in accordance with economic or political goals (in particular Barth 1969). In this view, ethnic identities are strategically created and shed in the course of political interactions – they are opportunistically imagined. However, it is one thing to criticize ethnicity at an ontological level – ethnic identities are not a fixed reality – and another to completely discard it at an epistemological level. As Ulrike Sommer (2011: 171) writes, 'even if the history and (homogeneous) composition of a group are entirely fictional, the moment members of this group decide to act together for common aims (or pretend the existence of common aims) ... this group does begin to exist'. These arguments draw on the emotional and social salience of ethnicity, which is often based on the belief in a shared common origin, whether objectively verifiable or not (Weber 1976 [1920/1]: 237). Through this, and the physical marking out of differences to perceived 'others', ethnic groups succeed in turning an instrumental association of common interests into a deeply felt sense of commonality (Weber 1976 [1920/1]: 237). Both situational and primordial aspects are important for its political efficacy (Damm 2010: 12–20; Fernandez-Götz 2013; Hu 2013: 376; S. Jones 1997: 77–81; Voss 2008: 18–19).

For archaeologists, a third and last problem remains – that of identification. Foundational publications like those by Sian Jones (1997: 74–9) or Stefan Burmeister (2000) have cast doubt on whether archaeological methods are sufficient to reliably identify ethnicity (see also Bellwood 2013: 32–3; Weik 2014: 294) and where it would be best visible. In the context of Andean archaeology, Emily Stovel (2013) contrasts two understandings of ethnicity: a passive one based on Pierre Bourdieu's concept of the habitus, according to which ethnic identity is most visible in unreflected aspects of daily life; and an active understanding, based on Fredrik Barth's work, in which ethnicity is consciously communicated in a situation of competition between groups. She proposes that the former level provides the framework from which certain aspects can be actively selected as core symbols in more active displays – the term 'ethnicity' should be reserved for these latter (Stovel 2013: 9). In this way, scholars can account both for a broad similarity in (cultural) lifeways across a region and the punctuated, temporary emergence of explicitly stressed differences (Stovel 2013: 6–8; also S. Jones 1997: 120–1). Similarly, Burmeister (2017a: 61–3; forthcoming) distinguishes between internally and externally performed identities, which can draw on two different cultural traditions.

Ethnicity and migration are also often linked. This can work in one of two ways – with reference to a territorialized notion of ethnic identity, in which 'original' inhabitants are seen to hold a birth right to land held 'since time immemorial' and into which others should be prevented from moving; or with the explicit mention of (mythical) migrations during which a group of people is said to have coalesced into an ethnos, often in the face of difficulties (Hu 2013: 372–6). Migration is not the only context in which new ethnic identities can emerge, but situations of frequent demographic (dis)aggregation, which bring new sets of people into contact and demand a renegotiation of boundaries, have been repeatedly flagged as important (e.g. Hu 2013; Voss 2015). This encompasses colonization, where actors compete for access to land and resources, but can also happen during smaller-scale processes, particularly where fission is an important strategy to mediate intra-group tension (e.g. Kopytoff 1987), or where people can routinely shift between ethnic groups (e.g. Fowles and Eiselt 2019). From an archaeological point of view, it is important to realize that ethnicity need not be something that is necessarily in place at the beginning of a migration event and then remains unaltered. Rather, it can also change or emerge during relocation, or indeed only after arrival in a new setting. Whether or not ethnicity is a useful concept to pursue depends on the analytical work this concept can contribute to a given analysis.

The spread of the Neolithic into the European fringes

In an archaeological context devoid of oral history, these patterns become more ambiguous. Albeit under very different geographical circumstances, a maritime expansion also brought Neolithic materials and ways of life into north-western-most Europe – the north-east Atlantic archipelago (present-day Britain, Ireland and the Channel Islands). Settling southern Scandinavia required no open-sea crossings. In these regions, hunter-gatherer populations persisted for more than a millennium after their more southerly neighbours had adopted agriculture, longhouses and a range of social and material technologies associated with Neolithic lifeways and sedentism. Archaeological debate about the emergence of the Neolithic in these regions has been a microcosm of broader arguments about the role of diffusion versus population migration. Were the elements of the Neolithic package (primarily agriculture and animal husbandry) adopted by local people in these peripheral areas, or did migrants set up their own settlements (see summaries of the debate from the two different perspectives in Rowley-Conwy et al. 2020; J. Thomas 2008)?

Following the archaeological common wisdom, prior to 4000 BCE people living in the north-east Atlantic archipelago followed hunter-gatherer subsistence practices and lived mobile lives. Although some houses and monumental structures were constructed, these are generally explained as consistent with seasonal occupation by small and dispersed groups (Conneller et al. 2012: 1005–7). Then, there was a watershed moment: within just a few centuries, by *c.* 3700 BCE, the full Neolithic package was present throughout the archipelago (though perhaps somewhat patchily both spatially and chronologically; Rowley-Conwy et al. 2020; Smyth et al. 2020). By 'Neolithic package' in this region, we mean:

- buildings of various sizes, including larger structures termed 'halls' that seem to have served a communal rather than residential function;
- agriculture and animal husbandry;
- cosmological innovations, such as monumental structures (both earthen and megalithic);
- production and use of ceramic and other novel technologies, including the circulation of polished and ground-stone axes, flint mining and new knapping sequences;
- dietary changes, including a shift from marine to terrestrial resources and the consumption of various domesticated products, such as milk and grain;
- perhaps also new kin or ethnic formations.

Biomolecular data have shown that this technological shift coincided with population mobility from the continent, resulting in considerable genetic turnover (Brace et al. 2019; Neil et al. 2020). This has been used to support the hypothesis of migrants bringing their Neolithic ways of life to the archipelago and culturally (and otherwise) replacing the resident hunter-gatherer population. However, while continental affinities exist for some artefacts and practices, no singular continental point of origin for the archipelagic Neolithic has been identified (Sheridan 2007). Indeed, considerable regional variation is present in even the earliest Neolithic phases (Anderson-Whymark and Garrow 2015; Smyth et al. 2020). Both radiocarbon and genomic data have been read to suggest episodic migration from different continental locations to different regions within Britain and Ireland, contributing to the formation of the Neolithic population and their regionalized lifeways (Brace et al. 2019; Whittle et al. 2011) (Figure 3.4).

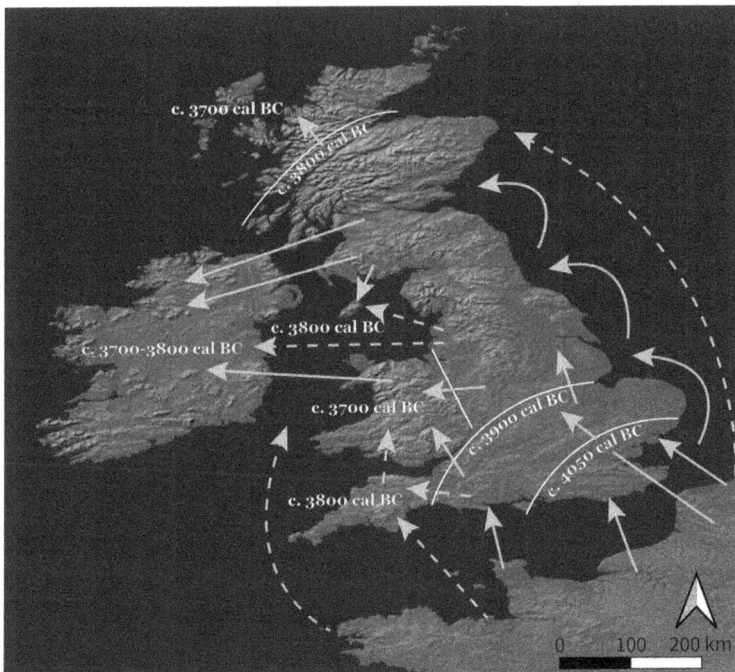

Figure 3.4 Schema for the spread of the Neolithic throughout the north-east Atlantic archipelago (re-drawn after Whittle et al. 2011: fig. 15.8).

Especially in Ireland, continuities in practice, landscape use and material culture are evident, such as the continued use and construction of shell middens and the circulation of fragmented human remains (Smyth et al. 2020: 428–32). This suggests that new groups of farmers were aware of, interacted with and defined themselves through pre-Neolithic practices and peoples (who may have been involved in early farming activities; e.g. Sheridan 2013). Hugo Anderson-Whymark and Duncan Garrow (2015: 68) further note that some practices typically understood as 'Neolithic', such as the deposition of axes in wet contexts, have Mesolithic parallels and may represent cultural continuities rather than introduced innovations, perhaps serving as 'boundary objects' (*sensu* Frieman 2012: 456; Star and Griesemer 1989) to ease frictions between resident and incoming populations. Chantal Conneller and colleagues (2012) argue that there is evidence for converging practices before 4000 BCE, such as the communal construction of timber monuments, as well as a significant investment in place-making seen in the elaboration of large sites like Star Carr over many generations.

Forager populations in this archipelago, as elsewhere in northern and western Europe, seem to have been seasonally mobile, and isotopic data testify to a diet high in marine foods, suggesting coastal groups were comfortable on the water as well as the land (Anderson-Whymark and Garrow 2015; Cramp et al. 2014; Garrow and Sturt 2011; Smyth et al. 2020). Ireland was already an island when it was settled (Chapple et al. 2022), so its inhabitants had the technology and knowledge to cross open water. Ephemeral traces of continental materials, including domestic cattle bones[3], in the archipelago before 4000 BCE indicate cross-Channel contacts prior to the local appearance of the Neolithic package (Anderson-Whymark et al. 2015; Elliott et al. 2020; Garrow and Sturt 2011; 2017). Still, the biomolecular data illustrate that, from about 4000 BCE, the genetic ancestries of people in the archipelago predominantly derived from continental European Neolithic peoples, especially those from what is now northern France (Brace and Booth 2023; Cassidy 2023).

However, it is still debated how many episodes of influx directly from the Continent there were. Based on comprehensive radiocarbon models, Alasdair Whittle and colleagues (2011: 853–64) argue for an extended process of Neolithization starting in the later fifth millennium BCE in the Thames estuary. After a few generations of standstill, this then expanded into southern central England via chain migration. Anderson-Whymark and Garrow (2015) propose overlapping contact zones or 'maritories' (*sensu* Needham 2009) in the fifth millennium seaways around the archipelago (Figure 3.5), leading to the movement of some continental people to Britain and Ireland, as well as the local adoption of agricultural practices, ceramic technology, etc. They argue that this pattern of overlapping mid-range mobilities contributed to the subsequent rapid

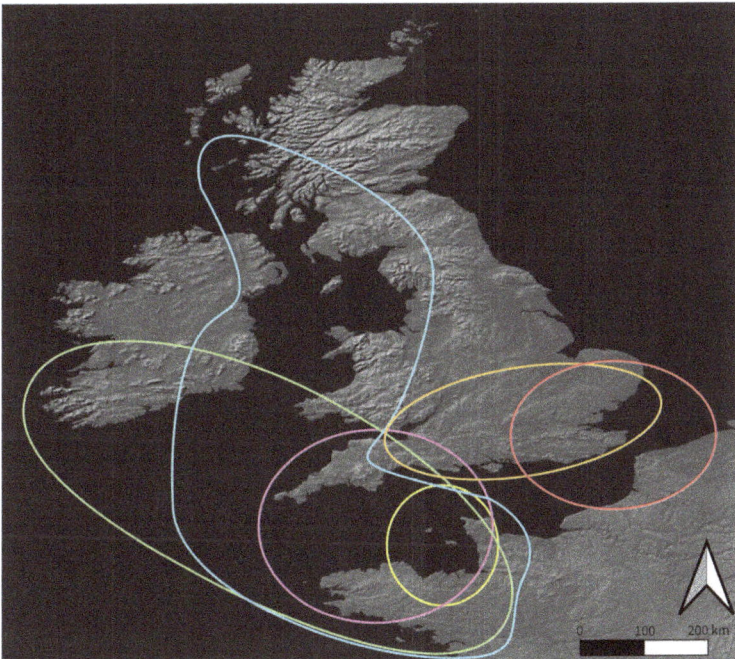

Figure 3.5 Overlapping interaction spheres in the late fifth and early fourth millennia BCE (re-drawn after Anderson-Whymark and Garrow 2015: fig. 5.5).

regionalization of Neolithic materials and ways of life. Julian Thomas (2022) builds outwards from these data to suggest that the emergence of distinctly Neolithic lifeways in the archipelago had two clear stages, an earlier 'minimal Neolithic' lasting 4100–3900 BCE that saw migration by a few smaller continental groups from north-east France and Belgium to south-east England, and a subsequent establishment phase with greater numbers of migrants and clearer affinities to Normandy, moving from the Continent to sites in southern and central England and Wales.

Indeed, even in the earliest phases of the Neolithic, archaeologists can distinguish clearly between practices and materials on the continent and across the archipelago, even where there are shared elements. For example, Anderson-Whymark and Garrow (2015: 70) note clear parallels between early fourth millennium leaf-shaped arrowheads in the archipelago and within the Michelsberg zone, but differences in technique may indicate that these latter were copied rather than directly transferred. Hélène Pioffet (2014) uses technological and stylistic analyses to suggest affinities in ceramic production and style between south-eastern England (and subsequently eastern England and Scotland) and the Scheldt valley (northern France and Belgium) from *c.* 3900 BCE, and between western Britain, the Isle of Man, Ireland, Brittany and Normandy from 3800 BCE. Across Britain and Ireland, she notes a rapid and regionalizing impulse creating clear distinctions between production zones within the archipelago as well as between the insular ceramics and their continental inspirations. While she sees hints of ongoing cross-Channel contact in regional pottery assemblages, from 3700/3650 BCE a distinctly archipelagic ceramic trajectory and interaction sphere had taken root. Vicki Cummings and James Morris (2022) have also suggested that viable cattle herds could have been built up from a small initial cohort within the first centuries of Neolithic arrival, without requiring continued influx of continental stock.

This mix of rejection and convergence echoes earlier patterns of relation between mainland and islands, as fifth millennium BCE foragers, who were likely at least occasionally in contact with ceramic-using continental neighbours, did not adopt pottery, perhaps in conscious resistance to aspects of agricultural society (Elliott et al. 2020). That newly arrived continental populations were quickly distinguishable from their neighbours through ritual practices, technologies and stylistic choices testifies to the complex patterns of identity and boundary creation enacted by these mobile populations as they established themselves in a new landscape, alongside (but perhaps not regularly intermingling with) its long-term inhabitants (cf. Garrow and Sturt 2017).

Certainly, both archaeological and genomic data indicate that separate populations persisted for some time after the early migrations of farmers from the continent. In Wiltshire near Stonehenge, a large pit referred to as the 'Coneybury Anomaly' was opened in the first quarter of the fourth millennium, perhaps between 3800–3700 BCE, and filled with the debris of a large gathering, including domestic and wild fauna, sherds and stone tools of both Neolithic and longstanding Mesolithic technological traditions. Based on this mix of materials, as well as osteological and biomolecular analysis of the animal remains, Kurt Gron and colleagues (2018) have suggested that this assemblage reflects a solidarity feast and food redistribution event that included several communities of farmers and at least one group of hunter-gatherers, all of whom likely lived within a day's walk of the site. The Coneybury Anomaly does, however, remain an isolated instance.

Similarly, the genomes of a handful of mid-fourth millennium BCE individuals buried in caves in western Scotland demonstrate recent Mesolithic-derived ancestry, indicating that such groups remained present despite the migration of new people from the continent (Patterson et al. 2022). These genomic patterns find parallels in the ongoing use of shell middens in western Scotland from the fifth into the fourth millennium BCE (Wicks et al. 2014). Other areas of the archipelago have so far not shown any such long-term survival of hunter-gatherer DNA, suggesting that this signal was quickly swamped (Brace and Booth 2023).

J. Thomas (2022) interprets these scant traces as evidence for parallel societies of farmers and hunter-gatherers, which eventually merged to create something *sui generis* in the archipelago. Indeed, for a few centuries after 4000 BCE, farming communities made up of various continental migrants and their descendants were probably small and perhaps clustered in specific locales, likely near major estuaries, while earlier hunter-gatherer populations persisted, especially in less accessible interior, upland and northern coastal regions (Griffiths 2014).

The uniquely insular development of Neolithic styles and practices could result from a concerted desire to cut ties with continental kin or from sustained interaction with local hunter-gatherers, but is perhaps more likely to stem from interactions between these heterogeneous Neolithic 'islands' as small agricultural enclaves struggled to survive in precarious conditions and on a landmass where they shared few kin connections to help them weather disasters. That is, we may be seeing the results of a rapid process of hybridization or ethnogenesis of migrants from slightly different backgrounds within the islands as a logical and necessary support network.

Southern Scandinavia shows some similarities to the processes just described. Being part of the same chronological 'horizon' of change, the introduction of Neolithic cultural elements in this region may have gone through partly similar phases and cultural dynamics as Britain and Ireland. The onset of the Neolithic in southern Scandinavia, however, was part of the emergence of the Funnel Beaker, or TRB, material culture complex that encompassed a large area of northern-central Europe where Neolithic ways of life had already been practised for many centuries. Within the century after 4000 BCE, communities with domestic crops and animals, polished flint axes and TRB pottery (Figure 3.6) established themselves across southern Scandinavia, forming the so-called 'northern TRB group' (Midgley 1992; Persson 1999). These groups settled slightly different landscapes from the predominantly coastal, Late Mesolithic forager sites, preferring well-drained, sandy soils at a slight distance from the coast and offering good spots for a new type of dwelling structure – longhouses – as well as easy access to areas suitable for agriculture (Johansen 2006; P. Nielsen and F. Nielsen 2020; L. Sørensen 2014). Since Henrik Tauber's (1981)

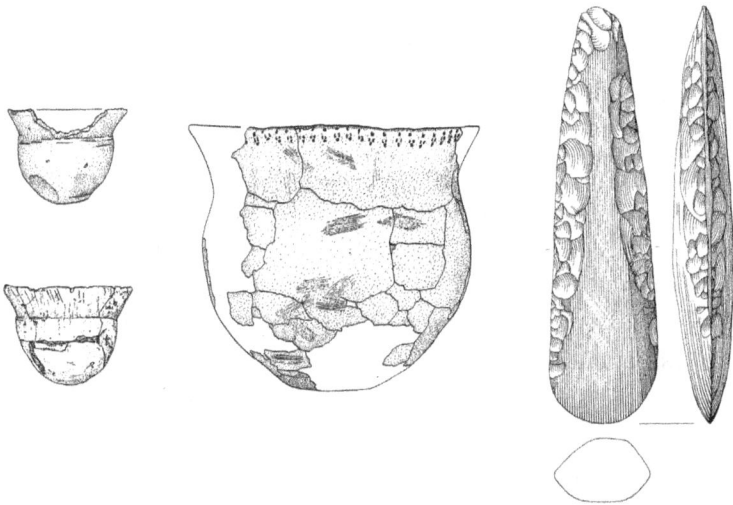

Figure 3.6 Artefacts from the earliest Neolithic of southern Scandinavia; *right*: pointed-butted polished flint axe, type 1; length: 26 cm (Petersen 1999: 103); *left*: Funnel Beaker ceramic vessels, type 0; height of small vessels *c*. 8 cm, height of large vessel *c*. 22 cm (Koch 1998: 84).

foundational work, stable isotope studies have made clear that this new way of inhabiting the landscape was accompanied by a marked shift away from the highly marine diet of the region's Late Mesolithic foragers to one that was much more based on terrestrial resources (Fischer et al. 2007; Shennan 2018: 169).

While these patterns of landscape occupation and subsistence seem to indicate a rapid transition from a forager to a farmer way of life in southern Scandinavia, other lines of evidence point to continuity and more gradual transition. These include parts of the flint tool inventory (Fischer 2002; Wadskjær 2018; although see Högberg and Berggren 2023) and the continued use of coastal shell middens – the core sites of the late Ertebølle forager groups – for several centuries into the fourth millennium BCE (S. Andersen 2008). Furthermore, the pollen record for that time reveals little overall impact of agricultural activities on the vegetation cover (Feeser et al. 2012; Rasmussen 2005), although this may in part reflect the limited population size pursuing the new types of activity in the landscape (cf. Johannsen 2023).

While the introduction of Neolithic culture into southern Scandinavia was commonly argued to have happened by diffusion – local foragers adopting a new way of life from their neighbours to the south (cf. Cummings et al. 2022; Fischer and Kristiansen 2002) – recent genomic studies have shown that migrants played a main role in introducing a new economy and culture (Allentoft et al. 2024b). This evidence has thus corroborated previous arguments that the change to an agricultural way of life was too complicated and fundamental to have resulted from imitation of groups residing elsewhere (L. Sørensen and Karg 2014).

However, while the genomic evidence is very clear on the scale of centuries – leaving no doubt that people with so-called 'Neolithic'[4] ancestry became demographically dominant in the region within a few hundred years – certain findings at the level of individuals provide glimpses of a more complex process. Notably, the genome of a female who lived approximately two centuries after the arrival of farming – preserved in a piece of birch pitch used as chewing gum, found at Syltholm – showed that, genetically speaking, she belonged to the population of foragers that inhabited the region prior to the Neolithic (Jensen et al. 2019). In other words, neither her parents nor any previous generations in her lineage had been migrants carrying biological ancestry linked to Neolithic communities in central Europe. Genomic and isotopic analyses on an adult male individual buried with Early Neolithic artefacts at Dragsholm during the early fourth millennium BCE similarly show that this individual, genetically speaking, only had forager ancestors; yet, he was clearly given a Neolithic burial. What is more, his diet had changed during the course of his life, from the highly marine diet of a Late Mesolithic forager when he was a child to the mainly terrestrial diet of a Neolithic farmer as an adult (Allentoft et al. 2024b).

Though such finds are rare, they do indicate that the cultural and demographic processes that unfolded when local foragers and immigrant farmer groups came into contact were multifaceted and more variable than a simple replacement scenario. Archaeologically, we struggle to discern and understand them due to the scale (of centuries) at which we typically operate. Nonetheless, Kurt Gron and Lasse Sørensen (2018) have suggested four phases of cultural transformation that they label and approximately date as follows:

1. The contact/scouting phase, from *c.* 4400 BCE
2. The introduction phase, from *c.* 4000 BCE
3. The negotiation phase, *c.* 4000–3700 BCE
4. The homogenization phase, after *c.* 3700 BCE

This framework raises a number of interesting questions. While southern Scandinavian foragers and farmers south of the region were neighbours (in a regional sense) and must have known of each other's existence for over a millennium before 4000 BCE (Klassen 2004; Koch 1998), contact across this forager–farmer frontier appears to have risen steadily through the second half of the fifth millennium BCE, during the suggested 'contact phase'. Gron and Sørensen (2018: 968) emphasize rare finds of domesticates in Ertebølle contexts, and though the chronology and cultural associations of these are not always entirely clear, it is plausible that (food products based on) domesticates were part of exchanges between foragers and farmers. While most cases of such exchange would have left no archaeological trace, a more reliable indicator exists in the so-called 'shoe-last adzes'. These stone artefacts were by far the most common southern import among Ertebølle foragers, and in spite of a positive preservation bias they are suitable as a proxy for the general level of contact. They unequivocally demonstrate exchange between foragers and farmers across the frontier and indicate that the intensity of this contact increased gradually during the final centuries of the fifth millennium (Klassen 2004), leading up to the profound changes that occurred during the decades around 4000 BCE.

The term used by Gron and Sørensen (2018) to describe the following period, the 'negotiation phase', in part reflects the aforementioned elements of continuity as well as the absence of certain Neolithic innovations, such as monumental architecture, during the first couple of centuries of Neolithic culture in the region. But it also reflects these authors' belief in a lengthy phase of population duality, during which groups with farming and foraging backgrounds occupied different parts of the landscape, while using broadly similar 'Neolithic' material culture. For this scenario to work in concert with more recent aDNA data (Allentoft et al. 2024a; 2024b), there would have had to be a relatively strict separation of these two populations with regard to reproduction (as Mesolithic biological lineages did not persist later into the Neolithic), even if other forms of exchange could have thrived. While there can be little doubt that there was such a phase of coexistence, as Gron and Sørensen (2018: 969) themselves acknowledge, we do not know its duration – and it is difficult to substantiate the idea that it would have lasted the two or three centuries until the appearance of monumental architecture (N. Andersen 1997; Andersson et al. 2022; Ebbesen 2011; Eriksen and Andersen 2017), copper import and metallurgy (Gebauer et al. 2021; Klassen 2001) and a significant, gradual rise in both population (Müller and Diachenko 2019) and activities in the landscape (Feeser et al. 2012; Rasmussen 2005).

Regardless, conceptualizing the first few centuries of the fourth millennium in this region as a process of 'negotiation' potentially misses what may have been one of the most important causal factors at play: the earliest communities that practised farming in southern Scandinavia attempted to do so in a landscape that was not well suited to an agricultural way of life at all. Learning about the local environment from members of the pre-existing forager population, who had been manipulating their natural surroundings long before farmers arrived (cf. Groß et al. 2019), is likely to have been key for Early Neolithic migrants. However, the very different economic strategies of these groups meant that farmers still had to establish their agricultural niche by carving it into the landscape themselves – thus engaging in what, in biology, is known as niche construction (cf. Odling-Smee et al. 2003). According to this perspective, the final phase proposed by Gron and Sørensen (2018) – the 'homogenization phase' – followed when Neolithic communities had become sufficiently consolidated to allow for economic and demographic growth and included what must be described as a truly extraordinary expenditure of resources on different forms of ritual activity. Establishing Neolithic culture in southern Scandinavia is unlikely to have been entirely a process of negotiation between or development of different cultural preferences; it was *also* a generations-long, arduous process of shaping local landscapes to better suit a new way of life (Johannsen 2023).

Complex affiliations among mobile communities: lessons from north-western Europe and the Pacific

The similarities between Neolithic migration in the north-east Atlantic archipelago and southern Scandinavia are striking. In both regions we see people who persisted in practising hunter-gatherer ways of life while their near neighbours were farming and building longhouses. Contact between farmers and non-farmers occurred during this period, but was small-scale and left only minor traces in the archaeological record (and almost none in the genomic data). In the centuries around 4000 BCE, groups of farmers began moving into what had been hunter-gatherer lands. No trace of mass violence is evident, perhaps because of this deep history of ongoing if transient interaction, but also likely linked to the choice by farming people to settle away from the rich coastal resources preferred by many of the existing inhabitants. However, some displacement from traditional lands must have occurred. Patchy but consistent evidence from the first quarter of the fourth millennium tells us that in at least some regions migrants and earlier populations coexisted, occasionally feasting together, rarely having children. Eventually the migrants became locals – possibly faster in the north-east Atlantic archipelago than in southern Scandinavia – and distinctly local Neolithic lifeways and sets of material culture emerged.

However, the two regions are distinct in the connections these migrants appear to have felt towards their ancestral kin. While more or less regionally distinct structures, practices and artefacts can be clustered into a 'northern' group, the Neolithic that developed in southern Scandinavia was part of the wider TRB, a group of archaeological objects whose traces can be found from the Elbe to the headwaters of the Dniester and the Bug. By contrast, the archipelagic Neolithic maintained no such ties. Even in its earliest manifestations, the ceramic technology in particular is not identifiable as coming from one specific place in continental Europe. Some affinities with the continent are present – constructing monumental funerary and gathering sites, building megaliths and using polished stone axes – but these items are primarily produced from locally significant stone sources and made in locally preferred styles. It is as if the Neolithic migrants, having moved into the archipelago, were more interested in developing local affinities with each other than maintaining or even acknowledging ancestral kin elsewhere, in spite of geographically much less challenging conditions for continued contact than was the case in the Pacific. Certainly, the genomic data suggest they preferred not to have children with continental cousins (Brace and Booth 2023). That the Channel formed a social rather than physical boundary is shown by archaeological and biomolecular data for mobility across the Irish Sea throughout this period (Frieman 2008; Pioffet 2014). This intensive interaction among archipelagic agriculturalists, who were from various natal communities and may not initially have shared a common language, may have been a necessary and intentional strategy of building solidarity and social resilience. In the first quarter of the fourth millennium, agricultural communities were enclaves of continental migrants and their descendants. They engaged in pioneer agriculture in a place where they had few or no kin ties to call on if an animal escaped, a house collapsed, or a crop failed. Building strong relationships with new neighbours who shared important aspects of their way of life may have been key to survival. Although difficult to detect archaeologically, we should also consider that some early settling attempts likely failed, due to a lack of economic success, disease, conflict with local groups or several such factors, potentially causing the immigrant groups in question to perish or attempt to return to their natal communities.

That migrants moved rapidly, in large numbers and nearly simultaneously into both southern Scandinavia and the north-east Atlantic archipelago likely speaks to social and cosmological changes among continental European populations. Migration became a desirable social strategy, and migrants introduced new subsistence practices, architectural forms and religious rites. As in the Pacific, the patterns of migration may have been shaped by demographic and geographical circumstances: a relatively small archipelagic Mesolithic population would have meant less conflict over arable land, while a larger and more settled Mesolithic population in southern Scandinavia may have necessitated more time to find a neighbourly footing – and consequently more trips back to natal communities for food, support and other supplies. While neither terrestrial nor maritime boundaries imposed isolation, migrants to the north-east Atlantic archipelago strategically severed ties with communities on the continent. Where northern TRB people developed a local identity and way of life in close contact with neighbours and kin to the south, the new islanders reinvented themselves, creating a hybrid cultural constellation that combined various ancestral ways of life and relied on complex patterns of communication and support amongst a heterogeneous migrant community. They made a separate, island identity.

As the Pacific case study showed, social and cultural affiliation are based on such interactions. Therefore, the resulting ethnic identities are not a simple and given aspect of existence, carried along on a migration like a snail carries its shell (as Robb and Miracle 2007: 102 have phrased it). Rather, they emerge during or after such an event as a result of interaction patterns. In the Pacific, migrations were initially accompanied by continued contacts, even over vast distances – but, like in Britain and Ireland, this was eventually discontinued. Aotearoa, Hawai'i and Rapa Nui were effectively isolated by the time of European contact (N. Thomas 2021: 195–6), either because changing weather patterns made them harder to reach or because interest in maintaining social links declined as newly established communities became more numerous (Anderson 2017: 6; 2018: 486). Myths often focus on one or a very limited number of voyages which established their communities (Sahlins 1985: 58; Suggs 1960: 173). Contact remained much more of a feature further west.

Migration did not involve closed ethnic groups from the start, but larger-scale identity groupings that might be termed 'ethnic' could result from a migration event. Thus, migration events became a kernel around which myths of origin could be woven. In the case of Aotearoa, the initial Māori settlers may have numbered 500 people as part of a 'strategic mass migration' to what must have been a known archipelago (R. Walter et al. 2017: 355). The impetus for this event appears to have been largely social, and as the settlers are not very closely related genetically, Richard Walter and colleagues (2017: 370) propose that charismatic leaders following visionary ideas (what Graeber and Wengrow 2021: 362–70 discuss as 'charismatic politics') convinced people from several communities to colonize a known, but as yet empty landscape. Rather than trying to find a specific origin point, the homeland of Hawaiki mentioned in the oral histories of Māori settlement would hence refer to the western Polynesian interaction zone more generally (R. Walter et al. 2017: 369). It could then have been strategically deployed to provide the sense of common origin necessary for ethnic group formation, as members of the Great Fleet began to differentiate themselves from their various origin communities. Internally, conflict between groups tracing their origin to specific canoe crews (Finney 1991: 384; R. Walter et al. 2017: 352) encouraged further fragmentation. In north-western Europe, too, the migration event was the catalyst for creating new identities; but, given the geographical realities, it was not the danger or difficulty of the journey that provided the background for this.[5] Rather, the glue holding these societies together was the choice to rely on tight networks with neighbours, some of whom may already have been kin while others were made kin through shared practices and intermarriage. It is in these daily and ceremonial ties that new ethnic identities were formed.

In the Pacific, ethnicity as a partly descent-based grounds for common action only emerges at specific historical points, but is not a significant feature in either causing voyaging events or explaining the composition of migrating groups. Similarly, in Britain and Ireland at least, when the initial migrations of continental agriculturalists seem to have ended around 3700 BCE, ritual practices and funerary rites focussed strongly on lineage, descent and affiliation as new identities and relationships were negotiated (Cummings and Fowler 2023). Ethnicity could sometimes emerge as a result of settlement events, drawing on the transformative effects of shared journeys, just as in the Migration Period in Europe (see Chapter 2). Alternatively, it could be the result of subsequent efforts at group demarcation within expanding settler societies or other interaction scenarios (e.g. Flexner et al. 2019). If we want to understand how migration events were organized and why they happened, we therefore need to look at factors such as personal leadership, local histories of conflict, the establishment of support networks among kin and other affiliated people, co-ordinating surplus production within households and lineages or drawing together people from several communities. Migration, even in these large-scale cases, was a consequence of particular small-scale power structures, which it also perpetuated. It is to these that we turn next.

4

The Middle Distance

Migrations within Regions

The US Southwest and the Pueblo migrations

US-American archaeological debates about migration provide fruitful points of comparison for prehistoric Europe, as ethnohistoric evidence and oral traditions (see e.g. Naranjo 1995) have encouraged a sustained engagement with the variable causes, processes and outcomes of migration. Although not limited to the US Southwest (see e.g. S. Alt 2006; Birch 2012; Cipolla 2013; O'Gorman and Conner 2023), the latter is chosen here as a particularly rich case study. Several larger-scale horizons of migration can be identified in this area, particularly after *c*. 800 CE (Table 4.1; Figure 4.1).

Table 4.1 Main horizons of migration events in the Pueblo area of the US Southwest

from *c*. 800 CE	migration into Chaco, from Mesa Verde or the south-west (e.g. Mills et al. 2018)
from 1050 into early 1100s CE	migration out of Chaco, likely into San Juan (W. Wills 2009)
1100s CE	migration from San Juan into Chaco (Mills et al. 2018)
after *c*. 1150 CE	Abandonment of Chaco itself, but presence in wider region (McElmo phase, e.g. Lekson and Cameron 1995; W. Wills 2009)
1200–1450 CE	multiple migrations, e.g. abandonment of Mesa Verde *c*. 1300 (e.g. Clark et al. 2019), migrations into Hopi area (e.g. Bernardini 2011a), from Kayenta area into Hohokam (e.g. Stone 2003), etc.

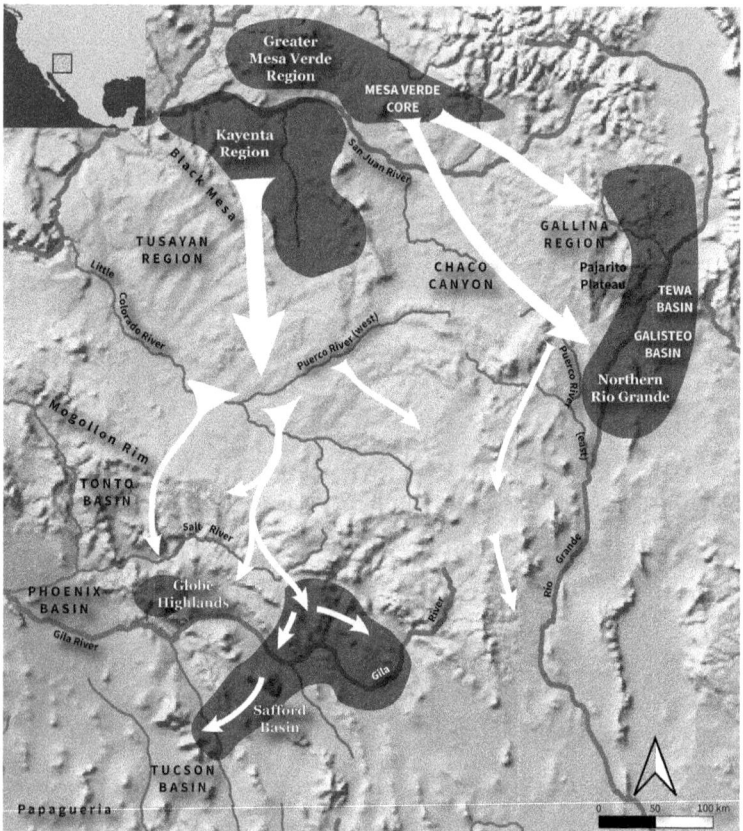

Figure 4.1 Map showing Kayenta and Mesa Verde homelands, migration routes, and resettlement areas with regions and sites mentioned in the text (re-drawn after Clark *et al.* 2019: fig. 1).

The coalescence of the big ceremonial centre at Chaco, but even more so the subsequent period of 'great migrations', persistently challenge another assumption of the culture concept: that group identity is in some way predicated on the existence of a stable place or clearly delimited territory (Bernardini 2005). The South-west experienced repeated migration events by groups of varying sizes moving longer or shorter distances into more or less densely settled areas that were culturally more or less similar to their areas of origin. As a result, the impacts of migration are highly varied, and only a few selected case studies can be covered here.

The emergence of the large regional centre at Chaco, beginning *c.* 800 CE and itself predicated on new patterns of mobility in a frontier zone (Mills 2023), saw the establishment of Great Houses with their corresponding kiva ritual spaces, forming the central points of dispersed and less permanent settlement sites (e.g. Lekson and Cameron 1995). Ritually important material culture, such as ornaments, was produced at a large scale, while other items flooded into Chaco from surrounding areas: macaws from Mexico (e.g. Lekson and Cameron 1995; A. Watson et al. 2015), foodstuffs and construction timbers from several locations (see e.g. Benson et al. 2003; English et al. 2001) and people (Mills et al. 2018; Wilshusen and van Dyke 2006), not all of whom may have arrived voluntarily (Cameron 2013: 225). All this went hand in hand with marked social inequality, visible in part in lavish grave goods (Akins 1986; Harrod 2012). This inequality could have caused a breakdown in social relations, triggering the abandonment of Chaco (W. Wills 2009: 309). When the area was resettled some generations later, no cultural continuity to Chaco is apparent (Lekson and Cameron 1995; Mills et al. 2018; W. Wills 2009). Indeed, it has been argued that the possible abuse of ritual power at places like Chaco led Native American communities to develop effective strategies for the avoidance of fixed and absolute status positions (Graeber and Wengrow 2021: 456–92). Migration can be interpreted as one of these strategies. However, how migration impacted both the migrants and the people whom they came into contact with depended on a number of factors, generally negotiated at the scale of individual sites and households.

The Kayenta migration, which started in *c.* 1260 CE, is an example of a demographically relatively small-scale event, with Kayenta migrants usually far outnumbered by local residents. For instance, only about 3,000 reached the Phoenix basin, where *c.* 60,000 people already resided (Clark et al. 2019). There, Kayenta settled in separate enclaves and small household clusters and continued their own cultural traditions (Clark et al. 2019; Hegmon et al. 2016). Local communities appear to have seen this as a threat and reacted by building highly visible platform mounds which proclaimed a ritual tradition very different from that of the Kayenta, as well as by concentrating food production in areas that were easier to control (Hill et al. 2004). In addition, there are more fortifications and violent clashes, notably at Point of Pines where a migrant enclave was burnt down (Stone 2003: 59–60), although the overall extent of violence is disputed (Clark et al. 2019; T.A. Rogers et al. 2021: 146–8). It took until *c.* 1325 CE to begin to surmount this rift. One key mechanism was the production by Kayenta potters of highly decorated Salado polychrome vessels (Figure 4.2), which depicted religious symbols valued by both ethnic groups. This ware was used for communal feasts, providing a counterpoint to the hierarchical ritual traditions centred on platform mounds (Borck and Clark 2021; Borck

Figure 4.2 Salado polychrome vessel of the Tonto Polychrome style, dating *c.* 1350–1450 CE; unknown finds location. Height *c.* 20 cm (ASM 2011-272-1; photo: Natalia Gabrielsen; © Arizona State Museum, The University of Arizona).

and Mills 2017). Communal feasting eventually broke down quotidian barriers to interaction as well, resulting in sites with a mixed population. Salado pottery styles became widespread in the Southwest (e.g. Mills et al. 2013), although some communities also deliberately rejected them (Borck and Mills 2017).

Where the Kayenta did not meet with fully established village communities, but arrived while the settlement system was relatively fluid, they were integrated more easily and differences between local and newcomer were subordinated to other social relations, for instance running along age and gender lines (Mills 2007; Stone 2003). The quick and deliberate effacing of differences between newcomers and locals was also achieved after the abandonment of Mesa Verde, when around 20,000 persons relocated to New Mexico, outnumbering the local population (Clark et al. 2019). After the likely institutional collapse and violence in Mesa Verde, migrant groups did not maintain their religious symbolism and the hierarchical social institutions which had so recently failed them. Instead, migrants and locals settled in the same communities and lineage ties were weakened by granting a relatively stronger role to ritual sodalities, which included both migrants and non-migrants (Clark et al. 2019: 274–9). This has also been flagged as an important strategy in other migration scenarios, as it allows for the flexible integration of people of different origins (Bernardini 2011a: 217; Fowles and Eiselt 2019).

As a final example, migration between communities in the Hopi area (e.g. Bernardini 2005; 2011a; 2011b) was a more or less constant process and seen as a spiritually important search for the world centre (Naranjo 1995). The decision to migrate was taken at the level of clan units consisting of several households. These were themselves compositionally unstable, as they coalesced around ritual objects and ceremonies, control of which could pass between various subclans over time, with consequent re-negotiations of membership (Bernardini 2011a: 38–9). A sense of continuity was therefore built around objects, ceremonies and stories, not places. Indeed, those in control of ceremonies and objects could generally negotiate a position of influence in a new community and retained a socially recognized clan identity. Those who did not command such resources embarked upon their journey 'with a much fuzzier idea of who they would be upon arrival' (Bernardini 2011a: 39–40).

Once again, ritual proved an important mechanism of integration, this time distinguishing those with shorter and longer migration histories and creating a sequence of seniority. Clans with long migration histories ('Nùutungkwisinom', meaning 'last people') probably arrived in the area during the fourteenth century. They can be contrasted to the 'Motisinom' (or 'first people'), who are considered the original inhabitants of the Colorado plateau and whose oral traditions of migration histories are less elaborate (Bernardini 2011a: 201; Bernardini and Fowles 2011). These groups had very different ritual priorities. The katsina cult of the Motisinom was 'democratic, public, and benign' (Bernardini and Fowles 2011: 259) – anyone could participate actively and the overarching principle was to stress a simple and co-operative life. In contrast, Nùutungkwisinom clans brought with them elaborate, 'restrictive, esoteric, and dangerously powerful' ritual traditions (Bernardini and Fowles 2011: 259) which allowed ranking according to control over sacred knowledge and arrival sequence. Most positions of spiritual authority at Hopi were thereby filled by Nùutungkwisinom (Bernardini and Fowles 2011: 259). In spite of the inherent inequalities of this system, which may have led to some fissioning (e.g. Fowles 2005), organization into ritual moieties (Figure 4.3) proved a stable strategy that often diffused tensions and facilitated intra-regional mobility (Borck et al. 2015). The central place of migration in oral traditions, alongside the well-established mechanisms for integrating newcomers, also enabled some Pueblo communities to react flexibly to Spanish incursions from the sixteenth century onwards (Trabert 2020).

In such a setting, settlements are at best temporary coagulations of several different clans, each with their own migration histories stretching backwards and forwards in time (Bernardini 2005). Even neighbouring villages could differ markedly in their composition. Although the cumulative effect of migration in the Hopi area is

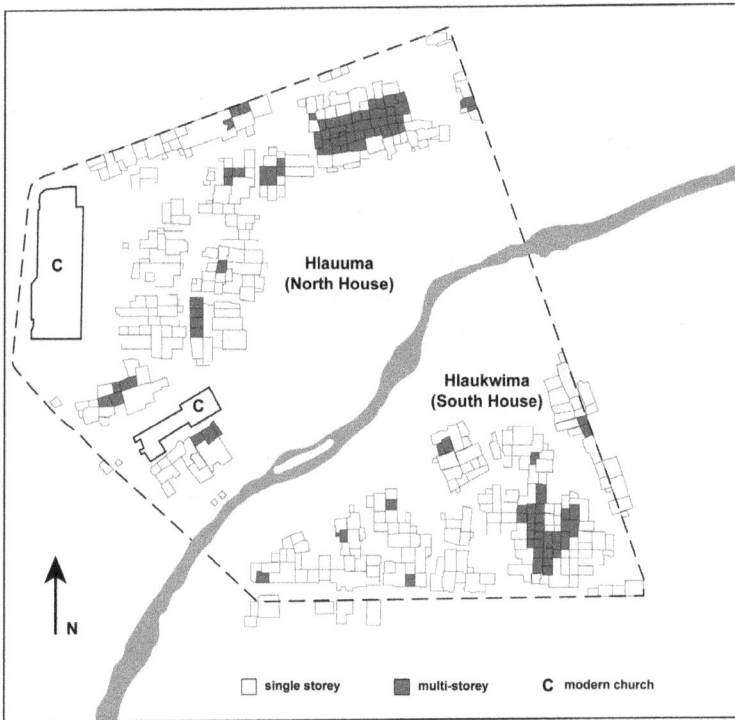

Figure 4.3 Map of Taos Pueblo showing the bipartition of the site into a northern and southern cluster, in this case also defined by a river. These clusters were inhabited by different moieties, integrated through ritual responsibilities (re-drawn after Bernardini and Fowles 2011: fig. 16.2).

considerable, this is not one wave-like, synchronized event for which one unified reason can be found (Bernardini 2005: 34), but rather a series of braided streams, or in Cordell's (1995: 205) words a 'spider web of paths', which divide and recombine multiple times. Bernardini (2011b: 37) has coined the term 'serial migration' to describe this way of life. Movement, as conceptualized by Puebloans today, is not an anomalous occurrence, but an activity essential to life (Fowles and Eiselt 2019: 187–91; Naranjo 1995; Villareal Catanach and Agostini 2019: 229–31).

The US Southwest and Neolithic Europe in dialogue

What can we take away from this case study when approaching migration in the European Neolithic? First, we are faced with Bernardini's (2011b: 13) challenge to write migration narratives that involve fuzzy boundaries crossed in multi-generational, sequential events driven by small-scale, unstable social units. This implies no common reason or purpose to migration, which in turn is not considered an atypical behaviour or last resort. Migrations of this 'braided stream' variety are harder to spot archaeologically, particularly as material culture traits change smoothly if people constantly amalgamate in new combinations (e.g. Cordell 1995: 206). Large-scale horizons of visible change may be the rare tipping points in a continuum of settlement relocation.

Second, new arrivals have to negotiate their position. The resources available for doing so will depend on whether the migration event was triggered by a crisis, was planned, involves a numerically large or a smaller, vulnerable group and so on (Cameron 2013). Successful integration will be facilitated where migrants join culturally similar areas, do not opt to maintain visible expressions of their separate identity and where host communities do not perceive them as a threat (Clark et al. 2019: 279–82). Internally heterogeneous migrant groups with a long history of splitting and recombining also form the networks through which new goods and ideas travel, causing lasting transformation in the host societies.

Third, in all the examples discussed here, shared ceremonies were central strands for integration, an aspect so far relatively neglected in narratives of prehistoric Europe, where ritual and religion are rather considered the domain of aggrandizing social elites (e.g. Hayden 2001; 2014). However, as Spielmann (2002) has pointed out, ritual feasts and exchanges are important for all members of a social group, as they support individual, household and kin projects (marriage, payment of blood debts, funerals etc.). Small-scale societies spend a good deal of surplus on maintaining ritual obligations, often using foodstuffs and other resources specifically produced for these activities years in advance (Spielmann 2002), while checks and balances may be in place to avoid appropriation by elites (e.g. Wiessner 2002).

Interpretative challenges: What makes a community?

If migration events are often decided on at the level of the 'community', and if community relations are central for the integration of migrants, then this relocation of analytical scales comes with its own problems. The community, too, is a fuzzy form of group identity. Communities share space, practices and a sense of mutual belonging but, as the term is used by archaeologists, they tend to be tethered to geographies (cultural and spatial) rather than temporalities. One is not born a community member; one joins. Communities are not innate features of an individual's sense of self and affiliation, but rather an emergent, transient phenomenon of their embodied interaction with others.

Communities are contested in archaeological research. Yaeger and Canuto (2000) provide a brief historiography of the concept in the twentieth century. They outline how, historically, communities have been implicitly treated as homogeneous, conservative, static social units – perhaps divisible into equally static and bounded households – and typically co-resident (see also Pauketat 2000; Souvatzi 2008: 7–30). There is also a danger of idealizing communities as harmonious, intimate and safe (Harris 2014: 77, 87).[1] Instead, Yaeger and Canuto (2000) argue we should treat communities as complex and dynamic, socially constituted, constantly in the process of being shaped by their members (both human and non-human) and based on co-presence, albeit not necessarily co-residence. In their words, a community is an 'ever-emergent social institution that generates and is generated by supra-household interactions that are structured and synchronized by a set of places within a particular span of time' (Yaeger and Canuto 2000: 5).

As with ethnicity, a shared community identity emerges from engagements between members (Harris 2014: 79). However, the two scales need not overlap: an ethnic or kin group may make up a single community or participate in several, just as a community may include people of one or many kin or ethnic groups. A community can contain other communities (neighbourhoods within a town, for example) and an individual can be a member of multiple communities. In contrast to ethnicities, communities do not require an idea of shared origins; they mainly coalesce through daily practices in shared spaces. This means that communities are able to cross-cut (and are themselves cross-cut by) other forms of affiliation, emerging and dissolving without threat to other dimensions of identity. This capacity for ready formation within and across other institutions lies at the heart of the well-known concept of 'communities of practice' (Frieman 2021; Roddick and Stahl 2016; Wenger 1998) – that is, formal or informal groups of practitioners with a shared set of aims, techniques or responsibilities that form to support these activities without necessarily respecting pre-existing institutional structures and hierarchies. This gives communities an element of subversive possibility: existing outside, encompassing or cross-cutting other forms of affiliation, a community may undermine hierarchical structures (e.g. Mehrer 2000).

Archaeologically, tracing fluid and multi-scalar communities is challenging. In how far, for example, are the limits of 'community' coeval with the limits of a settlement site, as opposed to a cluster of sites, or indeed concentrations of households within a site (e.g. Whittle 2003: 70–5)? For Alasdair Whittle (2003: 15–17), the question centres on shared values and affect, a 'moral community' whose members recognize each other as holding key attitudes and practices in common. As with the scale of ethnicity, this places great demands on archaeologists – how is one to recognize values and which are the ones that matter for self-identification? One fruitful starting point is to focus on those strategies that could have created social bonds between people during face-to-face interaction, be this larger-scale events such as feasts, rituals or monumental constructions (e.g. Johnston 2020; Yaeger 2000) or more mundane settings, such as settlement layout or the organization of discard practices (e.g. Birch 2012). In addition, one could trace potential faultlines within aggregations of people, such as increasing inequalities, outbursts of interpersonal violence or tendencies towards settlement fissioning (e.g. Beck 2006; Harris 2014: 81–4; McGuire and Saitta 1996; Whittle 2018: 179–85).

In the case of the US Southwest, therefore, the scale of co-resident communities can be fruitful in analysing migration events – sometimes, entire sites are abandoned more or less simultaneously – but most of the migration ventures described above involved smaller groupings, such as sets of households or those (temporarily) affiliated to a subclan. Focusing simultaneously on the level of community and of its constituent groupings is thus a good way to think through both the tensions that led to frequent out-migration and, at the other end of the journey, the social strategies necessary to integrate newcomers and those already resident at a place.

In many archaeological narratives, the household has taken centre-stage as a building block which makes up larger communities (e.g. Robb 2007; Souvatzi 2008). The household is, effectively, a social and economic unit (more or less bounded) with a key role in social and biological reproduction (Schuster 2023; Yanagisako 2015). This sometimes maps onto the modern concept of a co-resident family, but in practice often incorporates fuzzier and more complex relations and constellations. At the level of the co-resident household, decisions about whether to migrate will be taken based on the perceived benefits, economic or social, to at least some of its members and according to existing social ties to destination communities. This opens another, even wider field of potential variation in reasons for fissioning and re-aggregation. For many of the societies he observed in Africa, for example, Igor Kopytoff (1987: 5) suggested that temporary aggregations of household groups from several communities formed in the interstices of established polities, driven there variously by accusations of witchcraft, defeat in warfare or general dissatisfaction with their situation. Others joined particular communities to avoid aggression and the resulting impoverishment, as Raymond Kelly (1985: 250) has suggested for groups of Dinka fusing with the expansive Nuer. For yet others, and as in the Pueblo case, the multiple reasons for constant relocation may eventually have translated into a general moral equivalence of movement and survival.

To live is to move – the Neolithic in the northern Alpine foreland

In the European Neolithic, the place where the re-thinking of community structures has been pushed furthest is the Alpine foreland. The exceptional waterlogged preservation makes it possible to reconstruct year-by-year biographies for village sites, tracing the establishment, duration and abandonment of structures. This has revealed an extremely high degree of settlement mobility and resulted in extensive discussion on the nature of these Neolithic communities.

Sites established on marshy and boggy ground, as well as in shallow waters and flood-prone areas along lake shores, have been documented all around the Alps, from the Jura mountains in the west to Slovenia in the east. Here, we mostly focus on the north Alpine foreland, where lake village settlements are first attested in the forty-third century denBCE and continue into the Bronze Age. Episodes of intense lake-shore settlement are interrupted by phases with few or no sites, whether for reasons of taphonomy or due to temporary abandonment is still debated (e.g. Billamboz 2001; Heitz et al. 2021: 83–5; Magny et al. 2005a; 2005b; Menotti 2004). Neolithic lake village sites consist of wooden houses of varied size and layout, either with raised floors or constructed on piles. Compared to LBK longhouses, these are flimsy structures requiring constant repairs (e.g. Ebersbach 2010). Houses are generally built close together and little differentiated internally (Figure 4.4). Some sites also have communally maintained architectural features, such as walkways or palisades (e.g. Schlichtherle 2004).

Each house needed repairs after a mere six years or so and had an overall lifespan of only twelve to fifteen years, with sites as a whole rarely lasting more than twenty years (Bleicher 2009: 145–8; Hofmann et al. 2016: 17–18). Site sequences often began with one or two pioneer

Figure 4.4 *a*) Impressions from the reconstructed Schussenried culture village of Taubried at the Federseemuseum, Bad Buchau; *b*) The larger (back) room of one of the Schussenried culture houses (photos: D. Hofmann).

buildings, progressively joined by a few more each year, until a construction boom set in. After this, new houses were built at a reduced pace and some of the earlier ones began to be abandoned (Heitz et al. 2021: 80–1; Hofmann et al. 2016). Sites were therefore constantly growing and shrinking, and houses in various stages of construction and abandonment coexisted (Figure 4.5).

Often, groups of a few houses share economic preferences or specializations (e.g. Dieckmann et al. 2006: 236; Hafner and Suter 2000: 44–56; Strobel 2000: 302; Styring et al. 2016: 101). At Arbon-Bleiche 3 on Lake Constance (3384–3370 denBCE), this created a tight network of mutual exchange and dependencies (e.g. Doppler 2013: 108–88, 215–20; Doppler et al. 2011). Other authors interpret economic and architectural differences as expressions of (hereditary) inequalities (e.g. Bleicher and Harb 2018; Harb et al. 2017; Schlichtherle 2011).

Although there are also indications of longer-term commitments to particular landscapes, such as the multi-generational management of timber resources (e.g. Billamboz and Köninger 2008; Billamboz et al. 2010), the high frequency at which movement happens at the scale of households and household clusters is comparable to the Pueblo migrations sketched above. As in the US Southwest, there could be a variety of reasons for movement, from climatic deterioration to social factors, such as resistance to inequality. Indeed, there are few sites on which differences in layout or activity patterns are replicated over the longer term and several examples (such as Torwiesen or Zurich Parkhaus Opéra, Bleicher and Harb 2018; Schlichtherle 2011; Schlichtherle et al. 2010) where a phase of more marked differences is succeeded by either abandonment or reorganization.

It is difficult to track how far people moved in a particular instance. Where detailed data are available, for example in the Zurich area and along parts of Lake Constance (Bahss and Bleicher 2022; Bleicher and Harb 2018), distances were arguably small, so that access to resources could be maintained. Overall house numbers in a micro-region do vary between phases, so that some outside influx or out-migration are possible (Bleicher and Harb 2018), but most relocations likely happened

Figure 4.5 The development of Arbon-Bleiche 3, canton Thurgau, showing initial establishment by few settlers, construction boom and beginning of abandonment (re-drawn after Doppler 2013: 207 fig. 52).

within a tightly woven network that was facilitated, but not disrupted by the many individual movement episodes. This may have given this system its long-term resilience, both in terms of environmental adaptation (Heitz et al. 2021) and in alleviating potential social friction. The many household units must have negotiated regularly about the establishment of sites, the maintenance of communal resources and the organization of tasks. Where disagreements could not be overcome, dispersal within the region could have ensued, effectively limiting the control of individuals and groups over each other.

Perhaps because of this overarching framework of lake village mobility and the long-term persistence of its overall set-up, actual migration events are rarely discussed. In what follows, we focus on the Mesolithic–Neolithic transition as one situation in which migration occurred and argue that the Neolithization of the Alpine foreland was mainly made possible by fundamental changes in the political structures of earlier Neolithic societies. The resulting permanent fluidity in social relations also had an impact on how the later transformations of the third millennium panned out in the region. Yet in spite of considerable mobility at the individual and household level throughout the sequence, evidence for ritual or cosmological strategies for social integration is conspicuously absent, a fact that can be connected to a specific political style.

The Mesolithic–Neolithic transition of the northern Alpine foreland

The Neolithization of the northern Alpine foreland has often been cast as an example of local adoption by the Mesolithic population, based on for instance continuity in artefacts (such as chipped stone tools; e.g. E. Nielsen 1997; 2004), claims for Mesolithic experimentation with agriculture (e.g. Tinner et al. 2007) and with its own ceramic production possibly inspired by Mediterranean Neolithic traditions (e.g. Kirschneck 2021; Manen and Convertini 2009; Mauvilly et al. 2008; Pétrequin et al. 2009). Finally, the very mobility of lake villages themselves has been seen as a kind of continuity 'in spirit' with a foraging lifestyle (e.g. Stöckli 2016: 82–91; Whittle 2003: 144–5).

However, claims for Mesolithic agriculture have been sharply criticized (Behre 2007) and well-dated macro-remains from otherwise 'Mesolithic' contexts are so far absent (Jacomet and Vandorpe 2022: 11). Also, while new artefacts like pottery exemplify that Mesolithic Alpine groups were well connected, they did not cause widespread economic or social changes. In contrast, the Neolithic as a broad set of transformations across several aspects of life involved many entirely new activities, such as herding, clearance, planting, tending crops, harvesting, building and so on. In these respects, the foreland Neolithic looks no different to adjacent areas of central Europe at this time, where post-Linearbandkeramik developments had resulted in the demise of the longhouse, now replaced by much smaller structures. In addition, a change to shifting cultivation (e.g. Rösch 2005: 116; Schier 2017) and perhaps a greater emphasis on herding (e.g. Geschwinde and Raetzel-Fabian 2009), as well as overall dietary diversification (Asam et al. 2006; Münster et al. 2018; Perutka et al. 2021) all indicate more flexible economic choices than previously. These could have resulted in a geographically widespread pattern of periodic abandonment and re-establishment that was similar to the foreland (e.g. suggested by Seidel 2012; 2017).

These similarities, as well as genetic studies (Furtwängler et al. 2020), make it likely that the beginning of the foreland Neolithic was not solely a matter of the local adoption of selected exogenous traits,[2] but was part of a wider expansion of Neolithic lifeways at this time. Migrant groups now also reached the north European plain, while hitherto more neglected landscape zones, such as wetter areas and uplands, began to be used across central Europe. Compared to earlier phases, this kind of Neolithic must have involved the restructuring of existing social ties and interaction patterns (Klassen 2004). This is a process with deeper roots.

As described above, in the LBK the social position of households is believed to rely on the inheritance of land (e.g. Bentley et al. 2012; Bogaard et al. 2016; but see the discussion in Chapter 6 in the section on 'Consequences for our understanding of migration'), with mobility and migration consequently devalued. In contrast, the expansion into the Alpine foreland involved establishing new sites, driven by the out-migration of small groups of households. As a result, the importance of the house as a monument embodying the success and productivity of its inhabitants was mostly lost. What this means for the groups living in these less substantial buildings has not yet been discussed. Following Bradley Ensor (2021: 116–31) and Václav Hrnčíř and colleagues (2020), who base their arguments on cross-cultural comparisons of house sizes and village layouts, the smaller houses could indicate a larger role for patrilocality. However, this remains difficult to ascertain given the rarity of burials. Also, there are no evident indications that this regularly resulted in inherited status positions or that it limited the connections that household members could entertain to the inhabitants of other buildings or sites. Perhaps this process is best seen as one in which decision-making units became smaller and alliances between them potentially looser, making it easier to break old links and forge new ones. How this worked in detail remains largely unexplored. Spatially, it led to the further spread of a Neolithic way of life, as routine mobility and economic diversification expanded to take in new landscape zones.

If this scenario is correct, then the earliest evidence for settlement of the Alpine foreland should show small pioneer groups of a few households, who fine-tuned existing architectural or economic strategies to succeed in these new landscapes. Indications for this exist from both the southern and northern side of the Alps. Isolated, likely short-stay sites have been documented at Isolino Virginia north of Milan between 4950 and 4700 calBCE (Antolín et al. 2022) and at dryland sites in the Sion area in canton Valais, where pottery similar to that at Isolino has been recovered alongside domestic animal remains and hearths dated between 5200 and 4700 calBCE (Besse and von Tobel 2011: 20). Such low-level occupations are consistent with the initial arrival of small groups, perhaps making use of established networks involving foragers. Several centuries of these more tentative kinds of presence apparently preceded the lake village horizon proper.

North of the Alps, stray finds of LBK, Hinkelstein and Großgartach pottery have been recovered from later lake village locations, as at Hornstaad-Hörnle Ia (Dieckmann 1990: 105), a settlement site and small grave group have been documented near Hegne Abbey (Hald et al. 2020) and there are other isolated graves close to lake shores

(Moinat et al. 2007). The clearest case of a pioneer settlement is Zizerz in the Upper Rhine Valley, fifteen km south of the Swiss–Liechtenstein border and dated to around 4800 BCE (Brombacher and Vandorpe 2012; Seifert 2012). Pottery of a late Hinkelstein or early Großgartach style (Figure 4.6) was found in a dark brown humic layer interspersed with fireplaces and activity zones. There were no recognizable house plans. Local Alpine radiolarite and rock crystal were exploited for making stone tools (but not the *Ölquarzit* used in the Mesolithic) and there are imported lithics from Bavaria and northern Italy. While pottery shape and decoration are northern Alpine, the addition of handles and perforations under the rim are characteristic for contemporary groups further south (Seifert 2012). The cereal assemblage is dominated by barley, but wild plants are also attested (Brombacher and Vandorpe 2012). Four further sites provisionally dated as Epi-Rössen or Rössen and two further Middle Neolithic find spots are also known from the area, but so far uninvestigated.

0   5 cm Zizers, Friedau
                          ZF02_736

Figure 4.6 Zizers-Friedau, canton Grisons. Decorated sherd showing similarities to the south-west German Hinkelstein and Großgartach pottery styles (photo and ©: Archäologischer Dienst Graubünden).

The precise origins of Zizerz's residents are impossible to ascertain and may indeed be mixed, but in the course of interactions at the margins of more established, large-scale culture areas north and south of the Alps, hybrid forms of material culture appeared and patterns of dwelling and interaction changed. In such interstices, there was room to experiment with new ways of living together which may have acted back on the main cultural cores. Eventually, knowledge of potential contact partners in the circum-Alpine area and of its environmental and climatic conditions made it possible to expand ever further.

More and more sites documenting the transformation of economic strategies and architectural traditions are coming to light (e.g. Dieckmann et al. 1997; 2017; Hald et al. 2020; Rigert et al. 2005; Wegmüller et al. 2022: 359). The earliest attested Neolithic wetland settlements in the northern Alpine foreland therefore had roots in the societies of the Early and Middle Neolithic of central Europe, for whom the migration of households and groups of households had long formed a viable strategy, but had mostly involved similar kinds of landscapes. Initial colonization events in the Alps, in contrast, required greater adaptability, but also exposed migrants to new contacts and ways of life, in this case of a western or Mediterranean inspiration. In this dynamic interaction, and in line with wider transformations in central Europe as a whole, new ways of organizing communities were developed, which emphasized household-scale mobility further, creating the flexibility to cope with this new environment. This in turn enabled the large-scale settlement of the northern Alpine foreland in the second half of the fifth millennium BCE. In the longer term, the social structures created during these migration events cemented the role of mobility as a social strategy, which in this case helped to counter the creation of lasting social inequalities. This, however, required further transformations.

Moving against hierarchy?

Above, we have suggested that an increasing flexibility in economic adaptations and a change in the character of mobility enabled pioneer groups to migrate into unfamiliar territories, where new contacts then drove further change, making lake villages a phenomenon with multiple roots. Yet beyond domestic architecture and economy, what increasingly distinguishes the Alpine foreland Neolithic from that of adjacent areas is the radical toning down of potential axes of distinction, whether this involves lavish burials, prestige goods, feasting or monuments (see also Whittle 2003: 148). We will look at each of these points in turn.

Predating the lake villages, cist-grave cemeteries of the Chamblandes tradition were established from the first half of the fifth millennium, initially in the southern and western Alpine region and then spreading north- and eastwards (Steuri et al. 2023), but they faded in popularity when lake villages became numerous (Baudais et al. 2007; Beeching 2007: 71). While the idea of cist graves has precursors south of the Alps, other aspects such as body positions and the range of grave goods follow northern Alpine practices (Beeching 2007: 73; Degasperi et al. 2006; Steuri and Hafner 2022). The Chamblandes tradition therefore integrated stimuli from a broader interaction zone. Importantly, however, conspicuous single burials remain the exception. For instance, the male in grave 12 at Lenzburg was buried with two arrowheads, several bone tools, a knife, a rock crystal blade, a necklace of five dog teeth, a bone comb and some burnt human and animal bone (Wyss 1998: 64). Yet this burial did not form the starting point for a succession of similarly marked individuals in what could be interpreted as a hereditary hierarchy. In fact, it is the only one that did not attract further inhumations in the same cist. While there is site-based variation, the general trend is from more individual to more collective interments (Abegg et al. 2021: 4), later culminating in small dolmens in the western parts of Switzerland (e.g. Bleuer et al. 2012: 236–7).

Outside the Chamblandes zone, pre-Corded Ware burials are archaeologically virtually invisible, being limited to stray bones recovered from settlement sites (e.g. Harb et al. 2017: 246; Ulrich-Bochsler 2017) and the so far unique unfurnished Horgen culture cremations retrieved from post structures at Singen near Lake Constance (Hald et al. 2016).[3] The dolmen of Oberbipp in canton Bern, the easternmost such structure in Switzerland, is also associated with Horgen material culture. The people buried here (forty-two individuals of all ages and both sexes) showed no sex-based differences in diet and most came from the local or at most regional area. Compared to other regions, like the Jura, there was a strong reliance on plant consumption, and grave goods remain modest. All this suggests use by a small, local community which was not very differentiated internally (Lösch et al. 2020; Siebke et al. 2020).

This stands in contrast to developments further north, for instance in the Münchshöfen and Michelsberg cultures of southern Germany, where human remains were deposited as single and multiple interments and as scattered or partial remains (e.g. Meixner 2009; Nickel 1997). In particular, the deposition of manipulated human remains in storage pits and enclosure ditches has been used to argue for a strongly hierarchical society with captives and slaves (e.g. Gronenborn 2001; 2016; Lefranc et al. 2017; but see Hofmann 2022). All this is entirely absent from the Alpine foreland.

Similarly, there are few deposits of objects that could be interpreted as restricted status items, such as copper or polished stone artefacts. The few examples that have been retrieved – for instance the green serpentinite axe with decorated shaft from Cham-Eslen (Gross-Klee and Hochuli 2002), carefully crafted bows (Bahss and Bleicher 2022: 15) or the Hornstaad copper disc (Klassen 2010) – have come from cultural layers between or near buildings and cannot be attributed to a specific structure, nor does their context provide indications for deposition in the course of public ritual displays. The same is true of personal ornaments. Showier items, such as limestone bead necklaces or boar-tusk pectorals, are limited to the very early lake village horizon, with an impressive assemblage from Hornstaad (Heumüller 2009: 207–30). Over time, there is a shift towards perforated carnivore teeth (including dog, wolf and bear) and items such as fruit stones, generally found scattered across settlement layers (Hafner and Suter 2003: 19–22, 40, 50, 55–6; Maréchal et al. 1998). Copper, shell or other imported materials are virtually never used.

Finally, there are few monuments. The known western Swiss dolmens are small and never develop into passage graves or larger complexes (Moinat and Stöckli 1995). Enclosures, a staple of Neolithic life since Linearbandkeramik times, are absent. The few palisades surrounding villages are a far cry from the impressive earthworks constructed for instance at Michelsberg or Altheim culture sites (M. Meyer and Raetzel-Fabian 2006). There is also no evidence for the lavish destruction of pottery in the course of communal feasting, as has been tentatively identified in southern Germany (e.g. Hofmann 2022; Hofmann and Husty 2019). Rather, Christian Harb and colleagues (2017: 253) evoke the image of the large, undecorated coarse ware pots constantly bubbling on the fire for shared meals, but without any of the social display or special foods usually associated with competitive feasting (Kassabaum 2019).

Indeed, there are hardly any communal arenas of any sort, such as plazas or meeting houses where group solidarity could be created or distinctions reinforced. At Ludwigshafen-Seehalde and Sipplingen on Lake Constance, clothed female figures with three-dimensionally modelled breasts had been painted onto the walls of one building (Schlichtherle 2010); it is unclear whether 'regular' dwelling activities were also carried out in these houses. The motifs painted on and between these female figures, such as suns and tree-like motifs, are not restricted and are for instance also found on statue stelae, or on pottery (Harb et al. 2017: 251), so there is no indication of secret esoteric knowledge being monopolized by particular households. At Marin les Piécettes on Lake Neuchâtel, a building without regular occupation traces on an artificially raised area at the centre of the site may have functioned as a meeting place (Honegger 2005; 2007). However, buildings of this sort remain extremely rare, never reach monumental proportions and were constructed only at particularly large and/or long-lived sites, where they could have been needed to prevent the ubiquitous tendency to fissioning (Hofmann 2013).

Compared to contemporary societies elsewhere, then, the communities of the Alpine foreland seemingly underwent a process of progressive restriction of status display arenas. Differences between households and household groups did exist, notably in economic orientation or in access to certain goods, but whether these can be interpreted as socio-economic inequalities remains uncertain (Bahss and Bleicher 2022) and in any case these were not long-lasting or strictly institutionalized. Instead, the Neolithization of the Alpine foreland went hand in hand with an almost total suppression of marked forms of differentiation, as well as defined arenas for public gathering.

In light of the expectations derived from our Pueblo case study, this is surprising. Granted, in both cases migration can be connected to diminishing levels of hierarchy. Also, while migrations in the southwestern US covered longer distances than in the Alpine foreland, the composition of sites was fluid in both cases. However, for the lake villages we are missing any obvious mechanisms of integration, of fusing together people of diverse origins and migration histories. One possible explanation is that after the initial settlement of the Alpine foreland, movement became regionally more tightly circumscribed, so that people no longer needed to negotiate their position at a 'new' place. Another possibility is that mobility as a social strategy reduced the kinds of situations in which any existing differences in prestige or material wealth could be flaunted – if confronted by too obvious displays, people could 'vote with their feet' (Beck 2006; Rosenberg and Rocek 2019), even if such changes of residence did not cover large distances.

In contrast, at an individual level, migration crossing the boundaries of material culture areas was still taking place. For instance, pottery from different cultural traditions often coexists on the same site (De Capitani 2002: 209–16; Gross 2017; Heitz 2017: 261; Schröter 2009: 231–8; Stapfer 2017: 143–5, 157). As true 'imports' are rare, only detailed studies of pottery shapes, decorative motifs, clay sources and paste recipes (e.g. Stapfer 2017) can trace the complex combinations of different traits into 'hybrid' vessels that cannot be unequivocally assigned to one or the other culture grouping (see also Gross 2017). Such vessels embody a history of mobility: they were made either by persons who had travelled far and for long enough to learn how to produce pottery in new styles, or by people who, albeit using local materials, had originally been socialized in a different technological tradition (Heitz 2017: 282). At the Cortaillod culture settlement of Concise-sous-Colachoz (overall occupation in several phases between 3868–3516 denBCE; Burri 2007; Ebersbach et al. 2017; Stapfer 2017: 146–54), several of the tightly dated settlement horizons (generally covering a decade or less) see an influx of non-local pottery traditions. However, immediately adjacent households share clay paste compositions, even if they produce pottery of dissimilar styles. One possible interpretation is that potters cooperated during crucial production steps, in spite of their divergent traditions, creating new, hybrid combinations. Yet these did not result in lasting stylistic change (Burri 2007; Ebersbach et al. 2017: 7–8).

There are many other examples of translocal connections, involving plants, lithics, new technologies like wheeled vehicles and new ways of doing things (e.g. Dieckmann et al. 2016; Hafner et al. 2016; Harb and Bleicher 2017: 254–5). Together, these links formed a broader network of connections that kept relocations at the household level a realistic possibility – after all, one had ties elsewhere.

This system remained remarkably stable in spite of several short-term oscillations in terms of economic and material culture preferences. Even the arrival of Corded Ware ceramic styles did not fundamentally impact daily life beyond pottery production (Ebersbach et al. 2017). The cultural openness of the Alpine foreland network eventually led to the introduction of more transformative novelties, but only in the longer term. At the transition between the twenty-sixth and twenty-fifth centuries BCE, a wooden chamber containing the remains of at least twelve individuals was built at Spreitenbach in canton Aargau (Figure 4.7). It continues regional, south-west German and northern Swiss traditions of burial, contributing to a highly diverse picture even in Corded Ware times (Besse et al. 2012: 274–81; Bleuer et al. 2012: 264). The deceased shared a uniform diet and did not move far beyond the region during their lifetimes (Knipper et al. 2012). It is only with the arrival of Bell Beaker cultural traditions that there is more marked change, at least locally. In western Switzerland, sites like Sion Petit-Chasseur see the construction of groups of megaliths, which around 2600–2400 BCE are associated with new pottery technologies and increased personal mobility (e.g. Derenne et al. 2022), but such monumental complexes remain restricted geographically. Elsewhere, there was a shift in the preferred landscape niches used for grazing and agriculture (Lechterbeck et al. 2014). Soon after, the lake village way of life was abandoned. In contrast, the genetic evidence (Furtwängler et al. 2020: 4) shows that a larger-scale influx of steppe signatures begins before these changes and is followed by a long phase of resurgence of 'Neolithic' signatures and slow admixture over centuries.

The arrival of new burial rites and means of ritual expression may therefore in some regions have temporarily destabilized a centuries-old system that relied on a moral community based on the near-total suppression of visible expressions of difference. However, this is not a

Figure 4.7 The collective burial at Spreitenbach, canton Aargau, in its last phase of deposition (reproduced from Doppler *et al.* 2012: 303, © Kantonsarchäologie Aargau).

development that pitches 'migrant' against 'local'. Rather, in analogy with the Pueblo example, this could have served as a means of integrating mixed populations around new symbols of power (see also Derenne et al. 2022: 949), eventually creating genetically mixed populations – but also new avenues for distinction that ultimately led to the demise of the lake village settlement system.

Casting the Neolithic of the Alpine foreland through the lens of the Pueblo migrations has thus opened up new interpretative possibilities. We can now envisage a more explicit role for social strategies of mobility and mobile cosmologies, rather than exclusively environmental adaptations. The absence of clear arenas for communal ceremony and of ritual strategies of integration through much of the Alpine sequence does stand out, and was perhaps partly conditioned by the much smaller cultural differences that were encountered in most Alpine mobility settings. When ritual foci finally emerge, they are connected to new social formations. The resolution of the Alpine foreland evidence has also suggested that reasons to migrate were at least occasionally based on individual decisions and priorities which could differ in detail. Archaeologically, appreciating such very small-scale decisions is a challenge. Yet this scale of analysis may be particularly salient in situations of frontiers, migration and change, where established norms and behaviours may be disrupted and various alternatives emerge concurrently. It is to such scenarios that we turn next.

5

Mobile People

Interactions at the Small Scale

Frontier translators in the Americas

The destabilizing effects of European expansion into the Americas and Australia constitute one of the main – if largely implicit – inspirations for the way prehistoric migrations have been written about (see Chapter 2, in the section 'why do we talk about migration the way we do?'). Here, we focus in particular on the consequences that situations of cultural encounter and migration can have on gender relations, with subsequent re-negotiation of tasks, roles and autonomy. The narrowness of suggested gender relations is one aspect that has been repeatedly criticized for narratives of third-millennium BCE central Europe, where female agency is often seen as curtailed and women allegedly moved mainly to fulfil male power strategies (e.g. Kristiansen et al. 2017; for criticism see e.g. Bickle 2020; Frieman and Hofmann 2019; Frieman et al. 2019; Nash 2012). In contrast, Catherine Cameron (2013) has traced how the fate of captive women in small-scale societies can comprise anything from servitude to eventual acceptance as members of their new communities (for instance through marriage or adoption, e.g. Halbmayer 2004), to which these women contribute significant new skills and knowledge. In this chapter, we trace what opportunities existed during the highly disruptive colonial projects of the Spanish, French and English presence in the Americas. Armed with the kinds of actions that were possible to people even in these extreme settings, we can suggest alternative trajectories also for Neolithic Europe.

Among the best-known examples of captive and displaced persons
in the colonial Americas are translators who assisted early explorers,
traders and conquerors in their various endeavours. The role of
translator was open to both men and women, and indeed some of the
captives taken in early encounters by Columbus and others were
abducted with the express goal of training them as translators
(Greenblatt 1991: 106–7, 140; Ruiz Rosendo and Persaud 2016: 12–14).
Communication between indigenous peoples and newcomers was
fraught with possible misunderstandings (Greenblatt 1991: 89–102;
Merrell 1999: 182–202). While language eventually became a tool of
empire, imposing new patterns of thought and new cultural dependencies
(Greenblatt 1992: 16–39), in early encounters much depended on
translators, whom early colonists had no choice but to trust. Yet
frequently, these individuals pursued their own agendas, warning their
interlocutors against colonial vanguards, plotting against their captors
and escaping at the earliest opportunity (e.g. Greenblatt 1991: 108, 140).

Because of their adaptability and relative ease at learning new
languages, initially many translators were children. In the early part of
the sixteenth century, when Christianization of the conquered peoples
of New Spain began in earnest, Franciscan friars specifically removed
elite children to newly established schools to teach them Spanish and
Latin (as well as learning Native languages from them) and to
instrumentalize them in the missionary effort. Anna Maria D'Amore
and colleagues (2016) draw attention to the complex ideas concerning
the nature of divine power, salvation of the soul and so on that these
children were asked to translate, requiring not just in-depth knowledge
of highly abstract vocabulary in two languages, but a reframing of
unfamiliar ideas into understandable concepts. This process was fraught
with difficulties of communication, misunderstandings and emergent
hybrid readings, and sometimes resulted in rejection and violence
when these children returned to their natal communities. The use of
children and adolescents as cultural go-betweens continued throughout
the settler period, also in the US and Canada, where the forcible removal
of children to schools was an explicit strategy to break Indigenous

cultural continuity (e.g. Castañeda 1998: 238). The role of children in language brokering – translating and interpreting for their migrant parents in official situations from medical check-ups to legal controversies – remains to this day and can destabilize traditional expectations of gender or age roles in the child's original and/or host society (e.g. Bauer 2016; Faulstich Orellana et al. 2003).

However, it is particularly indigenous female translators who, in the absence of detailed historical sources (see also Ruiz Rosendo and Persaud 2016: 2), have attained a semi-mythical status. Between the sixteenth and eighteenth centuries,[1] several of them transgressed gender norms, often both in their society of origin and in settler societies. Well-known examples are La Malinche/Malintzin, an enslaved Nahua noblewoman who played a key role in Cortés' conquest of Mexico (Karttunen 1994: 1–43; Valdeón 2013), John Knight's translator Thanadeltur, a former slave who enabled exploration journeys north of the Hudson Bay Company's Fort York (Clarkson 2021), Sacajawea, an enslaved woman who accompanied Lewis and Clark on their 1805–6 expedition from the Missouri River to the Pacific (Karttunen 1994: 23–45), or the chief's daughter Pocahontas, who eventually travelled to and died in England in 1617 (e.g. Khelifa 2017; Rountree 2005). Many of these women were children or in their early teens when their interactions with settler societies began. At a time when hard boundaries between a unified 'indigenous' and a unified 'settler' identity had not yet emerged, and when alliances may still have been perceived as beneficial, their skill in negotiating unclear and ambivalent situations gained them positions of influence in spite of all restrictions, (gendered) power imbalances and violent encounters of the frontier.

This degree of fluidity was enabled by the particular historical conditions of the frontier at this time, which – in spite of the havoc wrought by disease and incipient economic exploitation – had not yet solidified into the nineteenth-century pattern of ruthless expansionism and forced removal (Cayton and Teute 1998; Mattioli 2017: 33–78). To examine one situation in detail, the Great Lakes area and adjacent regions were part of the 'Pays d'en haut', an area with scattered French settlement geared towards fur exploitation and, in contrast to British-dominated settlement areas, characterized by mixed marriages and multi-ethnic communities. Although some of these sites were the product of temporary alliances by the survivors of raids and epidemics, the situation stabilized somewhat after the 1690s, when inter-racial marriage between French and Native American individuals also became more common (White 1991: 14–50, 69). Still, this 'middle ground', as Richard White (1991) terms it, was characterized by complicated and conflicting loyalties, as different interest groups both within Native American societies and among the French settlers drew on different allies and loyalties, creating 'an evolving cultural logic that sprang from convergences, some accidental, some quite close, of two different cultural systems', neither of them internally homogeneous, 'faced with a common set of problems' (White 1991: 92).[2]

This broader region was home to the famous French-Algonquian translator Madame Montour (1667–1752; Delâge 2006; Hirsch 2000). Her biography bears many of the hallmarks of uprootedness and dislocation of other frontier translators, although it remains uncertain whether she was ever taken captive (Hirsch 2000: 82). As a fluent speaker of French, several Native languages and eventually English, she became a trusted and influential go-between for colonial authorities. Many of the events in Madame Montour's life, such as her decision to transfer her loyalties from the French to the English, were founded in personal experiences and relations (Hirsch 2000), but it was also a specific political and social landscape that made the realignments possible.

At this time, multilingualism was widespread, as especially Native women and children moved between groups due to marriage, adoption or capture (Hirsch 2000: 111). While absolute numbers are hard to come by, celebrated cases like that of Eunice Williams, a seven-year-old minister's daughter who was abducted by Mohawk warriors in 1704, can serve as illustration. Mohawk warriors frequently kidnapped outsiders to stand in for deceased relatives. Consequently, Eunice was fully adopted into the community, where she eventually married and became the head of a matriclan. Although she had several occasions to do so, she never rejoined New England settler society (Strong 2001: 472–3; for an example from a

Spanish colonial context, see Greenblatt 1991: 140–1). As Strong (2001: 471) points out, such acts of 'adoption' were thus both violent and generative of new kin relationships. In contrast to the much later practice of forcibly removing Native children to state boarding schools (Strong 2001) and to the prevailing modern Western view that adoption entails the severing of blood ties, this wider idea of adoption as expanding networks of kin is, in many societies, one of the primary means of establishing ties of mutual amity between groups (Gailey 2019; papers in Bowie 2004) – even where the initial experience of abduction was traumatic.

The seventeenth to early nineteenth centuries also saw the establishment of several multi-ethnic towns, with and without European residents, in what is now the eastern US (e.g. Hirsch 2000: 88; Levine 2020: 56–7). Murphy (1998) recounts the fate of Creole towns between Lake Michigan and the Mississippi in which French-Canadian fur trappers resided with their mostly Native wives of diverse backgrounds. Such marriages necessitated cultural negotiations, for example concerning different ideas regarding female sexual freedom (e.g. White 1991: 63–74) and the allocation of gendered tasks. The latter was unproblematic where European and Native ideas coincided, as when classifying sugar making as a largely female occupation (Murphy 1998: 277–9). In contrast, tasks such as milking and breadmaking were women's work in European communities, but unfamiliar to and often unloved by Indigenous women. Therefore, outside help was hired where possible, or these products were simply bought in (Murphy 1998: 279–83). Living in multi-ethnic towns thus required a degree of linguistic and cultural flexibility, with both Europeans and Indigenous inhabitants interested in finding mutually acceptable solutions. Gender roles were an integral part of this and women were important cultural mediators (Merrell 1998: 27; Murphy 1998: 275).[3]

This also concerns new spiritual ideas, as exemplified by contacts between female Moravian missionaries and Native women. In contrast to other denominations, Moravians – at least from the 1740s to the 1770s – were convinced that conversion should proceed through example, not preaching. Moravian husband-and-wife missionary couples lived in majority Native settlements for extended periods, sharing daily routines with locals and conversing with them on spiritual and quotidian matters. Female missionaries were crucial, as only women could build a lasting spiritual bond with other women (Faull 2019: 104–6; Richwine 2022). By sharing in daily tasks, helping Native women through the grief at the loss of a child, blessing crops and exchanging gifts, Moravians like Jennetje Mack (Figure 5.1) and Anna Margarethe Bechtel built up considerable linguistic skills and became some of the most successful missionaries of their time (Faull 2019).

Figure 5.1 Eighteenth-century portrait of Anna (Jennetje) Mack, one of the Moravian missionaries living in Shamokin. Painted by Johann Valentin Haidt; oil on canvas, 64.5 × 49.5 cm (Painting Collection (PC) 50, Moravian Archives, Bethlehem, PA).

Cultural negotiation also came with its darker sides. Moravian strategies of integration were far less successful where Native girls attended boarding school in majority Moravian communities (Lengvarsky 2009: 58–80). Similarly, at the multi-ethnic and multilingual town of Shamokin, where Madame Montour spent the latter part of her life, the resident Iroquois, Delawares and Tutelos and many of the Native and European traders that regularly passed through were susceptible to excessive alcohol consumption, resulting in violent confrontations, threats and disturbances (Merrell 1998; 1999: 87). As the town was primarily a trading and meeting place without extensive resources, the situation was often exacerbated by food shortages (Merrell 1998: 28). For instance, Madame Montour's daughter-in-law resented having to share her meagre stores with the Moravians, although tensions between a daughter-in-law from a matrilocal tradition having to reside in a patrilocal setting may also have had a role to play (Hirsch 2000: 108). Between the various Native groups, accusations of witchcraft were rife, while European missionaries and fur traders attempted to sabotage one another's plans (Merrell 1998: 25).

Undoubtedly, the extent of cultural diversity, the periodic breakdown of order and the linguistic patchwork at Shamokin could be unsettling. Famously, the Moravian missionary Martin Mack referred to the place as 'the very seat of the Prince of darkness' (Richwine 2022: 82). Nevertheless, Shamokin played a crucial role in regional geography for some time, becoming amongst others the residence of the Oneida go-between and diplomat Shikellamy in 1742 (Merrell 1999: 45). As James Merrell (1998: 21) puts it, it provided 'the enduring pull of disorder and the enticing prospect of an altogether new order, a fragile rearrangement of disparate peoples'.

In the end, however, culturally mixed towns did not form the template on which the subsequent history of colonialism was built (e.g. Mattioli 2017). As more and more European settlers moved in, there was less incentive to create lasting personal relations with Native residents. For instance, the lead mining boom of southern Wisconsin and northern Illinois attracted mostly young, single Anglophone males aiming to make as much money as they could and then settle elsewhere. This disinterest in longer-term commitments caused increased violence against Native men and particularly women (as is still the case in comparable situations today, see e.g. Grisafi 2020). Tensions were brought to an end only when the army moved in to quell Native unrest, ending with the eviction of the resident Native inhabitants by the colonial authorities (Murphy 1998: 287–300). A similar fate befell Shamokin (Merrell 1998: 29–59), while the mixed settlement established by Madame Montour's son Andrew – an official translator and negotiator in his own right – eventually had its residents evicted (Merrell 1999: 299–301). In these cases, attempts at creating cultural homogeneity proceeded by force and/or through substantial institutional support. Alongside the imposition of a more unified Anglophone culture among the colonists (e.g. Erben 2019; Lengvarsky 2009: 87) and more restrictive viewpoints regarding female missionaries (Richwine 2022: 76), this created the more rigid, segregated and ideologically charged frontier conditions of the nineteenth century (e.g. Cayton and Teute 1998).

For several generations, then, and in spite of considerable disruptions and violence wrought on Indigenous societies, what is now the eastern US was a patchwork in almost every aspect of life – settlement patterns, languages, economic activities, gender, religious ideas and views on kinship were all open to negotiation. The cultural hegemony of one subset of the settler population only came about through strong state and military support. In a prehistoric setting, structural conditions of experimentation, accommodation and hybridization can be expected to have lasted longer and to leave traces in the archaeological record. Particularly quotidian negotiations, during which intercultural relations were transported to the personal level, could have resulted in greater motivation to find workable compromises.

The Great Lakes and the European Neolithic in dialogue: the spread of Indo-European languages

In Neolithic Europe, perhaps as a remaining hang-up of the culture concept, those sharing a set number of material culture traits are generally also assumed to speak the same, or at least closely connected languages, an issue most explicitly discussed for the arrival of Indo-European languages. Yet this is unlikely to give the full picture. For example, the Iban longhouse communities on Borneo typically consist of dozens of one-roomed apartments occupied by individual households, which together form the longhouse. Communities are a product of countless episodes of fissioning, migration and re-aggregation of people, which means that people speaking quite different languages end up living together in the same longhouse and sharing in everything from routine tasks to important ritual events (Metcalf 2010: 69–72). Peter Metcalf (2010: 71) has coined the term 'speech communities' for these polyglot aggregations. In a historical setting, the frequent integration of captives from various other linguistic groups into the expanding Iban longhouse societies (e.g. Bellwood 2013: 12) would have contributed to this linguistic heterogeneity. For his own recent fieldwork, Metcalf has described his impressions of longhouse festivals, when there was 'lively discussion, full of good-natured interruptions, going on in a babel of excited voices, with simultaneous translation for the less adroit' (Metcalf 2010: 73).

Mechanisms for the integration of people speaking different languages most likely also existed in prehistory and must have involved individuals picking up new languages. Yet this remains poorly theorized even for Indo-European languages, whose spread is closely connected to third-millennium migrations. 'Linguistic palaeontology', i.e. the idea that things and concepts shared by all branches of a given language family must have been invented and familiar to speakers before any daughter languages emerged, was instrumental in suggesting a steppe origin for Indo-European some time after the mid fourth millennium, based on words associated with wheeled transport, horses and so on (see Anthony 2007; 2019; Anthony and Brown 2017: 32–7; Anthony and Ringe 2015; Mallory 1989; Pereltsvaig and Lewis 2015: 168–79). Fixing the geographical origin of Proto-Indo European (the root language of most contemporary European and some central and south Asian languages) was somewhat more difficult. Shared roots of words denoting common animal and plant species, suggested borrowings from other languages and so on, seem consistent with a steppe origin (Pereltsvaig and Lewis 2015: 182–202), although the precise area of origin remains disputed and perhaps ultimately unknowable.[4]

Recent models work on the assumption that Indo-European was imposed on an earlier Neolithic substrate in the course of military defeats and (sometimes forced) intermarriages with males of steppe origin (e.g. Kristiansen et al. 2017). These are said to have spread as part of a 'mass migration' (Haak et al. 2015) originating in the area of the Yamnaya culture. This suggestion has been moderated only slightly by the historical linguists Asya Pereltsvaig and Martin Lewis (2015: 208–13), who propose that any expansion out of the steppes would involve populations with a mainly pastoralist mode of life moving into areas largely populated by settled agriculturalists. In such a situation, agriculturalists would be more numerous, but nomadic pastoralists would be healthier (having a diet richer in protein, being able to move when resources are depleted and avoiding many water-borne diseases), leading to population increase and territorial expansion. Where this takes them into areas settled by agriculturalists, they would take over landscape niches (rough grasslands, open forests…) not heavily used by the farmers and from there raid the stock of their sedentary neighbours and acquire 'local wives, concubines, and female slaves, imposing their language on them' (Pereltsvaig and Lewis 2015: 213). The result would be a kind of enforced bilingualism, with the more prestigious language of the pastoralists eventually winning out.

The linguistic merits of this research notwithstanding, there are two main axes of criticism: linguistic method, and categorical opposition of societies. First, there is persistent and increasing scepticism surrounding the possibility of identifying a specific Indo-European homeland (e.g. Simon 2008). Proto-Indo-European language is pieced together from later derivatives and should not be equated with a language that really existed (Zimmer 2006: 191), but the methodological consequences of this are often not sufficiently considered. It is by no means clear whether the individual reconstructed elements can all be traced back to an area of common language and a single point in time (Schmitt 2000: 388; Seebold 2000: 410–11) and whether linguistic reconstruction therefore reflects a historical reality at all (e.g. Mallory and Adams 2006: 50–3; Untermann 1985: 148–50). Previous attempts to identify the Proto-Indo-European homeland by linguistic means have suggested everything between the Rhine and the Hindu Kush (see e.g. Dressler 1965; Simon 2008; Zimmer 1990b). As Wolfgang Dressler observes, '[w]hen important scholars obtain diametrically opposed results from the same material ... one question becomes paramount: the question of method' (Dressler 1965: 26). This question remains unresolved (Simon 2008). Proto-Indo-European language is a purely linguistic construct that has so far resisted methodologically and theoretically sound adaptation by other disciplines. Rüdiger Schmitt (2000: 389–90) therefore urgently warns against the unrestrained mixing of linguistic with archaeological and physical anthropological evidence – genetics, which he did not have in mind at the time, should be included here.

Part of the problem may lie in the near-exclusive use of branching tree diagrams, which visually suggest a clear origin point. As Jean-Paul Demoule (2023: 448) summarizes, the predictable branching of one language from another as part of gradual evolution is but one possible model, and has been particularly popular because it lends itself to ideas of original communities of speakers communicating in a unified language in an original homeland. These ideas fitted the nineteenth-century political conceptions that dominated when linguistics emerged as a discipline. They have gained renewed popularity because tree-like diagrammatic representations of linguistic branching look enticingly like aDNA trees (Demoule 2023: chapters 1–8). However, many of the core tenets of the tree-like branching model for Indo-European – that Indo-Europeans were conquerors imposing their language without any influence from the substrate, for example – are difficult to independently substantiate (Demoule 2023: 395–441), while statistical approaches and coding decisions have also come in for methodological criticism (e.g. J. Campbell 2008; Laks 2008; Pereltsvaig and Lewis 2015: 127; Robb

1991). Indeed, more recent models focus on longer-term and braided histories of the spread of Indo-European languages, including several episodes of dispersal over time (Heggarty *et al.* 2023).

In the current debate, an unrestrained mixing of genetic data with linguistic reconstructions and archaeological evidence has occurred, which James Mallory and Douglas Adams (2006: 454) diagnose as selective amnesia, suppressing everything that contradicts one's own statements. In this way, a seemingly conclusive and compelling chain of argument is created that overstrains the underlying data. We currently still lack both the methodological tools and the theoretical understanding to reconcile the evidence from genetics, linguistics and archaeology, and cannot therefore reliably evaluate hypotheses such as the expansion of Indo-European languages from the steppes at a particular time. As several reasonably probable assertions are progressively based on each other, each bringing their own disciplinary problems of method and theory, the degree of probability that the model is correct decreases with each step (e.g. Dressler 1965: 34).

Second, the model suffers from the potential weakness that it too neatly opposes a 'Corded Ware pastoralist' and a 'Neolithic sedentary farming' way of life, which can then be ordered hierarchically. For the third millennium in Europe, we are dealing with a highly variable situation in which societies with different degrees and forms of settlement mobility existed across the continent and came into contact (Furholt 2021). Moreover, it is far from certain whether out-migration from the steppes ever was 'wave-like', and alternative scenarios are worth considering. For example, Raymond Kelly's (1985) account of Nuer territorial expansion stresses that this was the result of a bridewealth system in which inflationary increases in the amount of cattle to be paid for a wife fuelled seasonal raids against neighbouring Dinka communities, destabilizing the food supply. Affected communities would either retreat, or themselves become members of a Nuer tribal segment through intermarriage or adoption. Instead of an inexorable wave of advance, Nuer expansion was driven by the local fall-out of social demands (the need for cattle to support individuals' and kin groups' marriage strategies) and by the decision of Dinka groups on how best to deal with this situation. As a result, pockets of Nuer and Dinka settlement existed as patchworks in immediate proximity to each other, with Dinka in the long run tending to be assimilated into Nuer society (Kelly 1985: 32).

Such patchwork scenarios open up interesting alternatives for how languages could have spread in prehistoric settings. Even if migration was one of the main factors driving linguistic change in Final Neolithic Europe, we do not need to reconstruct this process as wave-like, i.e. fast and all-encompassing from the beginning. It could instead also be conceptualized in terms of 'pockets' of language change, interspersed within a substrate of the many diverse, pre-Indo European languages of the Neolithic (Iversen 2019: 91). A series of smaller and medium-scale migration events of relatively mobile pastoralists would have led, at least initially, to such a more fragmented linguistic picture, not to wholesale replacement. The motivation to then switch permanently could be associated with status differences, or with simple expedience, as languages spoken over wider areas facilitate interaction (Pereltsvaig and Lewis 2015: 212). Today, languages disappear for a variety of reasons – for example as small speech communities are integrated into larger ones, or because one language is perceived as more socially advantageous than another (Evans 2022: 212, 215) – but a situation of multi-generational overlap between several languages is still common. Many adults in areas of high linguistic diversity speak between three to seven languages fluently (Evans 2022: 213).

A scenario of pervasive bi- or multilingualism (Comrie 2008: 60) and mutual influences, coupled with the absence of effective methods for imposing linguistic coherence (such as state schooling), would have resulted in multiple regional and local divergences. Processes of this kind have been documented in the emergence of mixed and Creole languages, although there are few examples in which these initial stages have been directly observed and analysed by linguists (McConvell and Meakins 2005; O'Shannessy 2019: 323). In the case of the emergence of Light Warlpiri (a mixture between English Kriol and Warlpiri) in modern-day Australia, Carmel O'Shannessy (2019; 2021) could trace how children began to regularize mixed-language input they received from their parents and to develop the resulting patterns (including grammatical changes and word substitutions) further, until a mixed language had emerged. What aided this processes was that children spent much time in their peer group, so that language took on an identity-marking function; that these peer groups were tightly-knit and numerically restricted, interacting across many contexts of daily life; that there is little written codification of Warlpiri; and that there is generally relatively little adult control of children's speech, especially given the propensity for linguistic creativity of Warlpiri itself (O'Shannessy 2019: 328–30). This constellation of factors is relatively rare today, but could have been more common in prehistory. Actors other than male conquerors could thus be instrumental for how language change pans out.

In our example, pre-Indo-European language elements could, for instance, have survived as a substratum, as recently argued for words connected to agriculture (Iversen and Kroonen 2017; Kroonen 2012), but innovations could also have extended to grammatical structures, especially if children were raised bilingually and had opportunities to create mixed registers (see also Pereltsvaig and Lewis 2015: 136). Complex concatenations of processes can follow from each other, including divergences, but also borrowings and convergences (e.g. Ringe and Warnow 2008). Even in a situation of migration, therefore, specific languages are unlikely to be linked to specific genetic signatures for very long. All these aspects make it relatively unlikely that the spread of language took the form of a simple, wave-like advance, or that their development can be adequately modelled using a neat, tree-like pattern – although possible alternatives (Figure 5.2) are often less intuitive. To the networks of hosts and institutions of guest friendship that have been suggested for third-millennium BCE Europe (Wentink 2020), we can add translators and multilingual individuals as key agents enabling the spread of innovation. This is an analytical scale with which archaeologists have long struggled.

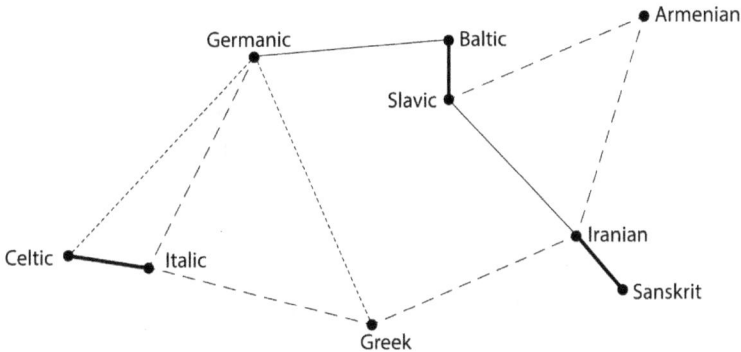

Figure 5.2 Kroeber's (1960: 4) alternative version of the relations between major Indo-European language families. Language families connected by thick lines show the closest similarities, those connected by dashed or dotted lines the fewest. Armenian is the least closely connected and projects outwards into three-dimensional space. As opposed to a tree-like structure, Kroeber's calculations highlight geographical closeness, pointing to the role of mutual influencing in language change.

Interpretative challenges: archaeology, agency and structure

While human life takes place at a variety of temporal and spatial scales, there are as yet few universally accepted attempts to bridge these analytical levels (Robb and Pauketat 2013). On the one hand, there are traditional approaches based on, broadly speaking, evolutionism, functionalism or environmental and climatic determinism, which see the main driving forces steering human life as firmly located outside the control of people themselves. On the other hand, some branches of post-processualism can be criticized for focusing too myopically on the very small scale. The most fruitful approaches have been those which in one form or another seek to balance 'agency' and 'structure', or put another way, individual small-scale actions and the wider framework within which they are effective. The most commonly used schemes, such as Michel de Certeau's (1984) dynamic interplay between strategies and tactics in modern capitalist societies, Pierre Bourdieu's (1990) habitus or Anthony Giddens' (1984) structuration theory, rely on this dialectic between wider structures and individual room for experimentation within circumscribed limits, although where to strike the balance is controversial. In Bourdieu's habitus, actions overwhelmingly have the effect of perpetuating structure and only in a direct challenge – an encounter with an unfamiliar habitus, a radical change in external circumstances – is this seriously questioned. Similarly, Giddens' structuration theory centres on practices: it is their reproduction that eventually cements individual acts of repetition into lasting structures, and it is at this level that structures can also be altered.

These schemes were criticized for not providing enough scope for the creative agency of individuals to resist and ultimately change structures (e.g. Farnell 2000; Robb and Pauketat 2013: 13). More recent post-humanist approaches have expanded this by focusing on the way agency is distributed across constellations of human and non-human actants (e.g. Olsen 2003; papers in Alberti et al. 2013). Yet while the boundaries may be slightly differently configured, both more traditional and post-humanist approaches agree that it is the relational interaction of many factors that drives change. Change is therefore at the same time constantly present, but also not equally noticeable in every part of the network at once. Where approaches differ is in their conceptions of power. Post-humanist approaches in particular have tended to privilege a kind of thick description, in which the interrelationships of several actants are traced in detail for specific case studies, but often at the expense of acknowledging power differentials between different kinds of actants, including different kinds of people (for criticism see e.g. Glørstad 2008; Ion 2018; Johannsen 2012). There is also often a choice about which aspects of Bourdieu's work to foreground – those where the focus lies on creating shared principles through practice, or those more directly concerned with different kinds of capital (social, economic etc.) that agents can use to cement and naturalize distinctions between them (e.g. Bourdieu 1984; 1986).

So far, then, and irrespective of where the limits between actors/actants and structures are drawn, the pace of most narratives of Neolithic life has remained sedate, leaving us theoretically ill-equipped to deal with the more episodic nature of prehistoric social life increasingly being revealed by tighter dating frameworks (see e.g. Whittle 2018) and by migration scenarios (although see Frieman et al. 2019). These are, after all, situations of potentially drastic upheaval in which symbols of identity and group belonging would need to be adjusted, as would the habitus, in other words, routines of daily interaction with other humans and non-humans. This can happen rapidly and irrevocably and may include episodes that are profoundly disruptive, whether through the use of violence or through the radical questioning of all aspects of social life.

As John Robb and Timothy Pauketat (2013) have argued, the challenge remains how to best trace the ways in which each individual act resonates at different scales. They envisage progressively more local and shorter-term nested fields. 'Historical ontologies' – the basic views of the world and how it functions – form the largest level, framing a succession of several 'genealogies of material practice', which in turn comprise multiple cycles of shorter-term political, ritual and social developments, material culture traditions and landscape configurations. The interplay of several of these strands of change, each with their own pace, causes the more dramatic tipping points we sometimes see archaeologically (Robb and Pauketat 2013: 24–8). Similar tipping points, at which trajectories distributed across different, partly overlapping networks intersect and create rapid, structural transformations, have also been identified in history, notably in William Sewell's (2005: 100–22, 225–9) notion of the event (which has also enjoyed some popularity in archaeology, e.g. Beck 2013; papers in Bolender 2010). Evolutionary archaeologists recognize a similar phenomenon in 'cascades' of change, when previously rare behaviours are suddenly adopted as a new norm (e.g. Bentley et al. 2011: 69).

All these authors agree that the complex and distributed causal factors involved in such tipping points are extremely difficult to trace. Trajectories playing out at different spatial and temporal scales must be documented and their intersection creates largely unpredictable outcomes. Yet the seeds for this kind of change are there all the time – in the power differentials between people, in the friction caused by different interests and in the emergence of new and surprising ways of doing things. This process is messy. Even during tipping points we do not see the smooth replacement of one coherent logic with another, as people struggle to make sense of new conditions using a mixture of old and new strategies. At the small scale of analysis at least, we should therefore give due interpretative weight also to those responses that do not fit the dominant trends and diverge from the average (as argued e.g. by Gero 2007; McGlade and van der Leeuw 1997: 5–6). Our narratives should reflect that people experienced processes of change as open-ended.

In what follows, we try to trace these smaller-scale reactions and individual biographies by contrasting two scenarios. One is the issue of agency and mobility of Neolithic children, who are not often considered as actors in their own right. Following on from this, we address one of the largest-scale 'tipping points' identified in Neolithic central and western Europe: the arrival of new cultural influences, genetic signatures and quite likely languages from the steppes, and how cultural symbols like axes were deployed in these processes.

Neolithic interactions – age, gender and the 'steppe migration'

Children buried far from home

As aDNA analysis makes it ever more affordable to trace biological relations in mortuary populations, the focus has been on recreating dominant patterns of relatedness and their social corollaries, such as patrilineal inheritance systems. However, these studies are also increasingly revealing individuals who are not biologically related to anyone else on site, and these include children and adolescents. In what follows, we outline examples from across the European Neolithic sequence to contrast the different treatments these individuals received.

In the first half of the fifth millennium BCE, at least 128 individuals were buried in a compact cemetery in what is now the Yonne Valley in north-central France at a site called Gurgy 'Les Noisats' (Rottier *et al.* 2005). This included sixty-six adults and sixty-two juveniles, ranging from a few months in age to late adolescence (Rivollat and Rottier in Rivollat *et al.* 2023). A recent genetic and isotopic analysis of this funerary community found many were biologically related in two distantly connected family trees several generations deep (Rivollat *et al.* 2023). Among the eighteen individuals not part of either tree were six children, including a double burial of a three- to seven-year-old girl and a six- to ten-year-old boy, GLN211A and GLN211B.

The two were buried together, one on top of the other, crouched on their left side with their heads to the south (Figure 5.3). An animal-tooth ornament and a flint implement were recovered from the burial and are thought to be associated with GLN211B. The excavators believe the children were buried at the same time, but in separate containers of

Figure 5.3 Double burial GLN211A and GLN211B from the Neolithic cemetery at Gurgy, département Yonne (reproduced with kind permission of Stéphane Rottier).

organic material, like small boxes (Le Roy 2015). Overall, this funerary rite was well within the norms practised at Gurgy. The pit in which these children were interred is one of a small cluster in the main set of burial plots.

When the children's DNA was analysed, they were shown to be siblings. Neither their parents nor any closely related family members are present in the cemetery. Based on the dietary isotopes, GLN211B may have had a somewhat more protein-rich diet than the other children in his age group (Rivollat *et al.* 2023), suggesting these children grew up in a different landscape zone. They were not wholly unrelated, however. Identity by descent analysis (IBD) suggests they were distant relations to the siblings GLN325, GLN256, GLN221B and GLN266. Their respective mothers are interpreted as having been second- or third-degree relatives (that is, half-sisters, aunt and niece, first cousins or granddaughter and grandmother; Rivollat *et al.* 2023).

Of the six children not or only distantly related to the main pedigrees, three were boys and three girls. The former seem to be somewhat older, being aged from about seven or eight to fourteen or fifteen, while the latter are younger children under eight. In common with other communities of this period (e.g. Bickle and Fibiger 2014), the age of seven to eight appears to be a threshold to a life phase typically referred to as 'middle childhood', lasting until early adolescence, during which children experience a range of physiological and cognitive shifts (B.C. Campbell 2011; Lancy and Grove 2011) as well as social and identity development (Del Giudice 2015; L.O. Rogers 2020). All three of the unrelated (or distantly related) boys, including GLN211B, would have been in middle childhood. Thus, their presence among the Gurgy dead may be linked to early opportunities for them to contribute in more adult ways to their own family or community, for example learning new skills as part of a fostering arrangement, taking responsibility for stock or acting as translators or language brokers for their older kin.

Although some of these mobile children, such as GLN211A and GLN211B, seem to have died far from home, they were not treated as outsiders in death, but buried with local rites in a central area of the site.

This is particularly interesting given the extreme variety of fifth-millennium funerary rites in the Paris basin (Chambon and Leclerc 2003; Cheung *et al.* 2021; Midgley 2005). Monumental funerary structures co-exist with flat cemeteries, which each have different structuring principles concerning who could be buried and in what manner. There were no universal norms for funerary treatment that crossed community – and perhaps familial – lines, and the cemeteries containing similar burials may themselves only have persisted for three or four generations (as at Gurgy). In other words, not only did GLN211A and GLN211B receive appropriate funerary rites upon their death, they received the very narrow range of appropriate rites followed by the small, heavily interrelated Gurgy community. This certainly seems to have marked them as fully integrated into that community.

This contrasts with other examples where children and young persons were interred far from their natal communities. A millennium after the use of the Gurgy cemetery, an enclosure of the so-called Salzmünde culture (*c.* 3400–3050 BCE) was built on the eponymous site, in what is now the German state of Saxony-Anhalt. The site displays an unusual variety of burial treatments over multiple Neolithic phases (Meller and Friederich 2014). In the Salzmünde phase, there are amongst others settlement burials in abandoned quarry pits and isolated skulls of individuals of all ages and both sexes placed at the base of the enclosure ditch. In the second half of its occupation, it is argued that the enclosure became increasingly embattled and was eventually taken over by a group who redeposited an entire megalithic grave and its former occupants in the ditches, ending the site's occupation. This episode has been interpreted as a hostile ritual 'decommissioning' (Schunke *et al.* 2013).

Among the more unusual Salzmünde-phase inhumations are the so-called sherd graves. These normally consist of burial in a round, straight-sided feature with a flat base with the body covered by the remains of burnt debris – burnt daub, large chunks of charcoal and so on. On top of this and after the deposition of some sediment, there is a thick layer of sherds, often deriving from secondarily burnt and intentionally smashed pottery. The individuals from these sherd graves are notable for their unusual biographies or circumstances of death – they are, for example, more likely to show evidence of traumatic lesions, including lethal injuries, than other individuals (Stecher *et al.* 2013). This combination of violent death, but substantial ritual investment has been interpreted as a consequence of 'bad death' (Schlenker *et al.* 2017: 39), that is to say individuals who died in circumstances considered particularly unfortunate or socially unacceptable and who needed extraordinary ritual treatment to complete their transition to the afterlife and/or to protect the living (Hertz 1960 [1907]: 85).

One sherd grave contained the multiple interment of four adult women and five children: two under twelve months old, one one-year old, and two individuals between two and four years of age (C. Meyer *et al.* 2013). They were tightly squeezed at the base of the feature, covered by burnt daub and charcoal, and by over 8,000 sherds belonging to around 150 vessels (Figure 5.4). The four women are each closely associated with one of the children, facing or even embracing them; the youngest immature individual – a child aged four to nine months – was found near the hip area of one of the females. Originally thought to represent a burial of mothers and their children, mtDNA data available for the adults and the three older children showed that only one of the women could have been related to the child she was holding, as both belong to haplotype H5 – however, as with any mtDNA-based assessment, the biological relationship between these two people need not actually be close. The other two children were classified as haplogroup U3a, which is generally rare in central Europe, with no examples from Neolithic Germany outside Salzmünde (Brandt 2017: 243–4; Lipson *et al.* 2017: S1; Mathieson *et al.* 2015: S1; M. Richards pers. comm.). The remaining women exhibited either haplogroup H5 or V (Brandt 2017; C. Meyer *et al.* 2013). These children were hence not the offspring of the women they were buried with, and while the younger children still have a breastfeeding signal, the three-to-four-year-old exhibits a rather low nitrogen signal compared to others on

Figure 5.4 Drawing of the multiple burial from feature 6582 at Salzmünde, Saalekreis (drawing: I. Müller/U. Leipelt, © State Office for Heritage Management and Archaeology Sachsen-Anhalt).

site (C. Meyer *et al.* 2013; Münster *et al.* 2018: S1). However, in terms of the strontium signature, the children all fall within the local range.

This contradictory constellation remains difficult to interpret. The Salzmünde material would clearly benefit from the kind of detailed kinship analysis, based on whole-genome studies, carried out at Gurgy. Three scenarios seem plausible. In the first, the children could still be related to the women they are buried with along the paternal line. Alternatively, like the children at Gurgy, they were born away from Salzmünde and could have reached the site by a variety of means, for instance during the raids and captive-taking that may have marked the conflict-laden later occupation phases prior to the ritual decommissioning. Even in this reading, the children could have been accepted into the local community, as suggested by their careful burial in close connection to others. As a third option, all the individuals in this multiple grave may have been considered outsiders, reflected in the unusual burial.

Another sherd grave contained a young female, twenty to twenty-five years of age, who had been subjected to sustained physical abuse for at least several months before her death and possibly longer, since childhood or adolescence. The individual exhibits stress markers in the form of enamel hypoplasias on nearly all teeth – a level unusual for this site, and documenting episodes of illness or malnutrition already in childhood. Strong muscle attachments and a healed fracture of the spinous process on a cervical vertebra (a so-called clay-shoveler fracture) indicate longer periods of hard physical work. There were also three healed skull traumata, but only a few weeks before her death the woman also sustained a multiple fracture of her mandible, possibly related to inter-personal violence, which had only partly healed. Her death was similarly violent – she died through at least three blows to the head and her body shows carnivore bitemarks, suggesting exposure before interment in the pit (Stecher *et al.* 2013).

The depositional sequence begins with a layer of burnt debris and daub, overlain by a layer of broken pottery. This is followed by the burial horizon, another layer of burnt daub and finally more broken pottery – nineteen kilos of sherds were recovered in total. At some point after burial, the woman's body was disturbed and the bones partially scattered (Stecher *et al.* 2013). This individual hence held a subordinate position for a protracted time before her death, and could be interpreted as the victim of a raid, potentially abducted from her natal community while still relatively young. In contrast to the Gurgy children, while she likely spent some time at Salzmünde, there are no indications that she was integrated as an equal into the burial community.

In spite of their ambiguities, sites like Gurgy and Salzmünde open for discussion on how children and adolescents may have been incorporated into Neolithic communities away from their natal kin, an aspect rarely discussed before the availability of aDNA analysis. The form this incorporation took could evidently vary widely – from the kind of integration that entitled these individuals to formal burial alongside others in the community, as at Gurgy, to the much more ambiguous evidence from the Salzmünde multiple grave, to the outsider status of the young woman at the same site. The fact that both of the latter were buried in unusual sherd graves further heightens this ambiguity.

Together, these examples document a long-term trend in the European Neolithic to incorporate outsiders into a community, and they suggest that this often happened at a young age. This creates a background mechanism that can help us understand some transitional phenomena connected to the expansion of pastoralist societies from the Eurasian steppes just after the turn to the third millennium BCE. In much of Europe, this process has been cast as a disruptive mass migration (see above). In contrast, both archaeological and aDNA sources have identified the north-western Black Sea area as an interaction zone with complex histories of population admixture (e.g. Penske *et al.* 2023). Similarly, in modern-day Bulgaria, Romania and Hungary, there is evidence for more gradual interaction scenarios, with isolated graves in a steppe tradition appearing as early as 4500 BCE and present throughout the fourth millennium (Anthony 2019: 41; 2022; Czebreszuk and Szmyt 2011; Dani and Kulcsár 2021; Gerling et al. 2012: 1099; Heyd 2011: 543–4; Kaiser and Winger 2015: 130; Preda-Bălănică 2021; Preda-Bălănică and Diekmann 2023: 112). Eventually, in the Carpathian basin persons of steppe or mixed steppe and 'Neolithic' ancestry could be buried according to either local or steppe-derived burial rites, while people without clear steppe ancestry increasingly incorporated elements of the steppe burial rite, even before the main 'Yamnaya' migration, and more so afterwards (Preda-Bălănică and Diekmann 2023: 112–17). This created high variation in funerary rituals, which combine elements of diverse cultural origins (Preda-Bălănică 2021) in a situation of long-term cultural admixture.

The extensive burial mound at Sárrétudvari-Őrhalom (Hungary) with its eight interments spanning from the last centuries of the fourth to the mid-third millennium BCE is a case in point. The mound was constructed in stages, with the initial burial of an unfurnished, possibly female adolescent in grave 12 according to a Late Copper Age rite. Over the subsequent centuries, a further six individuals were placed into the expanded mound, now around fifty metres in diameter, with the latest grave dated to between 2860 and 2470 calBCE. These were mostly adult males, although one child of five to seven years is also included. The burial rites show a mixture of widespread, Yamnaya-associated features (such as body positions and metal items) and local elements, notably pottery (Gerling et al. 2012: 1101–2). Strontium and oxygen isotope analysis of all individuals revealed at least three people who spent their childhood at higher altitudes or in a colder region. Combined with the grave good inventories, an origin in the Apuseni Mountains, some 200 km away, can be suggested (Gerling et al. 2012: 1104–7). These individuals all date late within the mound sequence and were buried with some grave goods with steppe affinities. They are interpreted as possible 'traders' or transhumant pastoralists integrated into the local community, with a role as marriage partners explicitly excluded (Gerling et al. 2012: 1107), although one of the non-local males is buried in a double inhumation with a young child with local isotopic signatures. While only aDNA analysis could prove any biological relationship between these two individuals, the integration of males with steppe lifestyles into the more sedentary communities of the Carpathian basin could after all have proceeded through marriage and shared parentage. The power relationships involved in such transactions remain to be further elucidated; it is certainly striking that no further adult females were included at Sárrétudvari-Őrhalom after the foundation burial.

A longer-term pattern of interaction between steppe populations and resident groups is also evident in Bulgaria, where Elke Kaiser and Katja Winger (2015) identified a regionally differentiated pattern of hybridization in burial rites. Yamnaya-style kurgan burials (here identified as crouched burials containing ochre and deposited in a pit) are present from about 3300 BCE (see updated dating in Kaiser 2021: 92) and sometimes included Pontic-style copper daggers and personal ornaments as well as pottery made in local styles. The amount of grave goods differs between regions, with graves in the southern zone more richly furnished than would typically be seen in a Yamnaya setting. In the northern zone, these burial rites coexist with other, locally derived customs for several centuries (Kaiser and Winger 2015: 121–5, 129). Overall, Kaiser and Winger (2015: 136) reconstruct a slow process of integration in which both 'foreign' and 'local' traditions were changed. This has parallels in other areas of eastern central Europe (Ciugudean 2011; Kaiser 2016: 35–8). The 'classic' central European Corded Ware burial assemblage, with its battle axes and other material rarely found in steppe contexts, may well have been created in similar processes of protracted interaction between the practitioners of two or more different funerary customs (Anthony 2022; Kaiser 2016: 39–40).

Preda-Bălănică and Diekmann (2023: 115–16) also report the burial of a nine or ten year-old boy with over 50 per cent steppe ancestry from the eponymous Vučedol site. We are still awaiting cases of children who definitely travelled a significant distance from their natal kin on their own. However, with regards to the discussion of frontier zones in the Great Lakes area and the longer-term pattern of Neolithic children and young persons who likely were buried away from close relatives, we hypothesize that the movement of children and juveniles is an aspect that has been under-researched to date, but one that would have been crucial in exchanging knowledge and driving culture change in situations of cultural contact and mosaic processes.

Here, we would like to suggest two possibilities this contact may have taken: abduction; or adoption and fosterage. These need not be mutually exclusive. Adoption, where a child's allegiance, name and rights switch permanently to their adopted family, can be extremely common in some societies, particularly where it is considered the preferred way of bringing up children. Alber (2004: 34) observes that up to 50 per cent of children in some northern Benin societies spend at least part of their childhood away from their natal home. In other cases, adopting a female child from her lineage improves a woman's standing in her post-marriage residence and is part of conjugal political negotiations (e.g. Notermans 2004; Talle 2004). Elsewhere, adoption of adults to ensure, amongst other things, inheritance succession or ritual obligations is frequent (Roesch-Rhomberg 2004). Fostering, where individuals grow up away from their natal family, but maintain affiliation with them, can help cement alliances between groups, for example where early medieval elites in north-west Europe exchanged foster children in order to consolidate patron-client relationships (Parkes 2006: 365). Finally, adoption can integrate the victims of abduction into the society of their captors (e.g. Halbmayer 2004; Metcalf 2010: 25). Famously, Romans also often took the children of conquered elites as hostages, providing them with education in Rome and returning them to their native societies as Romanized adults (J. Allen 2006).

There is hence more than one mechanism by which children could have travelled away from their parents and been integrated into societies with different diets – as well as potentially different customs, different expectations of gender and other social roles, and different languages. As with the historical situation on the American frontier, such children could have come to act as language and cultural brokers, their pliability and adaptability creating lasting contacts and facilitating social and cultural change. While we do not know how, for example, the Gurgy and Salzmünde children and adolescents reached the site, the fact that the former were interred at the cemetery is not consistent with a low social position at the time of their deaths. In this case, then, fosterage or adoption are likely possibilities, even if these children were captives originally. The situation at Salzmünde is more ambiguous; at least the young individually buried female could have been abducted in childhood or adolescence.

All these scenarios remain highly speculative, and further targeted work is needed. It will also remain challenging to combine isotopic, DNA and artefactual data in non-essentializing ways. Yet the crucial role of children in alliance building is more than a remote possibility.

The importance of ritual action as one arena of social integration also remained salient during the spread of the Corded Ware culture into western and central Europe, as shown by the situation of cultural syncretism in Bulgaria. However, in our last case study we turn to the interplay between ritual and everyday activities.

Symbols in action: appropriating pottery and axes in the Netherlands

In the Corded Ware and Bell Beaker culture of central Europe, burial rite has long been seen as one key strategy of integration, and for a while as an alternative to migration when it came to explaining material culture patterning over wide areas. These are not either/or options. In what follows, we briefly introduce a case study from the Netherlands to show the potential of integrating ritual and domestic evidence in the context of third millennium transformations.

The background is formed by widening interregional networks, including the exchange of technologies, material objects and probably new social values that brought into contact several, previously more separate large-scale networks, notably Rinaldone in Italy, Maikop in the Caucasus region (Jeunesse 2020), Boleráz-Baden in southern central and south-eastern Europe (Furholt 2008; 2009), Globular Amphorae in eastern central Europe (Müller 2023; Szmyt 1999; Woidich 2014) and Funnel Beakers in northern central Europe and southern Scandinavia (Frieman 2012; Johannsen and Laursen 2010; S.K. Nielsen and Johannsen 2023). Many of the features seen as defining for the 'post-migration' Corded Ware and Bell Beaker groups – specialized weapons and male warriorhood, the marking of individuals in burial, binary gender differentiation, the prominence of drinking vessels and the lack of substantive remains of houses, among others – are already present or emerging in large parts of Europe prior to the genetically tangible migration event (Jeunesse 2020; Schultrich 2022) and are brought together into a new kind of package around 2900 BCE when contact networks expand (Furholt 2021).

The result are the new Corded Ware or Bell Beaker burial rituals, which prominently display individual, armed males, follow a binary gender model and contain drinking vessels (Furholt 2019b). This could well represent a more formalized religion – more formalized at least than in most previous European societies (Ahola 2020) – which provided a new layer of common identity for heterogeneous migrants and people with local backgrounds alike. Specific objects became emblematic of this identity, notably stone battle axes and the corded beaker or corded amphora, all of which originated in different regions and incorporated various pre-existing traditions (Furholt 2008; 2014; Hallgren 2008; Hübner 2005). These object types were involved in negotiating new burial rites, in particular also the differentiation of Bell Beaker from Corded Ware traditions. This was certainly a politically and ideologically charged process. Yet they were also used in non-burial contexts, particularly where funerary evidence is rare, as in Switzerland, parts of the Netherlands, Norway and the eastern Baltic. New evidence from these areas, the Netherlands in particular, highlights the diversity in individual encounters with the new ideas, values and practices.

Looking at the integration of new pottery forms, Sandra Beckerman's (2015) study of settlements in the coastal Netherlands traced how local and regional styles (Funnel Beaker or Vlaardingen pottery) were combined with new, transregional Single Grave (i.e. Corded Ware) ones. In sites such as Zandwerven, elements of both are combined, with Corded Ware-looking vessels emerging slowly over a matter of generations. Across the region, a distinction develops between coarse ware vessels executed in the local Vlaardingen style and fine ware ones manufactured according to the Single Grave/Corded Ware style (Beckerman 2015: 202; see also Kroon et al. 2019). This pattern is echoed all over Europe, appearing in mid-fourth millennium Bajc-Retz-Gajary and Boleráz-Baden contexts (Furholt 2009) and then in the Corded Ware (Larsson 2009) and Bell Beaker (Besse 2003; Vander Linden 2006) horizons: new transregional styles are largely confined to fine wares and serving vessels, while cooking and storage vessels continue to be produced in the traditional, local style. Where new transregional objects meet local traditions, the result is variable, ranging from total replacement of the old by the new (such as in eastern Switzerland: Hafner and Suter 2003; Winiger 1993), via selective incorporation of some traits (such as in western Switzerland: Suter et al. 2017), to a successive integration of traditions (such as in the southern Baltic region: Rimantiene 1989, or western Norway: Nyland et al. 2023).

This negotiation took place across different domains of social action. The coarse-ware cooking and storage vessels could be connected to food preparation, while the serving vessels rather refer to more outwardly directed social interaction, for instance in organized hospitality or feasting. Following Stefan Burmeister (2000), one could argue that significant numbers of migrants were involved only in those cases where both the coarse and the fine ware switched to the new style, while a change only in outwardly visible styles may indicate the acceptance of new norms by locals, implying restricted numbers of migrants and some form of accommodation.

But we should be wary of a too schematic application of this distinction. Even in cases in which new objects were adopted into daily life, there was the possibility of individual deviation, maybe even resistance to the new social or political values they embodied. While Corded Ware and Bell Beaker vessels are designed as drinking vessels, possibly connected to alcohol consumption and an elite drinking culture (Sherratt 1987), food crust and lipid analyses (Theunissen et al. 2014) from the Netherlands have documented a much broader range of functions, including cooking stews and fish soups.

A similar process can be traced for battle axes. These are even more visibly connected to new values, being associated mainly with male burials (Bourgeois and Kroon 2017) and the emergence of a male warrior identity. With few exceptions, specialized weapons are not encountered frequently in earlier funerary contexts in Europe (Schulting 2013; Vandkilde 2006). Daggers and halberds, and most frequently battle axes, then become prominent in several regions during the late fourth millennium BCE, with battle axes further increasing in Corded Ware single graves in the third millennium BCE. This is often

seen as leading to the rise of a Bronze Age warrior elite in the second
millennium BCE (Vandkilde 2007).

In stark contrast, Karsten Wentink's (2020) study on reproducing
use-wear marks on Corded Ware battle axes from the Netherlands
found that they were mostly used as a mundane working tool for
essential agricultural work, specifically for digging out tree roots
(Figure 5.5).[5] This highlights the processes of negotiation that took
place when people of diverse backgrounds interacted in daily practices,
as well as in situations of hospitality, feasts or rituals. Local traditions
could be upheld, transformed or replaced, while transregional
innovations were variously rejected, integrated or merged with existing
practice. Where the most consequential social innovations, such as fine-
ware drinking vessels or specialized weapons, were decontextualized
and repurposed, this could strip them of much of their political power.
Potentially, we are faced with a conscious political act of opposition to
or rejection of the emerging social values, such as heroic individualism
or the kind of elite networks that the new burial rites are supposed to
reference (Wentink 2020: 239–47). Using battle axes for one of the most
profane agricultural chores – uprooting trees – calls to mind James
Scott´s (1985) 'weapons of the weak', the notion of peasants' resistance
through small everyday acts of deviation. It shows where power – in the
sense of Arendt's collective consensus – actually rests. At the very least

Figure 5.5 Karsten Wentink performing experimental tasks with a Corded
Ware battle axe to match use ware traces observed on prehistoric examples.
Digging up tree trunks, shown here, turned out to yield the closest match
(reproduced from Wentink 2020: 124 courtesy of Karsten Wentink; photo:
Maaike Wentink).

we will have to rethink the often implicit assumption that elites and commoners formed two separate strata, one of which lived off the labour of the other. Perhaps the individuals and households that commanded the new kinds of resources were not leading radically different everyday lives, but held an elevated position only in some, strictly circumscribed, contexts.

Overall, this illustrates the possibilities of individual and collective actors in the ongoing political negotiations of the third millennium, fuelled by a rise of transregional mobility and the tension between traditions and innovation, between the local and transregional. Decisions of whether to adopt novelties, and for what, are taken at the small scale, in daily interactions, where renegotiations of gender roles, the components of a 'good life' and the use of new things and practices were acted out. In both of our Neolithic case studies, individual factors had a strong impact on the adoption of new practices, even in situations of power imbalance. Over the several centuries that it took to reach the archaeologically visible 'tipping point' of the appearance of the Corded Ware culture, multiple negotiation processes were ongoing, building on existing networks and ways of accepting newcomers. Creative adaptation and resistance also continued for some time after, involving people of all ages and both sexes. These micro-political models seem more informative than the initially proposed large-scale and monocausal explanations, which relied on a massive increase in violence or on pandemics to explain 'the' Corded Ware culture spread and which have since been shown to be overly simplistic (see e.g. Fuchs et al. 2019; Trautmann 2021).

6

Re-orienting Migration Studies
in Archaeology

In this book, we have investigated the archaeology of migration in order to improve our understanding of more widespread patterns structuring migration processes and to use that knowledge to better understand specific archaeological cases. We have done this through a deep dive into the idea of migration, what it is and how it operates from the individual to the supra-community scale. Crucially, we have emphasized the political dimensions of migration in the past to inspire new archaeological models. In this chapter, we draw this out through a structured comparison of the different case studies highlighted in this volume. These represent different parts of the world, different research traditions and reliance on different sources and materials. They have given us insights into human movements as social practices of an inherently political nature. As we have shown, even the biggest scale of interaction requires an understanding of the complex social relations underlying it.

Comparing the case studies

The structures of migration processes – a visual comparison

The settling of Pacific islands, population movements in the US Southwest, historical biographies of US frontier translators and the spread and regionalization of the European Neolithic are historically specific and culturally contingent processes which we study using divergent materials in distinct ways. Nevertheless, as we have demonstrated, juxtaposing these well-known contexts allows us to identify questionable premises, blind spots and neglected questions in our understanding of migration in each of these areas. Referring back to Table 2.1, these examples can all be classified as migrations; but they differ in the composition of the migrating group, the distance travelled and the temporalities involved, as well as the cultural distance between source and destination areas.

In order to clarify the distinctive characters of our different migration case studies, we have produced a series of streamgraphs over various temporal extents (Figure 6.1). Streamgraphs are a visualization method for exploring qualitative data with a strong temporal element (Byron and Wattenberg 2008; Nelson and Chatfield 2022). Here, they provide a graphic summary of the migration processes compared in this volume by plotting the group size involved, the geographical distances traversed and the cultural difference between the incoming and resident populations. We have adopted a seven-point scale to characterize qualitatively the extent or scale of each of these variables – none, small, small to medium, medium, medium to large, large, very large – and used this as the basis for our visualization. These are simplifications, evidently. Migrations, as shown throughout this volume, have social impacts at various scales simultaneously, so any classification depends on the stance taken – do we wish to privilege the longer-term, aggregate impacts of an event (e.g. a large amount of new settlers, even though few may have been involved in each migration episode), or are we looking at the individual scale? The graphs here generally work with longer time scales and assessments of 'average' behaviours, but we have consciously omitted any numerical definition of 'large' or 'small' populations, distances and so on – these would lend a fake aura of objectivity to what is essentially a subjective process.

For the Pacific migrations, our graph shows the starburst pattern of punctuated phases of expansion, which is largely an effect of the chronological model we have adopted (see Chapter 3, 'Settling Remote Oceania') and may change with further research. Also, within each period of apparent stasis, there would be continued migration and

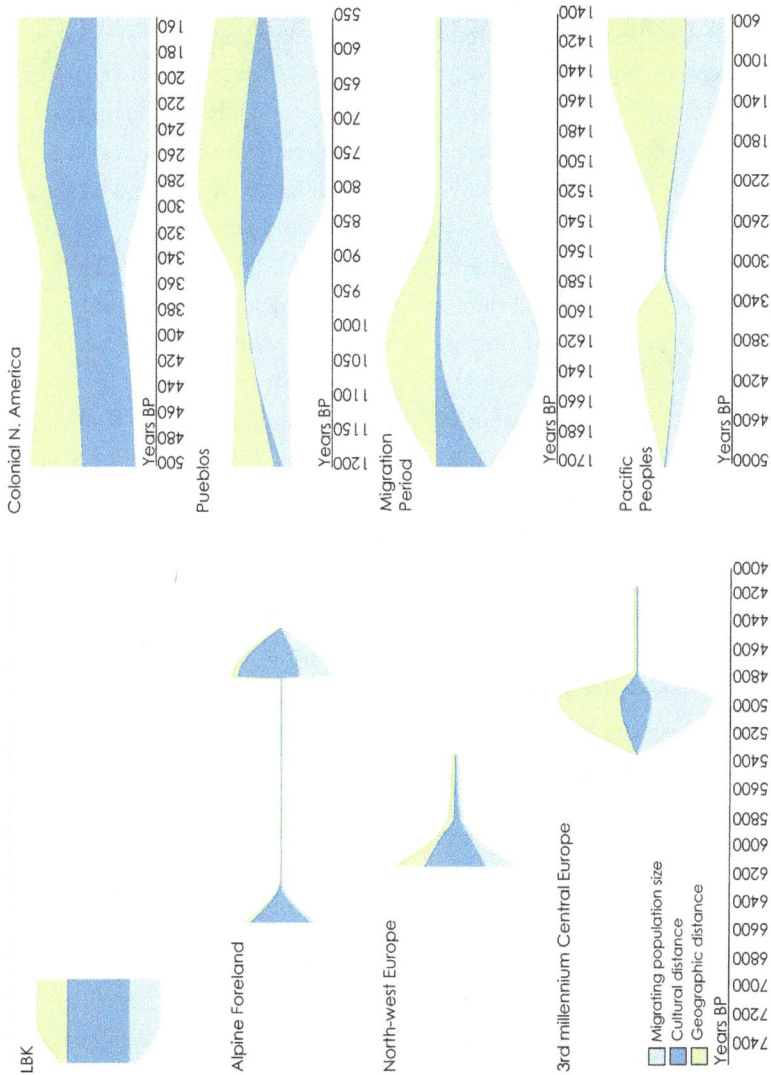

Figure 6.1 Streamgraphs of all case study areas treated in this volume, each on their own temporal axis. *Left:* European Neolithic case studies; *right:* global case studies. The different migration events are compared in terms of the geographical and cultural distances covered, and the number of people on the move. These assessments (large, medium, small) are not defined numerically, but relatively within the terms of each case study (see text). Created with flourish.studio.

mobility of smaller groups and individuals between places already settled, including westwards towards New Guinea, the south-east Asian mainland and adjacent islands, leading to continuous interaction between populations speaking different languages and practising different cultures. Yet, while covering vast geographical distances in aggregate, Pacific maritime migrations show that this large-scale process is the result of many smaller-scale ones, involving different groups of people. The composition of voyaging groups varied from dozens to hundreds and was made up of various members of the community – from young men looking for fame to older people following a charismatic leader to the children following parents out to sea. Each of these events was initiated by different triggers and motives. As the geographical distances increased, however, cultural distance was not immediately affected. People settled largely familiar and well-understood island biomes with no prior human occupants and with a gradient of climatological and environmental similarities and differences. This resulted in a largely uniform agricultural package, adapted to local circumstances. Moreover, scouting parties had already identified suitable islands and the routes to and from them prior to any larger movement of people. Polynesian sailors had deep astronomical and oceanographic knowledge, making extensive maritime journeys predictable and repeatable. Smaller scales of regular mobility – shorter episodic voyages, trips to join family, the departure and return of scouting parties with the seasonal winds and overland movement into island interiors – are set within many separate and situationally unique longer voyaging events, deconstructing any totalizing idea of the (singular, homogeneous) Polynesian migrations.

Similarly, in north-west Europe around 4000 BCE, we have detailed a migration process which extended the habitual movements and interactions of people and communities at the regional scale. Against the background of an already relatively mobile Neolithic settlement system in central Europe, the Funnel Beaker culture emerges and considerably extends its range. In southern Scandinavia, areas within which there had been contact and exchange for many generations were now settled by agriculturalists, perhaps initially following the paths opened by old alliances, but eventually fundamentally altering the region's settlement system and demographic composition. While hunter-gatherers survived alongside farmers for several generations, new, visible material culture, such as monuments and longhouses, proclaimed a migrant identity. In Britain and Ireland a contemporary phase of migration kicked off the local Neolithic, but a distinctly different trajectory emerged. There is less clear evidence for prior contact between island hunter-gatherers and continental farmers, and the reduced size and settledness of the local hunter-gatherer populations likely also led to a faster swamping of their genetic signal (Brace and Booth 2023). Yet migrants' distance from natal communities, and the choice not to rely on them for longer-term support, also played a part in this divergence. Migrants quickly established an identity materially distinct from the continental origin points. Expansion into the further reaches of the archipelago subsequently encouraged further processes of ethnogenesis within the islands, in spite of relatively reduced cultural differences. As in the Pacific, breaking down the model of a one-off wave reveals the variety, temporality and complexity of these diverse migrations. This echoes our Migration Period example (see Chapter 2, 'Identifying migrants and migrant identities'), where the traditional historic perspective on Germanic peoples and their alleged role in the fall of the Roman Empire has overshadowed more extended histories of movement, social re-configuration and ethnogenesis. Here, initial cultural differences between migrants were large but they were reduced by forming alliances along the way and by bi-directional acculturation.

The Pueblo migrations, in contrast, show a much more episodic pattern of migration events, as chronological resolution is more precise. We see first the establishment of Chaco as a central community, quickly drawing in people and goods from a substantial area. Once Chaco is abandoned, however, migrations of different geographical reach and involving varying numbers of people become commonplace. These include longer-distance relocations into areas settled by groups with different worldviews, so that elaborate strategies of coalescence were required. In our analysis, we have focused on the scale of households and groups of households, as these provide a stable background fluidity that persisted beyond the larger-scale migration pulses. Even migrations at this level required considerable efforts at integration.

The Alpine foreland sequence is similar in structure – larger-scale pulses of migration on a long-term background of individual, household and settlement mobility. This 'thin middle' on our Figure 6.1a appears much spindlier than for the Pueblo case, because the timescale overall is longer and because the migration pulses at either end of the sequence – respectively initial Neolithization and the Corded Ware horizon – involve greater cultural distance. In contrast, during the intra-regional mobility separating these two horizons of change, culture difference is lower than in the Pueblo case. Perhaps because of this, attempts at large-scale integration – for instance through monuments and rituals – were never attempted in this area.

In our final set of case studies, we compare one of the most destructive migration events on historical record – the arrival of Europeans in the Americas – to the Final Neolithic Corded Ware. Lethal violence has often been suggested as a fundamental characteristic here as well (e.g. Kristiansen and Earle 2022, 136), but this interpretation has also been resisted. Comparing these two case studies on the graph shows that much hinges on the nature of initial contact, which in both cases precedes the 'wave' of large-scale demographic impact. Modern colonial situations were characterized by violence and mistrust from the start, leading to a historically richly documented wave-like pattern of expansion across the American continent, driven by ever greater numbers of settlers and attendant subsequent land rushes. This pattern of overwhelming force is less evident in the record for Neolithic Europe. As we show with our Dutch example, the demographic and cultural effects – from hybridization to replacement – would have varied regionally, also depending on the varied influences of Bell Beaker and Corded Ware impulses. However, this period of mutual interaction eventually created a new and relatively stable system, although this accommodation was probably not without a human cost.

The various examples of non-local child burials illustrate this more ambiguous process, and show that such practices were active throughout the Neolithic sequence. Some were treated as locals in the funerary sphere, others were marked out in death. In their various rites and treatments, we see a tension between the foreign and the local. How these identities were inscribed or effaced depended on cultural, familial and incidental factors, most of which are outside the grasp of archaeologists. Nevertheless, centring children is valuable because they played central roles in processes of cultural and linguistic change and culture contact, although current archaeological migration models do not often account for them.

When looking at all the graphs at a comparable scale (Figure 6.2), it becomes evident that the processes of our different case studies unfurl over very different durations. Thus, while there are structural similarities underlying many of our case studies – the importance of a background level of smaller-scale migrations and the existence of social mechanisms for integrating newcomers, for example – the lived experience of these processes at the scale of human generations was hugely different. It is for this reason we see dialogue between our paired case studies rather than direct analogy. These pairings have, however, been successful in pointing out divergences and those aspects in scholarship that require more research. Interestingly, at the macro-scale, the aggregate of all our European Neolithic case studies (although involving different regions each time) replicates the two-peak structure of the Pacific migrations. The difference is not only in the overall duration, considerably longer in the Pacific (which also encompasses an incommensurably larger geographical area), but also in the complex patterns of interaction between resident and incoming populations in the European case. Here, migration patterns occasionally brought into contact people with very diverse lifeworlds, and understanding strategies of accommodation and interaction in all their variety should be a future research priority.

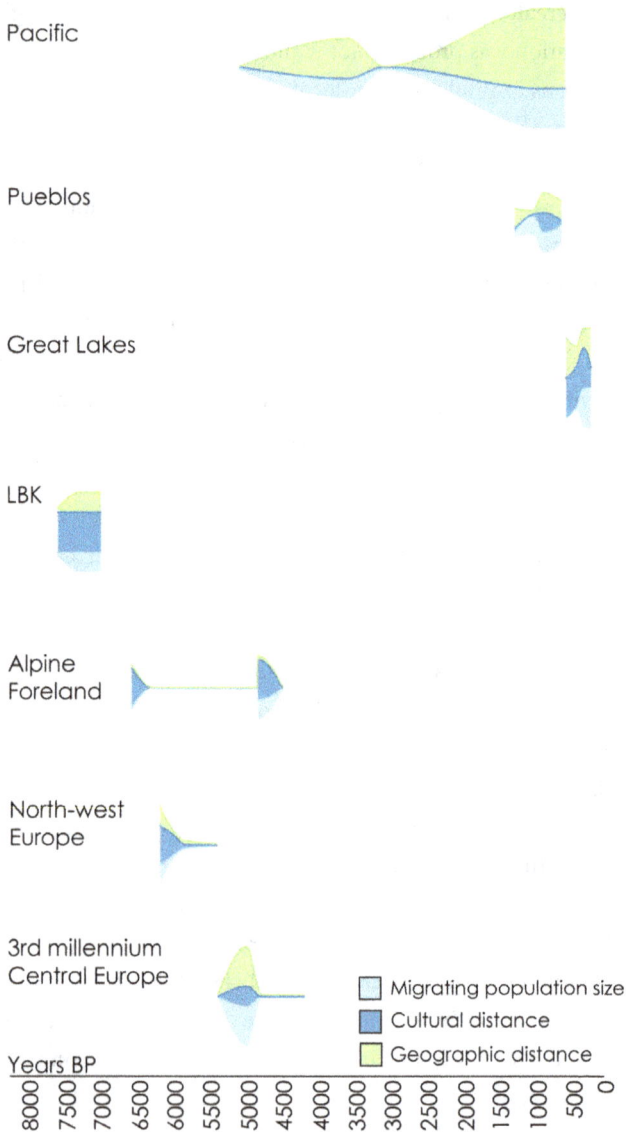

Figure 6.2 Streamgraphs of the case study areas treated in this volume on a combined temporal axis. The different migration events are compared in terms of the geographical and cultural distances covered, and the number of people on the move. These assessments (large, medium, small) are not defined numerically, but relatively within the terms of each case study (see text). Created with flourish.studio.

Common themes

In spite of all their diversity and historical contingency, in aggregate our case studies also highlight common methodological and interpretative themes. For the Pacific, economic push and pull factors and inter-community warfare played a role in some cases, but the main drivers of migration – and potentially the reason why migration was chosen as a preferred option – lay elsewhere. In Peter Bellwood's (2013) model of Polynesian migrations, 'founder rank enhancement', whereby ambitious junior group members emigrated to seek better opportunities elsewhere, was a socially incentivized strategy that necessitated considerable resources: production of surplus, ritual investment and the calling-in of social capital to bind people of various origins together into a new migrating group. Migration was not a last resort; and, as a result, one-off, single-direction migration events were not the end of the story. However, many crucial components of migration processes, such as return migrations, are usually archaeologically invisible. Similarly, the genetic signature of migrations is limited to events in which previously existing separations between populations are bridged for the first time, while later and continuous intermixing is harder to identify and thus often undervalued. This provides important lessons for Neolithic Europe, where migration events themselves, their planning and the composition and motivations of the social groups involved have rarely been an explicit focus.

These points are underscored by the evidence from the US Southwest, with its rich background of ethnographic information and traditional knowledge. The pattern of migration as a 'spider web of paths' (Cordell 1995: 205), as well as the diversity of social and ideological interactions structuring movement at the intermediate scale, give a dynamic picture of how these large-scale patterns emerge. Both the Pacific and Pueblo cases actually involved a range of group sizes at various points in their migration sequences. However, in the latter case, after the initial larger-scale population movements initiated by the disbandment of Chaco it was more achievable – and therefore more often practised – for single households or small groups of households to migrate, often into communities with which they already held social ties. As a result, migration at one level or another was a constant. This is likely the way of life also experienced by people in the Alpine foreland during the fourth and third millennia BCE. Here, regular mobilities linked communities across space and time and provided important social infrastructure to shape political relationships and resist power disparities.

Both the Pacific and US Southwest examples also show that migration should not be analytically isolated from wider concerns of ritual, cosmology or identity. In these two case studies, as well as, perhaps, the European Final Neolithic (the Corded Ware and Bell Beaker phenomena), migration events seem deeply enmeshed in ritual activities and cosmological values. These, in turn, might have been perceived as core motivations for or organizing principles of that migration, as well as important strategies for integrating individuals and groups of diverse origin. Migration was an integral cultural practice anchored in cosmological systems and a viable social strategy for at least some segments of society. This is an especially useful, but underexplored angle for the Neolithic of Europe. Ritual and ceremonial strategies for integration played a rather subdued role in the Alpine foreland, where co-residence and shared economic activities were apparently more important for creating cohesion. In contrast, the importance of burial rites for the European Final Neolithic has been repeatedly observed and sometimes used to stress the exclusive social role of invading elite male warriors (e.g. Bourgeois and Kroon 2017; Haak et al. 2023; critically Furholt 2019b; Wentink 2020). Bianca Preda-Bălănică and Yoan Diekmann (2023) instead demonstrate that the composition of the buried group and the biological identity of primary interments can vary from this alleged norm, with DNA signatures of both 'locals' and incomers represented. Whether and how these ritual practices were employed in strategies of integration or distinction is hence something that needs to be investigated in each case.

Our case studies also document the formation and re-formation of identities as an integral part of migration processes, as people who are mobile and those around whom they settle are confronted with new or differing habits and values, and rearrange social relations and power structures accordingly. Indeed, such processes may be much more important while on the move. As people come together to form migrating groups, internal differences can be suppressed for the benefit of creating a new, shared identity that takes its origin in the migration itself and fuses various traditions. As noted above, there is a tendency in European archaeology to see ethnic identities as stable and as premises for migration, or as something that forms after a migration event is concluded. But, as we have already suggested with reference to the Early Medieval Migration Period (see Chapter 2, 'Identifying migrants and migrant identities'), as well as the Pacific and the north-west European Neolithic (Chapter 3), it seems ethnic identities may often also emerge along the way.

At the small scale, our case studies caution against the equation of individual social status and power, and indeed, to return to Hannah Arendt (1970; see Chapter 2), of power and violence. Our foray into the early colonial situation around the Great Lakes showed that low-status individuals, such as captives and victims of violence, can be powerful social agents in situations of contact, especially in their ability (sometimes cultivated as a survival strategy) to adapt culturally and quickly learn languages. Particularly at initial contact, where boundaries could be blurry and loyalties confused, situations of coexistence and mutual accommodation, as well as conflict, would have been frequent. Whether multi-ethnic, composite communities like Shamokin could become viable models for new ways of living together depended on the capacity of individuals to negotiate relations of power in interpersonal settings. Yet, in the longer term, the presence of a wider colonial endeavour with extremely unequal means of asserting authority eventually cut this trajectory short in the Americas.

The process developed very differently in the central European Neolithic, although narratives have often been biased towards violent men as agents of history – horse-riding, Indo-European-speaking raiders, whose dominant position is reflected in an enforced conversion to their language and social conventions among those they encounter. Our case studies, by contrast, showed the power of adopted or captured women and children or pragmatic farmers and their role in shaping what became social reality. This regular, small-scale interaction is the crucial social infrastructure that creates large patterns of gene flow and population movement. Further, we emphasize the likely multilingualism of these past individuals, not just to highlight the variable power dynamics that emerge in acts of translation and border-crossing, but also to push back against totalizing models of migration and language change. Even where those violent men, hereditary rulers or exogenous push factors do play a role in a given migration process at the broad scale, the results cannot be understood without reference to individual positionality, relationships, access to resources and local power dynamics.

Being able to focus simultaneously on these different scales is an underutilized strength of archaeological model building, in which broad narratives are made up of tiny, well-studied fragments. If we want to understand migration, we can and should also look at that social process through the lens of children, women, slaves and other people who have played a marginal role in our narratives so far, but all of whom had potential impacts on cultural change (e.g. Cameron 2013).

Consequences for our understanding of migration

For many decades, Neolithic Europe was presumed to be a world of small-scale, highly regionalized and somewhat isolated communities whose way of life persisted with few local innovations for centuries or millennia (as critiqued by Robb 2014: 27–8). The recent focus on the two large-scale horizons of genetic influx, one at the beginning and one near the end of the Neolithic period, has not fundamentally changed this picture. Rather, two somewhat isolated waves – tsunami-like in their impact – are separated by a long, almost eerie calm. Here, we have harnessed a range of case studies to explore the prevalence of mobility, interconnection and migratory practices. In choosing to highlight the political dimension of migration, we have re-oriented our perspective towards a bottom-up focus on dynamic aspects of identity formation, interpersonal and inter-community relationships and individual experiences of complex social processes. In this section, we will outline the significance of this approach for both the continuities and the innovations we see at different times and places in Neolithic society.

Three main points can be made. The first is that what are described as big-picture, continental patterns usually result from an accumulation of many diverse events and processes taking place at the regional level and involving many equally diverse individuals and communities. Second, we must examine identity formation processes *during* migration events in greater detail. As we have seen across our case studies, integrating local and newcomer is potentially a crisis point, and much hinges on the shape these relations take. Migrating groups may need to work hard to create a functional social unit from diverse members, while much effort – often, but not always involving elaborate ritual sequences – accompanies interaction between existing and new settlers. Third, in spite of claims to the contrary, archaeological models often remain biased to the 'victors'' point of view, according most agency to the violent and out-of-the-ordinary while neglecting the many smaller-scale interactions in which the subaltern, too, leave their mark on events.

Adding this sense of politics can make a big impact even on established case studies. To illustrate this, we return briefly to our rough sketch of the migration and mobility patterns of the Linearbandkeramik and the new consensus model outlined in Chapter 2, 'A migration event in search of politics – the Linearbandkeramik', rethinking it through the lens of politics.

Fractal logics: the LBK finds politics

According to the current consensus, the earliest LBK expansion, which effectively displaced local hunter-gatherers, may have proceeded according to a kind of founder rank expansion, where migration itself was a status-enhancing behaviour. In the middle and later LBK, this situation is said to have changed completely and migration became a crisis response, undertaken by either lower-status groups within settlements or in the form of individual migrations, such as wife-exchange. High status is supposedly associated with those (mainly males) who remain in the location of their birth (see Chapter 2, 'A migration event . . .', for references). However, this model explains only part of the data. Introducing a perspective attentive to small-scale politics draws out the existing gaps with a view to further refining our models.

First of all, evidence is mounting that hunter-gatherer societies existed in parallel with expanding LBK communities for some time, even though they apparently did not intermix much (see summary in Hofmann 2015; 2016; Mathieson et al. 2018). Although it is uncertain how long this situation lasted, this leads to a new set of questions in need of further investigation. For example, how were social boundaries between these different groups maintained? Did their existence in the same or adjacent landscapes lead to mutual avoidance or hostility, or was there adaptation and accommodation? And does this explain the increasing diversity of LBK material culture?

Second, new (occasionally controversial) dating programmes have shown that the initial migration of the LBK beyond its core zone, further into central western Europe, may have begun substantially later than 5500 calBCE, rather closer to around 5350 calBCE (Bánffy et al. 2018; Jakucs et al. 2016; Strien 2017b). Instead of two distinct waves, we are thus faced with a smoother, continuous process linking earliest LBK and mid LBK expansion. This makes it less likely that people's attitude to migration as a social strategy would have changed so very radically. Seeing migration as a continuously valued practice helps to introduce new readings.

As shown throughout the volume, migrations destabilize alliances and affiliations, allowing these to be renegotiated and reformed. Further, they can drive identity formation, such as the creation of ethnic identities through an emphasis on cultural difference and boundaries.

In some regions, a deliberate redefinition of identity apparently occurred between the earliest LBK and subsequent phases, such as Flomborn or Notenkopf, which involved the abandonment of earlier settlements and a change in ritual expression (Petrasch 2020). From then on, frequent discontinuities in the biographies of longhouses and whole settlements suggest that relocating was relatively common, although it is hard to reconstruct how far people actually travelled. In the traditional *Hofplatz* or yard model (e.g. Zimmermann 2012), it was stipulated that the longhouse formed the core of the farm and was renewed once every generation to demonstrate the continuity of the patriline. However, while there was substantial continuity within some yards, others showed evidence for in- and out-migration (Figure 6.3). At a micro-regional level, not all settlements in a given site cluster were occupied in all phases; instead, there were episodes of dispersal and abandonment, followed by re-occupation, for example in the Rhineland and in Bavaria (e.g. Balkowski 2017; Hofmann 2016; 2020; Pechtl 2011; 2020). Finally, there is increasing evidence for the routine use of uplands by LBK communities, both in the isotopic data (Turck 2019) and on the ground in the form of pasture indicators, stray finds and some initial excavations (summarized in Hofmann 2020).

Therefore, we can see the budding-off of households and the abandonment of villages as parts of the same processes that also enabled initial LBK migration. There was always the expectation, at least for some people, that one could move on. Economic choices may have been made accordingly. The Vaihingen 'clans' that placed less emphasis on agriculture apparently also invested more energy into the husbandry of ovicaprids as opposed to the more stationary pigs (Bogaard et al. 2016: 17), while at sites in the Paris basin, some households relied substantially on wild animal meat (Hachem 2018: 912). These routine aspects of mobility ensured that LBK actors were aware of landscapes and opportunities beyond their settlement. Leaving a given site remained a viable strategy, for example to alleviate inter-household tensions or to react to challenges such as bad harvests. This sort of normative mobility also has a political dimension, since migration is

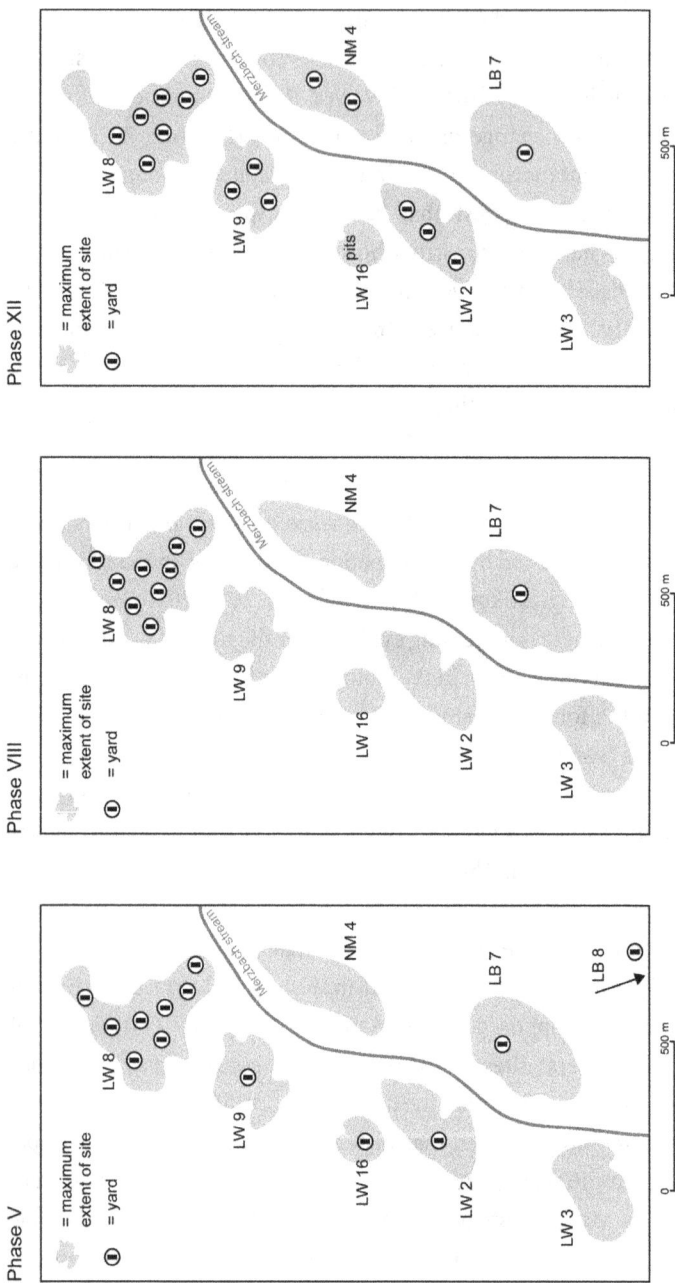

Figure 6.3 Number of inhabited houses on sites in the middle Merzbach valley in phases V, VIII and XII. The fluctuation in numbers is seen as indicative of migration. LW Langweiler; LB Laurenzberg; NM Niedermerz (Hofmann 2016: fig. 5).

one solution to conflicts of power (Beck 2006). Using the same line of thought, Graeber and Wengrow (2021) argue that the freedom to move is one of the three key freedoms underlying the resistance to hierarchy and permits individuals to opt out of perceived control. The substantial investment in fields, through manuring and weeding (e.g. Bogaard et al. 2013), was only one of several accepted LBK lifeways. Considerable numbers of people in this sedentary society were just as ready to be on the move again. The flipside is that mechanisms encouraging cohesion or integration of newcomers deserve more explicit study, be they monumental earthworks, changes in village plans or communal, everyday installations such as wells.

An important future research challenge is to work through the implications of this scenario. How can continued mobility and migration be combined with increasing regionalization in material culture? How did the use of uplands and other non-loess areas by LBK groups impact the remaining hunter-gatherers? Still, it is already clear that there was considerable dynamism throughout the LBK sequence and that this cannot be understood purely with reference to large-scale environmental upheavals or demographic pressures. Rather, as Leppard (2014; 2021) already argued for the Cardial expansion along the Mediterranean shores, this set of migrations is fuelled by the inherent contradictions between small-group interests and community solidarity, between attempts at aggrandizement and strategies of resistance, which make conflicting demands on people's resources. Balancing these opposing pulls is a fundamentally political act that involves rights and obligations, aspirations and failures.

At the smallest scale, patrilocality has been frequently proposed to explain both isotopic and aDNA patterns (for recent criticism, see e.g. Ensor 2021; Hrnčíř et al. 2020), but – perhaps because it conforms neatly to 'traditional' gender roles of active males and passive females – it is rarely explored what this would have meant in terms of gendered relations, the potential diversity of female experience and possibilities for women to pursue own agendas (for criticism, see Bickle and Hofmann 2022). This is in spite of the fact that there is no clear difference in grave-good provision or burial rites for isotopically local and non-local women (Hedges et al. 2013), so that 'outsiders' were evidently integrated effectively. Patrilocality has become the end point of an explanation, rather than the beginning of further investigations. Yet, where sample sizes are sufficient, practice emerges as more varied.

At the Slovakian cemetery of Nitra, for example, where forty-seven individuals were sampled for aDNA, several groups of genetic relatives could be reconstructed. The data are consistent with patrilocality as the majority strategy, but it was not the only one. There are many gaps in the family trees, also for males, suggesting out-migrated individuals. At the same time, those without particularly close genetic relationships were included in the burial community, indicating social strategies for making kin. In particular, no lines of biological relation could be revealed for persons buried with 'high-status' grave goods like axes or *Spondylus* shells, so that the inheritance of wealth and/or social status must have been negotiated beyond biological relations (Gelabert et al. 2023; Hofmann and Bickle submitted). Putting politics at the heart of Neolithic migration studies foregrounds these processes.

Taking these often overlooked data into account, a different narrative emerges. New communities are established first within the heartland of earliest LBK formation in western Hungary, Slovakia and eastern Austria; further expansion is then accompanied by landscape infill in already settled regions. While the size of migrating groups varied – from individuals, to households, to whole communities establishing new settlements – generally quite a number of people were on the move at any one time. However, the level of cultural distance would have differed considerably between situations where people moved within an already partially infilled settlement area, and events that saw them push further into hunter-gatherer territory, as across north-western France and the north European plain. Several processes were thus active simultaneously and may have been driven by different logics and experienced differently by various segments of the population. All of this cannot be reflected in a single, simple narrative.

Life beyond the wave

Migration was therefore an undercurrent of social life throughout the duration of the LBK, although there may have been shifts in speed and direction. Expansion into territories previously settled only by hunter-gatherers decreased as the limits of loess soils were reached and larger hunter-gatherer-fisher societies with more dependable resources were encountered. At the same time, LBK communities focused increasingly on settling non-loess areas in the regions they already occupied, and this could have contributed to the creation of ethnic boundaries between groups now competing for resources. However, whether this ultimately rather mechanistic model is plausible will depend on additional research, not least better dating. What is clear is that migration and mobility were not marginal, but quite common – even desirable – behaviours. The social position of migrating individuals was not necessarily one of lower status.

Similar aspects are visible in the diffusion of Neolithic practices, ways of life and populations into Europe's north-west fringes. In both southern Scandinavia and the north-east Atlantic archipelago, we see a rapid shift from primarily forager lifeways to primarily agricultural practices, coinciding with the adoption of new tools, structures and cosmologies. These are accompanied by clear evidence of population mobility. The current dominant model suggests that agriculturalists from elsewhere moved into these areas, bringing with them a suite of ways of doing, being and relating that we categorize as 'Neolithic'. Yet, despite the clear similarities in the temporality and tempo of migration, underlying subsistence practices and elements of shared cosmology between agricultural migrants in Scandinavia and the north-east Atlantic archipelago, these two regions see quite distinct processes of integration, identity formation and social development. The former maintained ties with their natal communities, manifested in shared technologies, styles and ways of life; the latter intentionally distinguished themselves, leading to the development of a distinctly insular Neolithic within just a few generations. We argue that these differences likely reflect the demographics and scale of relations with local hunter-gatherer populations, as well as mutual support strategies among the incoming agriculturalists that saw people emphasize certain affiliations over others. Whether the Alpine foreland situation of constant small-scale mobility, documented there thanks to exceptional preservation conditions, was more generally applicable for societies at this time needs to be examined further. If so, we again have a pattern in which punctuated migration episodes bubbled up from a consistent background of mobility. Moving on was a suitable choice in many situations.

Similarly, the changes of the third millennium in Europe have been portrayed as the result of a textbook example of a singular, clear-cut process with a single cause (e.g. steppe migrants sparking the formation of Corded Ware and Bell Beaker cultures). Yet the more accurate interpretation is as a patchwork of regionally and locally different political processes of migration, integration, negotiation, adoption or rejection of new practices, symbols and values that formed through interaction between regionally new and pre-existing identities (e.g. S.K. Nielsen and Johannsen 2023). The result is that we see some use of Corded Ware material culture and burial rituals among Jutlandic heathland pastoralists, Norwegian and Baltic fisher-gatherers, central German and Bohemian mixed farmers, and the partial adoption of Corded Ware vessels and battle axes in Swiss lakeshore settlements, Dutch coastal sites and eastern Danish megalith-using societies, among others (Furholt 2020). So far, archaeological debates have overemphasized initial migration processes and neglected successive human movements, return migrations and phenomena of population circulation or translocality. The example of so-called battle axes being used for field-clearing tasks in the Netherlands, as well as the long and sometimes uncomfortable history of how individuals reached new communities, show that there is a largely untapped potential for studies uncovering the individual level of political negotiations.

Migration is not just about the impulse (or incentive or imperative) to depart and the world people made after arrival, but is a complex, culturally contingent and temporally variable social phenomenon in its own right. Thinking of migration in this manner has forced us to ask new questions and look for new solutions to problems we did not previously realize existed. How, for example, could rituals be part of social integration processes that allowed migrants to join and remain part of new communities? Why engage in the complex kin-building and affiliation practices that underlie ethnogenesis? How were 'migration events' lasting generations or centuries experienced at the scale of the individual? How do small-scale mobilities and inter-personal politics drive broader social phenomena? How does all of this change our understanding of emerging archaeological and biomolecular data and how might we move forward from here?

Migration and politics – a new research agenda

While push and pull factors such as climate, war, disease and demography often play a role, migration phenomena are always social processes with their own politics. They emerge in specific structural settings and are shaped by the ways in which power rests within and between communities or is contended between individuals or groups. In addition, they are subject to collective negotiations, conflict or struggles between people with different interests and values, resulting in diverse decisions being taken. As our case studies highlight, such political processes are dynamically interlinked with layers of identity, such as ethnicity or gender, that were created, shaped or rearranged in the course of migration. Politics emerge as a fundamental part of any migration, bridging narratives on the large, continental scale, the middle, regional scale and the small individual one across regions and periods.

Lessons from the politics of migration

From our comparison of the case studies, we would now like to draw out three key points that we think future studies of migration in archaeology need to take into account: the choice of analytical scale; the importance of outliers and apparent contradictions in our data; and the acceptance of migration as a strategy beyond times of crisis. These points have been made before, but we argue that a focus on politics as a connecting theme allows us to bundle them together more effectively, multiplying their interpretative impact.

Beginning with scales of analysis, in Chapter 2 we argued that scholars use the term 'migration' to describe quite separate social phenomena with distinct political and social implications. These range from the movement of large groups of people to nearby locales where they have previously established kin or other ties to the movement of individuals or single families far from their homes to almost any combination in between (Table 2.1). While most studies of migration concentrate on the more extreme end of these criteria – large groups of people travelling, travellers moving over large distances, singular or exceptional mobility events, voyages to alien or unknown lands – the actual composition of any identified migration is much muddier and often less extreme.

Yet our scales of analysis affect our interpretations profoundly. This is not a new observation, but it is important to unravel if we are to address the politically fraught topic of past (and present) migrations. Archaeology tends towards multi-scalar interpretation because our fragmentary data often demand multiple forms of analysis (Frieman 2023; cf. Currie 2021). So a single site, individual or feature with a good (and well-funded) history of investigation may see multiple phases of scientific study and contextual analysis, from microscopy to dating to biomolecular analysis to taphonomic study, including associated materials and parallel practices in nearby locales. This affords us a uniquely rich body of data, but also tends to create individualized narratives that focus on unique qualities and particular histories. At the same time, the nature of looking back at a not-always-well-dated past viewed through the pinholes of reliable (often disconnected) data points can push us towards generalizing models (as in the case of the Polynesian migrations). Between these two scales of the singular object of study and the widespread and long-term pattern is the scale of generations, habitual practice, human memory and daily life. It is on this scale that our mobile past people experienced and engaged in the politics of affiliation, interpersonal violence, religious adherence, wonder and adventure.

Several consequences follow from this multi-scalar mode of working. In general, when we feel that our data are too contradictory or contain too many gaps, we tend to switch to a larger-scale analytical level in an effort to even out the discontinuities. This has the effect of making patchwork situations hard to spot. Where divergent modes of life co-exist in space and time, as might be the case in a migration situation, and especially where they do so for a limited time, we tend to more or less confidently assign them to successive periods, editing out the confusing overlap (Tutchener and Claudie 2022). This, in turn, creates situations of artificially defined boundaries, where change appears stark, catastrophic and uncompromising – migration as a sudden wave, rather than a process that may have built up over its own, longer-term timescale and that subsides slowly.

Following on from this is our second point, the importance of a diversity of actors and perspectives, including greater attention to situations that buck the statistical trends and averages. It is these situations that alert us to the possibilities for change that are inherent in social contradictions, divergent interests and political relations (e.g. McGlade and van der Leeuw 1997; Wobst 1997). In terms specifically of an archaeology of migration, this shifts the narrative perspective to the relations between incomers and residents and to problematizing this duality. Rather than contrasting two essentialized groups we can study how interactions unfolded dynamically over time. Processes of confrontation, but also integration, creative admixture and syncretism, should take as much room as migration itself. Thinking with a greater diversity of actors, including those to whom we have traditionally afforded little agency or power, is essential. We must also be aware that migration events often change the way people (both those moving and those who are not) think about their own identities, and that this will have its own material outcomes. Acknowledging the diversity of perspectives will make migration a far less unsettling concept to deal with.

As our third point, we would therefore like to return to the issue of migration as an 'out of the ordinary' behaviour, an assumption already criticized by David Anthony (1990). Migration is a term that overshadows and renders exceptional what are habitual (or at least familiar) patterns of mobility and the power flows that shaped them (for habitual mobilities, see e.g. Gibson 2021; Leary 2014). In this way, an overly narrow focus on migration, lacking the conceptual unpacking we have undertaken in previous chapters, actually obscures our ability to interpret any given migration by decoupling it from its wider setting of mobility and social relations. Looking at Table 2.1 through these eyes, we might re-organize it from a table of discrete attributes to a less differentiated, watery spectrum of practices, out of which bubbles emerge on occasion, causing ripples and splatters of varied size. Migrations can be profoundly transgressive events, but not necessarily in the sense of a destructive or problematic mass migration. Rather, migrations have the potential to bring into contact ways of life and people in new constellations. The outcomes of this are varied.

An archaeology of politics and mobility

Using politics as an analytical concept effectively helps to frame these three points into a coherent approach. As we have demonstrated across previous chapters, the scales of analysis we choose will inevitably shape our conclusions. Here, we advocate a highly mobile method that allows plenty of room for divergences, dialectics, conflicting pulls and changes. By letting the concept of politics seep into the past in this way, we do fuller justice to the lived reality of all migration processes. These were after all not played out following the arrows on our neat maps, but in an open-ended process whose outcome, even when planned, remained uncertain. It also shows the many ways in which migration was interconnected with other forms of mobility and was part of social and economic strategies throughout the human past, rather than being an option of last resort.

However, politics is not just at work in the past, but also in our writing in the present. We walk through a landscape of data, gathering some and leaving others. As such, we do not wish to advocate that any scale of analysis or narrative focus is necessarily 'wrong' – that it would be morally objectionable, for example, to write about migration events that extend over large scales, or to focus on the negative consequences for some of their actors. However, all these aspects are not neutral reflections of a single past 'reality', but analytical choices which must be reflected as such and *actively* made. Doing so may lead to a greater diversity of narrative options and to more experimentation with recording, mapping and describing migration processes, something long advocated (e.g. Anderson-Whymark and Garrow 2015; Frieman and Hofmann 2019), but so far rarely realized.

An archaeology of migration centred around the concept of politics also offers overlap with disciplines beyond archaeology. One project of this book has been to re-integrate migration into wider discourse on past mobilities, in dialogue with contemporary studies that re-imagine social relations on the move rather than situated at static points (e.g. Blunt 2007; Cresswell 2006; 2010; Glick-Schiller and Salazar 2013; Urry 2007). Uniquely among the social sciences, archaeology provides insight into human practices across temporal scales, from the moment to the epoch. Our necessarily multi-scalar methodology, once allowed to display messiness and ambiguity, can turn into a mode of analysis that is able to connect a single event to a pattern of practice to the *longue durée* of history without defaulting to teleological reasoning. Moreover, by juxtaposing outliers and oddities with habitual practices, we can trace the multiple potentialities inherent in each migration event and document that the currently known outcomes were not the only possible ones. In this, we have built the tools to tell complex, messy, deeply human and contested migration stories without projecting the present into the past. If the past was not inevitable, then neither are the present or the future.

This does not mean that archaeological models are less prone to error or bias than those developed in any other field, especially given how fragmentary our data often are. Nevertheless, the framework we have built around the act and concept of migration, informed by numerous archaeological case studies of different periods and scales, offers a richness and time depth that migration studies rooted in the present often lack. It finds migration, mobility and flux at the very roots of human experience. As such, it could be applied equally to unravel experiences and impacts of migration in the recent past and our contemporary world, to contextualize them with regard both to their own written and unwritten histories, and to draw out threads of implication into the future.

7

Conclusions

The interdisciplinary scholarly focus on migration and mobility over the last two decades is unsurprising when we consider the wider social, political and environmental context of the contemporary world. Not only have conflict and climate change forced thousands to flee to new homes, but cynical politicians have been alleged to have capitalized on migration events to destabilize rivals and neighbours (Braghiroli and Makarychev 2018). Migration has become big business, not only for traffickers and the private security firms patrolling state borders, but also for Western economies relying on the cheap labour of undocumented migrants in precarious life situations and not least for the NGOs tasked with housing and feeding refugees, and the journalists, academics and artists profiting from migrant stories (Hamilakis 2018b: 6). For all that the majority of us live quite settled lives, the disruption of potential migrations looms large and feels ever more possible. As catastrophic weather events become more extreme and more common, we are all of us taking stock of our ability to pack up and leave, to travel to family on higher or drier ground and to pick up the pieces once the crisis is past.

That said, among the results of all this scholarship is the appreciation that migration is not just a pathological antonym to settled life. Migration is and has always been a frequent, multi-scalar and deeply human process. People travel. In fact, high mobility and an ability to thrive in a range of biomes and climates is one of the defining features of our genus (Daniels 2022; Rutherford 2016: chapter 1; Shah 2020). From *Homo erectus* onwards, and before then within Africa, we have made journeys and, subsequently, made tools and made lives and made families just about anywhere our feet could carry us (Bellwood 2022). The proliferation of newly identified hominin species from Iberia to Siberia to Island South-east Asia demonstrates the time depth and significance of hominin dispersal. Mobility ceased to be the dominant pattern of life for (the majority of) our own species only a few thousand years ago (about the most recent 2–4 per cent of our existence as a species, if the date of *c.* 300,000 years currently given to our origin is correct). Even after settling down, mobility was constant, both the small-scale movements inherent in regular activities and the medium- and long-distance journeys to visit family, go on pilgrimage, engage in subsistence activities or simply see a new place (Cresswell 2006; Urry 2007).

Migrations, as we outlined in Chapter 1, form one facet of this dynamic flow, and they too are variable. As our meandering narrative has detailed, the word 'migration' enfolds many processes, but as used today tends to obscure the variable, complex and negotiated experience of mass and/or massive mobility. In response, with our multi-scalar approach we have tried to develop a holistic understanding of these sorts of social processes from the perspective of the people who experienced them. While we argue that migration is a normative feature of human society from the deep past through to the present, we also acknowledge that it often is transformative, changing large-scale social topography, the cultural geography of communities and community members and individuals' own sense of self and belonging. If, instead of picturing discrete and overwhelming waves of migrants, we visualize migration as the ebb and flow of water along an endless river bank – often constant, occasionally violent – then the diasporic communities who emerge from it are the delicate foam crests – not quite liquid, not quite solid – that cling at the same time to the water and the sand.

Social scientists and culture studies scholars have detailed the complex and often contradictory redefinitions of self and society that emerge from cross-cultural contact and connection (Bhabha 1994; Bhatia and Ram 2001; Hall 1990). Often studied through the lens of violent cultural coupling – colonialism, slavery and their aftermath – hybrid or diasporic identities take shape through the sort of small-scale power flows and personal politics we explore in previous chapters. Historical processes of forced migration and invasion lend themselves to narratives of cultural extinction, but the persistence of colonized and formerly enslaved people, their ongoing cultural development and their canny negotiations between a powerful past and a better future document resilience in the face of unplanned migrations and existential threats (Frieman and May 2020; May et al. 2020; Schneider and Panich 2022; Wilcox 2010).

Yet, not all migration is catastrophic – in impulse, experience or impact. Catherine Nash (2002; 2005) has written extensively about the potential of migration to spawn new cultural geographies of belonging among diasporic communities. Ties of lineage and descent are crucial here. Nash for example details the ways that European diasporic communities engage in genealogical thinking, creating concrete pasts and circumscribed ancestral homes for themselves to counteract the emotional and cultural dislocation of migration. In this way, a given process of migration does not just lead to new ways of being or identifying, but also recreates the migrants' own affective landscape.

These long and highly fluid afterlives of migration make clear that the temporality of migration extends beyond both the initial setting out and the eventual settling down. This long-term view, which archaeologists often pride themselves on, is something the field can contribute to interdisciplinary discourse on migration. Following David Anthony (2023), the archaeological study of migration should not begin when two monolithically defined 'cultures' come into contact and should not end when we have found out whether these 'cultures' do or do not correspond to a recognizable genetic signature. Rather, to stress the open-ended and historically situated, long-term process of migration, our studies need to begin with the pre-existing connections between people, their knowledge about 'others' and other places. This approach allows us to then trace migration itself with its many multi-generational movements in diverse directions, and to end with questions of accommodation, integration and the creation of new social formations, both while on the move and after arrival.

These data do not always cohere. Archaeological data are incomplete, aDNA much the same, and the way we make meaning from these various, overlapping and non-contiguous sources means that single totalizing narratives are impossible. The scales at which we study the past, the quality and completeness of our data, and the choices we make in defining e.g. regional or temporal bounds, all affect our conclusions. We suggest that, instead of attempting to delineate a singular narrative of any given migration event, we should accept the disconnected strands. An element of fragmentation or raggedness is characteristic of archaeological data and, we argue, more representative of the messy human underpinnings of this type of social process. Indeed, intertwining all these threads of various lengths and widths gives our lumpy, sometimes fraying narrative rope a tensile strength no single strand could match.

This more open-ended archaeological way of writing migration and mobility should also translate into new narratives for wider dissemination. Migration, with its insistence on fluidity and change, challenges dominant received notions of heritage as static, origins-based and rooted (Harrison et al. 2018). There have been attempts to record the material culture of recent migrations, including undocumented migration (e.g. De León 2013), and to incorporate 'migrant heritage' into exhibits (Kiddey 2023), sometimes at dedicated migration museums. Yet not all of these attempts have been successful, perhaps because the exhibition-makers knew little about their intended audience (Prescott 2019), because exhibits focused on the humanitarian crisis of migration, rather than foregrounding the agentive power of migrants, or because migrant heritage can be framed as being 'about them', rather than concerning everyone, thus sidelining migrant contributions within a heritage concerned with the history of bounded nation states (Hamilakis 2018b: 4–5, 16; Harrison et al. 2018: 215).

In addition, radical redefinitions of what makes 'heritage' are required, often against the reluctance of established heritage bodies to become involved in what are politically divisive issues (e.g. Schofield 2018). This process is under way, amongst others with plans for floating museums (Hamilakis 2018b: 16), detailed guidelines for European museums on re-thinking their focus of collection and display (MeLa project 2015) and critical engagement with the museum as a space for promoting social justice (e.g. Kiddey 2023; Labadi 2018; Whitehead et al. 2015). Archaeology, through both its deep-time perspective and its focus on materiality, has much to offer to this wider discourse.

There is also great value to us as archaeologists in revisiting our understanding of the past in light of new models of social practice, newly uncovered evidence and new forms of interpretation. Just as the emergence of ancient DNA analysis offered archaeologists the opportunity to think more carefully and more extensively about migration, so our ongoing engagement with our sibling fields in the social sciences is helping us make sense of the patterns we are finding. All of these build a richer understanding of the many ways of life experienced by past people. This, in turn, gives us a messier and more three-dimensional view of the world as it once existed, not just for adult men or elite leaders, but for children, people with disabilities, junior wives, younger sons and people who lived in the liminal spaces between other, more common identities. The result is an increasingly detailed and complicated story, elements of which fit more or less neatly with grand narratives of ethnogenesis and collapse or smaller stories of change and continuity.

The archaeological past is not, and never will be, fixed and certain. It is forever in the process of being created, understood and uncovered, and only ever exists in dialogue with our present. As we build our narratives of past people's actions, including the ways they travelled, constructed communities and understood their worlds, we not only gain a better understanding of how things were, but also develop new tools to see how things are now. Moreover, as migration is a universal human experience with important social and political implications in the present and near future, its past is deeply salient. The pasts we construct through archaeological research have enormous power to help us navigate our complex and contested future. Understanding the practices, relations and circumstances that both gave rise to and emerged from past migrations offers us insights into what we see around us. More importantly, it should give us tools to shape the future we want to live in. How we conceptualize migrants, how we treat each other, how we encourage or attempt to limit mobility, all of these are shaped by the history of sedentism and migration, nationalism and colonialism, disruption and peace. But histories – especially the really old ones – change all the time, and we can change with them.

Recognizing the deep histories of migration, we can rebuild our idea of community to include people on the move, instead of seeing migrants as outsiders. We can prioritize finding common ground among neighbours old and new, no matter how diverse our ethnicities and ways of life. We can question the boundaries – personal, cultural, linguistic and geopolitical – that separate us from others, and look for ways to bridge them. If migration is among the oldest and most human of activities, then finding affinities, building communities and sharing ideas across cultural divides must also be part of what has made our species so resilient when confronted with new environments, new people and new challenges.

Notes

1 Introduction

1 Isotopic data, with its emphasis on individual, site and micro-regional scales, caused less of an acceptance problem, perhaps because the explanatory models involved were broader from the start and included more routine behaviours, such as transhumance (Gerdau 2019).

2 Why a Politics of Migration?

1 '. . . jede Chance, innerhalb einer sozialen Beziehung den eigenen Willen auch gegen Widerstreben durchzusetzen, gleichviel worauf diese Chance beruht' (translation in main text: M.F.).

3 Migration at the Large Scale

1 This also appears to have happened on Rapa Nui in the seventeenth and eighteenth centuries, fuelling narratives of a society on the edge of collapse (Ingersoll *et al.* 2018).

2 Note that both these texts suggest migration events from South America to Polynesia. In line with Suggs (1960: 206–7; also N. Thomas 2021: 197), we think that current evidence rather supports a scenario of Polynesians reaching the South American coast and interacting sporadically, but not setting up permanent sites in this already settled landscape.

3 The domesticated status of this animal has been confirmed by archaeozoological analysis. There are in any case no aurochs in Mesolithic Ireland, so this animal must have been introduced by humans.

4 The south-west Asian signature referred to as 'Anatolian Farmer' in many archaeogenetics texts.

5 While we know little about Neolithic boating technology (see e.g. Cummings and Morris 2022: 21), the technological solutions required were far less challenging than for the Pacific.

4 The Middle Distance

1 In contrast, Mary Douglas (1991) characterizes the home as a dystopian place of tyrannical control of body and mind.

2 The evidence for a gradual transition between Mesolithic and Neolithic lifeways is much clearer south of the Alps (see e.g. Becker 2018: 157–71; Cristiani et al. 2009; Degasperi et al. 2006; Perrin 2009).

3 Recently, an enigmatic Pfyn and Horgen culture alignment of 170 stone cairns spread over several kilometres along the shore of Lake Constance has been documented. At the time of construction, the cairns would have been under several metres of water. They have been tentatively connected to a previously undocumented funerary rite, but this needs confirmation (Leuzinger et al. 2021).

5 Mobile People

1 In the second half of the eighteenth century, as relations between the emerging US states and Native Americans became more formalized, women played an increasingly restricted role as translators in official settings (Merrell 1999: 68–71), although this likely continued in more ad-hoc and private situations.

2 Similar processes are documented also e.g. in Dutch–Mohawk relations (Gorgen 2021).

3 It has also been argued that closer attention to the perspectives of the working classes may reveal many more examples of mutual accommodation and compromise, and indeed shared resistance against colonial economic and military policies (e.g. Greenblatt 1991: 146).

4 Most famously, Colin Renfrew (1987) proposed Anatolia as an alternative source area, but other options were discussed (for a summary, see Demoule 2023: 257–317). It has recently also been argued that important branches of the Indo-European family, notably Celtic, had an origin along the Atlantic façade and spread as part of the Bell Beaker network (Cunliffe 2018: 395), but this scenario has been critiqued (Sims-Williams 2020). Celtic most likely emerged in second-millennium BCE Gaul (Pope 2022).

5 This somewhat profane use of supposedly prestigious weapons had already been suggested for battle axes from Funnel Beaker contexts (Frieman 2012).

References

Abegg, C., J. Desideri, O. Dutour and M. Besse (2021), 'More than the sum of their parts: Reconstituting the paleopathological profile of the individual and commingled Neolithic populations of western Switzerland', *Archaeological and Anthropological Sciences,* 13: 59. https://doi.org/10.1007/s12520-021-01278-4

Abdellaoui, A. [+15 others] and D. I. Boomsma (2013), 'Population structure, migration, and diversifying selection in the Netherlands', *European Journal of Human Genetics,* 21: 1277–85.

Adas, M. (1989), *Machines as the Measure of Men: Science, Technology and Ideologies of Western Dominance,* Ithaca, NY: Cornell University Press.

Ahola, M. (2020), 'Creating a sense of belonging: Religion and migration in the context of the 3rd millennium BC Corded Ware complex in the eastern and northern Baltic Sea region', *Norwegian Archaeological Review,* 53 (2): 114–34.

Akerblom, K. (1968), *Astronomy and Navigation in Polynesia and Micronesia,* Stockholm: Ethnographical Museum.

Akins, N. J. (1986), 'The burials of Pueblo Bonito', in J. E. Neitzel (ed.), *Pueblo Bonito: Center of the Chacoan World,* 94–106, Washington, DC: Smithsonian Institution.

Alber, E. (2004), '"The real parents are the foster parents": Social parenthood among the Baatombu in northern Benin', in F. Bowie (ed.), *Cross-cultural Approaches to Adoption,* 33–47. London: Routledge.

Alberti, B., A. M. Jones and J. Pollard, eds (2013), *Archaeology after Interpretation: Returning Materials to Archaeological Theory,* Walnut Creek: Left Coast Press.

Aldred, O. (2020), *The Archaeology of Movement,* London: Routledge.

Allen, J. (2006), *Hostages and Hostage-taking in the Roman Empire,* Cambridge: Cambridge University Press.

Allen, M. S. (2014), 'Marquesan colonisation chronologies and post-colonisation interaction: Implications for Hawaiian origins and the "Marquesan Homeland" hypothesis', *Journal of Pacific Archaeology,* 5 (2): 1–17.

Allentoft, M. E. [+64 others] and E. Willerslev (2015), 'Population genomics of Bronze Age Eurasia', *Nature,* 522: 167–72.

Allentoft, M. E. [+!!! others] and E. Willerslev (2024a), 'Population genomics of post-glacial western Eurasia', *Nature*, 625: 301–11.

Allentoft, M. E. [+66 others] and E. Willerslev (2024b), '100 ancient genomes show repeated population turnovers in Neolithic Denmark', *Nature*, 625: 329–37.

Alt, K. W. [+14 others] and U. von Freeden (2014), 'Lombards on the move: An integrative study of the Migration Period cemetery at Szólád, Hungary', *PLoS ONE*, 9 (11): e110793.

Alt, S. (2006), 'The power of diversity: The roles of migration and hybridity in culture change', in B. M. Butler and P. D. Welch (eds), *Leadership and Polity in Mississippian Society*, 289–308, Carbondale: Southern Illinois University Press.

Altena, E., R. Smeding, K. J. van der Gaag, M. H. D. Larmuseau, R. Decorte, O. Lau, M. Kayser, T. Kraaijenbrink and P. de Knijff (2020), 'The Dutch Y-chromosomal landscape', *European Journal of Human Genetics*, 28: 287–99.

Amborn, H. (2019), *Law as Refuge of Anarchy: Societies Without Hegemony or State,* Cambridge, MA: MIT Press.

Ammerman, A. and L. Cavalli-Sforza (1979), 'The wave of advance model for the spread of agriculture in Europe', in C. Renfrew and K. L. Cooke (eds), *Transformations: Mathematical Approaches to Culture Change*, 275–93, London: Academic Press.

Amorim, C. E. [+22 others] and K. R. Veeramah (2018), 'Understanding 6th-century barbarian social organization and migration through paleogenomics', *Nature Communications*, 9: 3547. https://doi.org/10.1038/s41467-018-06024-4

Andersen, N. H. (1997), *The Sarup Enclosures: Sarup vol. 1*, Højbjerg: Jutland Archaeological Society.

Andersen, S. H. (2008), 'The Mesolithic–Neolithic transition in western Denmark seen from a kitchen midden perspective: A survey', in H. Fokkens (ed.), *Between Foraging and Farming*, 67–73, Leiden: Leiden University.

Anderson, A. (2006), 'Islands of exile: Ideological motivation in maritime migration', *Journal of Island & Coastal Archaeology*, 1 (1): 33–47.

Anderson, A. (2009), 'The rat and the octopus: Initial human colonization and the prehistoric introduction of domestic animals to Remote Oceania', *Biological Invasions,* 11: 1503–19.

Anderson, A. (2017), 'Changing perspectives upon Māori colonisation voyaging', *Journal of the Royal Society of New Zealand*, 47 (3): 222–31.

Anderson, A. (2018), 'Seafaring in Remote Oceania: Traditionalism and beyond in maritime technology and migration', in E. E. Cochrane and

T. L. Hunt (eds), *The Oxford Handbook of Prehistoric Oceania*, 473–92, Oxford: Oxford University Press.

Anderson, A. and S. O'Connor (2008), 'Indo-Pacific migration and colonization – introduction', *Asian Perspectives,* 47 (1): 2–11.

Anderson, A. and P. White (2001), 'Prehistoric settlement on Norfolk Island and its Oceanic context', *Records of the Australian Museum, Supplement*, 27: 135–41.

Anderson-Whymark, H. and D. Garrow (2015), 'Seaways and shared ways: Imagining and imaging the movement of people, objects and ideas over the course of the Mesolithic–Neolithic transition, *c.* 5000–3500 BC', in H. Anderson-Whymark, D. Garrow and F. Sturt (eds), *Continental Connections: Exploring Cross-Channel Relationships from the Mesolithic to the Iron Age,* 59–77, Oxford: Oxbow Books.

Anderson-Whymark, H., D. Garrow and F. Sturt (2015), 'Microliths and maritime mobility: A continental European-style Late Mesolithic flint assemblage from the Isles of Scilly', *Antiquity,* 89 (346): 954–71.

Andersson, M., M. Artursson and K. Brink (2022), 'The Funnel Beaker culture in action: Early and Middle Neolithic monumentality in southwestern Scania, Sweden (4000–3000 cal BC)', *Journal of Neolithic Archaeology*, 24: 61–97.

Anthony, D. (1990), 'Migration in archaeology: The baby and the bathwater', *American Anthropologist,* 92 (4): 895–914.

Anthony, D. (2007), *The Horse, the Wheel, and Language: How Bronze Age Riders from the Eurasian Steppes Shaped the Modern World*, Princeton: Princeton University Press.

Anthony, D. (2019), 'Ancient DNA, mating networks and the Anatolian split', in M. Serangeli and T. Olander (eds), *Dispersals and Diversification: Linguistic and Archaeological Perspectives on the Early Stages of Indo-European*, 21–53, Leiden: Brill.

Anthony, D. (2022), 'Migration, ancient DNA, and Bronze Age pastoralists from the Eurasian steppes', in M. J. Daniels (ed.), *Homo migrans: Modeling Mobility and Migration in Human History*, 55–78, New York: State University of New York Press.

Anthony, D. (2023), 'Ancient DNA and migrations: New understandings and misunderstandings', *Journal of Anthropological Archaeology,* 70: 101508.

Anthony, D. and D. Brown (2017), 'Molecular archaeology and Indo-European linguistics: Impressions from new data', in B. S. S. Hansen, A. Hyllested, A. R. Jørgensen, G. Kroonen, J. H. Larsson, B. Nielsen Whitehead, T. Olander and T. M. Søborg (eds), *Usque ad radices: Indo-European Studies in Honour of Birgit Anette Olsen*, 25–54, Copenhagen: Museum Tusculanum Press.

Anthony, D. and D. Ringe (2015), 'The Indo-European homeland from linguistic and archaeological perspectives', *Annual Review of Linguistics*, 1: 199–219.

Antolín, F. [+9 others] and D. G. Banchieri (2022), 'Neolithic occupations (c. 5200–3400 cal BC) at Isolino Virginia (Lake Varese, Italy) and the onset of the pile-dwelling phenomenon around the Alps', *Journal of Archaeological Science: Reports*, 42: 103375.

Arendt, H. (1970), *On Violence*, San Diego: Harvest HBJ Books.

Arnold, C. J. (1984), *Roman Britain to Saxon England*, London: Croom Helm.

Asam, T., G. Grupe and J. Peters (2006), 'Menschliche Subsistenzstrategien im Neolithikum: Eine Isotopenanalyse bayerischer Skelettfunde', *Anthropologischer Anzeiger*, 64 (1): 1–23.

Augé, M. (1995), *Non-places: Introduction to an Anthropology of Supermodernity*, London: Verso.

Bade, K. (1994), *Homo migrans: Wanderungen aus und nach Deutschland. Erfahrungen und Fragen*, Essen: Klartext.

Bade, K. (2003), *Migration in European History*, Oxford: Blackwell.

Bahss, A. and N. Bleicher (2022), 'Stability through movement: Theoretical and practical considerations of social space in central European Neolithic lakeside settlements', *Journal of Archaeological Method and Theory*, 30: 1378–403.

Baker, B. J. and T. Tsuda, eds (2015), *Migration & Disruptions: Towards A Unifying Theory of Ancient and Contemporary Migrations*, Gainesville, FL: University Press of Florida.

Balkowski, N. (2017), 'From Merzbachtal to the Graetheide? Mobility at the end of the Linear Pottery culture', in S. Scharl and B. Gehlen (eds), *Mobility in Prehistoric Sedentary Societies*, 119–28, Rahden: Marie Leidorf.

Ballard, C. (2020), 'The lizard in the volcano: Narratives of the Kuwae eruption', *The Contemporary Pacific*, 32 (1): 98–123.

Bánffy, E. [+9 others] and A. Whittle (2018), 'Seeking the Holy Grail: Robust chronologies from archaeology and radiocarbon dating combined', *Documenta Praehistorica*, 45: 120–37.

Bartels, I., I. Löhr, C. Reinecke, P. Schäfer and L. Stielike, eds (2023), *Umkämpfte Begriffe der Migration*, Bielefeld: transcript.

Barth, F. (1969), 'Introduction', in F. Barth (ed.), *Ethnic Groups and Boundaries*, 9–39, Boston: Little, Brown.

Bashford, A. and P. Levine, eds (2010), *The Oxford Handbook of the History of Eugenics*, Oxford: Oxford University Press.

Baudais, D., with E. Gatto, J.-L. Gisclon and S. Saintot (2007), 'Coffres en pierre – coffres en bois: La nécropole Néolithique moyen de Genevray (Thonon-les-Bains, Haute-Savoie, France)', in P. Moinat and P. Chambon (eds), *Les cistes de Chamblandes et la place des coffres dans les pratiques funéraires du Néolithique moyen occidental: Actes du colloque de Lausanne, 12 et 13 mai 2006*, 155–76, Lausanne: Cahiers d'Archéologie romande.

Bauer, E. (2016), 'Practising kinship care: Children as language brokers in migrant families', *Childhood*, 23 (1): 22–36.

Beck, R. (2006), 'Persuasive politics and domination at Cahokia and Moundville', in B. M. Butler and P. D. Welch (eds), *Leadership and Polity in Mississippian Society*, 19–42, Carbondale: Southern Illinois University.

Beck, R. (2013), *Chiefdoms, Collapse and Coalescence in the Early American South*, Cambridge: Cambridge University Press.

Becker, V. (2018), *Studien zum Altneolithikum in Italien*, Berlin: Lit Verlag.

Beckerman, S. M. (2015), *Corded Ware Coastal Communities: Using Ceramic Analysis to Reconstruct Third Millennium BC Societies in the Netherlands*, Leiden: Sidestone Press.

Bedford, S. and M. Spriggs (2008), 'Northern Vanuatu as a Pacific crossroads: The archaeology of discovery, interaction, and the emergence of the "ethnographic present"', *Asian Perspectives*, 47 (1): 95–120.

Beeching, A. (2007), 'L'affaire "Chamblandes": Ramifications chrono-culturelles et géographiques du dossier', in P. Moinat and P. Chambon (eds), *Les cistes de Chamblandes et la place des coffres dans les pratiques funéraires du Néolithique moyen occidental: Actes du colloque de Lausanne, 12 et 13 mai 2006*, 69–74, Lausanne: Cahiers d'Archéologie romande.

Behre, K.-E. (2007), 'Evidence for Mesolithic agriculture in and around central Europe?', *Vegetation History and Archaeobotany*, 16: 203–19.

Bell, M. (2020), *Making One's Way in the World: The Footprints and Trackways of Prehistoric People*, Oxford: Oxbow Books.

Bellwood, P. S. (2013), *First Migrants: Ancient Migration in Global Perspective*, Chichester: Wiley Blackwell.

Bellwood, P. S. (2022), *The Five-Million-Year Odyssey: The Human Journey from Ape to Agriculture*, Princeton: Princeton University Press.

Benson, L. V., L. S. Cordell, K. Vincent, H. Taylor, J. Stein, G. L. Farmer and K. Futa (2003), 'Ancient maize from Chacoan great houses: Where was it grown?', *Proceedings of the National Academy of Sciences*, 100 (22): 13111–15.

Bentley, A., M. Earls and M. O'Brien (2011), *I'll Have What She's Having: Mapping Social Behaviour*, London: MIT Press.

Bentley, R. A. [+13 others] and A. Whittle (2012), 'Community differentiation and kinship among Europe's first farmers', *Proceedings of the National Academy of Sciences,* 109 (24): 9326–30.

Bernardini, W. (2005), 'Reconsidering spatial and temporal aspects of prehistoric cultural identity: A case study from the American Southwest', *American Antiquity,* 70 (1): 31–54.

Bernardini, W. (2011a), 'North, south, and center: An outline of Hopi ethnogenesis', in D. M. Glowacki and S. van Keuren (eds), *Religious Transformation in the Late Pre-Hispanic Pueblo World,* 196–220, Tucson: University of Arizona Press.

Bernardini, W. (2011b), 'Migration in fluid social landscapes', in G. S. Cabana and J. J. Clark (eds), *Rethinking Anthropological Perspectives on Migration,* 31–44, Gainesville: University Press of Florida.

Bernardini, W. and S. Fowles (2011), 'Becoming Hopi, becoming Tiwa: Two Pueblo histories of movement', in M. C. Nelson and C. Strawhacker (eds), *Movement, Connectivity, and Landscape Change in the Ancient Southwest,* 253–74, Boulder: University Press of Colorado.

Besse, M. (2003), 'Les céramiques communes des campaniformes européens', *Gallia Préhistoire,* 45: 205–58.

Besse, M. and C. von Tobel (2011), 'Le site du Petit-Chasseur, ses occupations – du Néolithique moyen au second Âge du Fer – et son contexte régional', in M. Besse and M. Piguet (eds), *Le site préhistorique du Petit-Chasseur (Sion, Valais) 10: Un hameau du Néolithique moyen,* 17–28, Lausanne: Cahiers d'Archéologie romande.

Besse, M., E. Bleuer and T. Doppler (2012), 'Das endneolithische Kollektivgrab von Spreitenbach im europäischen Umfeld', in T. Doppler (ed.), *Spreitenbach-Moosweg (Aargau, Schweiz): ein Kollektivgrab um 2500 v. Chr.,* 267–86, Basel: Archäologie Schweiz.

Bhabha, H. (1994), *The Location of Culture,* London: Routledge.

Bhatia, S. and A. Ram (2001), 'Rethinking "acculturation" in relation to diasporic cultures and postcolonial identities', *Human Development,* 44 (1): 1–18.

Biana H. T. (2020), 'Extending bell hooks' feminist theory', *Journal of International Women's Studies,* 21 (1): 13–29.

Bickle, P. F. (2020), 'Thinking gender differently: New approaches to identity difference in the central European Neolithic', *Cambridge Archaeological Journal,* 30 (2): 201–18.

Bickle, P. F. and L. Fibiger (2014), 'Ageing, childhood and social identity in the Early Neolithic of central Europe', *European Journal of Archaeology,* 17 (2): 208–28.

Bickle, P. F. and D. Hofmann (2022), 'Female mobility patterns in prehistory: Patrilocality, descent and kinship of the Linearbandkeramik (LBK)', in R.-M. Arbogast, A. Denaire, Š. Grando-Válečková, P. Lefranc, M. Mauvilly and S. van Willigen (eds), *D'Oberlarg à Wesaluri, itinéraire d'un préhistorien: Mélanges offerts à Christian Jeunesse,* 105–22, Strasbourg: AVAGE.

Bierbrauer, V. (2004), 'Zur ethnischen Interpretation in der frühgeschichtlichen Archäologie', in W. Pohl (ed.), *Die Suche nach den Ursprüngen: Von der Bedeutung des frühen Mittelalters,* 45–84, Wien: Österreichische Akademie der Wissenschaften.

Billamboz, A. (2001), 'Beitrag der Dendrochronologie zur Frage der Besiedlungsdynamik und Bevölkerungsdichte am Beispiel der Pfahlbausiedlungen Südwestdeutschlands', in A. Lippert, M. Schultz, S. Shennan and M. Teschler-Nicola (eds), *Mensch und Umwelt während des Neolithikums und der Frühbronzezeit in Mitteleuropa,* 53–60, Rahden: Marie Leidorf.

Billamboz, A. and J. Köninger (2008), 'Dendroarchäologische Untersuchungen zur Besiedlungs- und Landschaftsentwicklung im Neolithikum des westlichen Bodenseegebietes', in W. Dörfler and J. Müller (eds), *Umwelt – Wirtschaft – Siedlungen im dritten vorchristlichen Jahrtausend Mitteleuropas und Südskandinaviens: Internationale Tagung Kiel 4.–6. November 2005,* 317–34, Neumünster: Wachholtz Verlag.

Billamboz, A., U. Maier, I. Matuschik, A. Müller, W. Out, K. Steppan and R. Vogt, with J. Affolter and A. Feldkeller (2010), 'Die jung- und endneolithischen Seeufersiedlungen von Sipplingen "Osthafen" am Bodensee: Besiedlungs- und Wirtschaftsdynamik im eng begrenzten Naturraum des Sipplinger Dreiecks', in I. Matuschik and C. Strahm (eds), *Vernetzungen: Aspekte siedlungsarchäologischer Forschung. Festschrift für Helmut Schlichtherle zum 60. Geburtstag,* 253–86, Freiburg i. B.: Lavori.

Binford, L. R. (1980), 'Willow smoke and dogs' tails: Hunter-gatherer settlement systems and archaeological site formation', *American Antiquity,* 45 (1): 4–20.

Birch, J. (2012), 'Coalescent communities: Settlement aggregation and social integration in Iroquoian Ontario', *American Antiquity,* 77 (4): 646–70.

Bleicher, N. (2009), *Altes Holz in neuem Licht: Archäologische und dendrochronologische Untersuchungen an spätneolithischen Feuchtbodensiedlungen Oberschwabens*, Stuttgart: Theiss.

Bleicher, N. and C. Harb (2018), 'Settlement and social organisation in the late fourth millennium BC in central Europe: The waterlogged site of Zurich-Parkhaus Opéra', *Antiquity*, 92 (365): 1210–30.

Bleuer, E., T. Doppler and H. Fetz (2012), 'Gräber im näheren und weiteren Umfeld von Spreitenbach', in T. Doppler (ed.), *Spreitenbach-Moosweg (Aargau, Schweiz): ein Kollektivgrab um 2500 v. Chr.*, 233–66, Basel: Archäologie Schweiz.

Blunt, A. (2007), 'Cultural geographies of migration: Mobility, transnationality and diaspora', *Progress in Human Geography*, 31 (5): 684–94.

Bocquet-Appel, J.-P. (2008), 'Explaining the Neolithic demographic transition', in J.-P. Bocquet-Appel and O. Bar-Yosef (eds), *The Neolithic Demographic Transition and its Consequences*, 35–55, New York: Springer.

Bocquet-Appel, J.-P. (2011), 'When the world's population took off: The springboard of the Neolithic demographic transition', *Science*, 333 (6042): 560–1.

Boersema, J. J. (2018), 'An earthly paradise? Easter Island (Rapa Nui) as seen by the eighteenth-century European explorers', in S. H. Cardinali, K. B. Ingersoll, D. W. Ingersoll Jr. and C. M. Stevenson (eds), *Cultural and Environmental Change on Rapa Nui*, 156–78, London: Routledge.

Bogaard, A., R. Krause and H.-C. Strien (2011), 'Towards a social geography of cultivation and plant use in an early farming community: Vaihingen an der Enz, south-west Germany', *Antiquity*, 85 (328): 395–416.

Bogaard, A. [+17 others] and E. Stephan (2013), 'Crop manuring and intensive land management by Europe's first farmers', *Proceedings of the National Academy of Sciences*, 110 (31): 12589–94.

Bogaard, A., R.-M. Arbogast, R. Ebersbach, R. A. Fraser, C. Knipper, C. Krahn, M. Schäfer, A. Styring and R. Krause (2016), 'The Bandkeramik settlement of Vaihingen an der Enz, Kreis Ludwigsburg (Baden-Württemberg): An integrated perspective on land use, economy and diet', *Germania*, 94 (1–2): 1–60.

Bolender, D. J., ed. (2010), *Eventful Archaeologies: New Approaches to Social Transformation in the Archaeological Record*, Albany: State University of New York Press.

Borake, T. L. (2019), 'Anarchistic action. Social organization and dynamics in southern Scandinavia from the Iron Age to the Middle Ages', *Archaeological Dialogues*, 26 (2): 61–73.

Borck, L. and J. J. Clark (2021), 'Dispersing power: The contentious, egalitarian politics of the Salado phenomenon in the Hohokam region of the US Southwest', in T. L. Thurston and M. Fernández-Götz (eds), *Power from Below in Ancient Societies: The Dynamics of Political Complexity in the Archaeological Record*, 247–71, Cambridge: Cambridge University Press.

Borck, L. and B. J. Mills (2017), 'Approaching an archaeology of choice: Consumption, resistance, and religion in the Prehispanic Southwest', in C. Cipolla (ed.), *Foreign Objects: Rethinking Indigenous Consumption in American Archaeology*, 29–43, Tucson: University of Arizona Press.

Borck, L. and M. C. Sanger (2017), 'An introduction to anarchism in archaeology', *The SAA Archaeological Record*, 17 (1): 9–16.

Borck, L., B. J. Mills, M. A. Peeples and J. J. Clark (2015), 'Are social networks survival networks? An example from the late Pre-Hispanic Southwest', *Journal of Archaeological Method and Theory*, 22 (1): 33–57.

Bourdieu, P. (1984), *Distinction: A Social Critique of the Judgement of Taste*, London: Routledge.

Bourdieu, P. (1986), 'The forms of capital', in J. Richardson (ed.), *Handbook of Theory and Research for the Sociology of Education*, 241–58, New York: Greenwood.

Bourdieu, P. (1990), *The Logic of Practice*, Stanford: Stanford University Press.

Bourgeois, Q. and E. Kroon (2017), 'The impact of male burials on the construction of Corded Ware identity: Reconstructing networks of information in the 3rd millennium BC', *PLoS One*, 12 (10): e0185971.

Bowie, F., ed. (2004), *Cross-cultural Approaches to Adoption*, London: Routledge.

Brace, S. and T. Booth (2023), 'The genetics of the inhabitants of Neolithic Britain: A review', in A. Whittle, J. Pollard and S. Greaney (eds), *Ancient DNA and the European Neolithic: Relations and Descent*, 123–46, Oxford: Oxbow Books.

Brace, S. [+25 others] and I. Barnes (2019), 'Ancient genomes indicate population replacement in Early Neolithic Britain', *Nature Ecology and Evolution*, 3 (5): 765–71.

Bradley, R. (1993), *Altering the Earth: The Origins of Monuments in Britain and Continental Europe*, Edinburgh: Society of Antiquaries of Scotland.

Braghiroli, S. and A. Makarychev (2018), 'Redefining Europe: Russia and the 2015 refugee crisis', *Geopolitics*, 23 (4): 823–48.

Brandt, G. (2017), *Beständig ist nur der Wandel! Die Rekonstruktion der Besiedlungsgeschichte Europas während des Neolithikums mittels paläo- und populationsgenetischer Verfahren*, Halle: Landesmuseum für Vorgeschichte.

Brandt, G. [+16 others] and the Genographic Consortium (2013), 'Ancient DNA reveals key stages in the formation of central European mitochondrial genetic diversity', *Science*, 342 (6155): 257–61.

Brandt, G., A. Szécsényi-Nagy, C. Roth, K. W. Alt and W. Haak (2015), 'Human paleogenetics of Europe – The known knowns and the known unknowns', *Journal of Human Evolution*, 79: 73–92.

Brather, S. (2000), 'Ethnische Identitäten als Konstrukte der frühgeschichtlichen Archäologie', *Germania*, 78 (1): 139–77.

Brettell, C. and J. Hollifield (2015), 'Introduction', in C. Brettell and J. Hollifield (eds), *Migration Theory: Talking Across Disciplines*, 1–26, London: Routledge.

Brombacher, C. and P. Vandorpe (2012), 'Untersuchungen zur Wirtschaft und Umwelt aus der mittelneolithischen Fundstelle von Zizers GR–Friedau', in A. Boschetti-Maradi, A. de Capitani, S. Hochuli and U. Niffeler (eds), *Form, Zeit und Raum: Grundlagen für eine Geschichte aus dem Boden. Festschrift für Werner E. Stöckli zu seinem 65. Geburtstag*, 95–104, Basel: Archäologie Schweiz.

Brück, J. and D. Fontijn (2013), 'The myth of the chief: Prestige goods, power and personhood in the European Bronze Age', in H. Fokkens and A. Harding (eds), *The Oxford Handbook of the European Bronze Age*, 197–215, Oxford: Oxford University Press.

Burmeister, S. (1998), 'Comment on Heinrich Härke, Archaeologists and migrations: A problem of attitude?', *Current Anthropology*, 39 (1): 27–8.

Burmeister, S. (2000), 'Archaeology and migration: Approaches to an archaeological proof of migration', *Current Anthropology*, 41 (4): 539–67.

Burmeister, S. (2017a), 'The archaeology of migration: What can and should it accomplish?', in H. Meller, F. Daim, J. Krause and R. Risch (eds), *Migration und Integration von der Urgeschichte bis zum Mittelalter*, 57–68, Halle: Landesmuseum für Vorgeschichte.

Burmeister, S. (2017b), 'One step beyond: Migration als kulturelle Praxis', in A. Dietz, A. Hidding and J. D. Preisigke (eds), *Migration and Change: Causes and Consequences of Mobility in the Ancient World. Distant Worlds Journal*, 3: 3–18.

Burmeister, S. (forthcoming), 'The migrants' home: The dual world of migrants as archaeological field of investigation', in V. Heyd and M. Ahola (eds), *Moving and Migrating in Prehistoric Europe*, London: Routledge.

Burri, E. (2007), 'Concise (Vaud, Suisse). Les vestiges céramiques d'un village du Néolithique moyen (3645–3636 av. J.-C.): répartitions spatiales et interprétations', in M. Besse (ed.), *Sociétés néolithiques: Des faits archéologiques aux fonctionnements socio-économiques. Actes du 27e colloque interrégional sur le Néolithique (Neuchâtel, 1 et 2 octobre 2005),* 153–63, Lausanne: Cahiers d'Archéologie romande.

Byron, L. and M. Wattenberg (2008), 'Stacked Graphs – Geometry & Aesthetics', *IEEE Transactions on Visualization and Computer Graphics,* 14 (6): 1245–52.

Cabana, G. S. and J. J. Clark, eds (2011), *Rethinking Anthropological Perspectives on Migration,* Gainesville: University Press of Florida.

Cameron, C. M. (2013), 'How people moved among ancient societies: Broadening the view', *American Anthropologist,* 115 (2): 218–31.

Campbell, B. C. (2011), 'Adrenarche and middle childhood', *Human Nature,* 22 (3): 327–49.

Campbell, J. (2008), 'What can we learn about the earliest human language by comparing languages known today?', in B. Laks (ed.), *Origin and Evolution of Languages: Approaches, Models, Paradigms,* 79–111, London: Equinox.

Capelli, C. [+13 others] and D. B. Goldstein (2003), 'A Y chromosome census of the British Isles', *Current Biology,* 13 (11): 979–84.

Cassidy, L. M. (2023), 'Islands apart? Genomic perspectives on the Mesolithic– Neolithic transition in Ireland', in A. Whittle, J. Pollard and S. Greaney (eds), *Ancient DNA and the European Neolithic: Relations and Descent,* 147–67, Oxford: Oxbow Books.

Castañeda, A. (1998), 'Language and other lethal weapons: Cultural politics and the rites of children as translators of culture', *Chicana/o Latina/o Law Review,* 19 (1): 229–41.

Cauvin, J. (2000), *The Birth of the Gods and the Origins of Agriculture,* Cambridge: Cambridge University Press.

Cayton, A. R. L. and F. J. Teute (1998), 'Introduction: On the connection of frontiers', in A. R. L. Cayton and F. J. Teute (eds), *Contact Points: American Frontiers from the Mohawk Valley to the Mississippi, 1750–1830,* 1–15, Chapel Hill: University of North Carolina Press.

Césaire, A. (2000 [1955]), *Discourse on Colonialism,* New York: Monthly Review Press.

Chambon, P. and J. Leclerc, eds (2003), *Les pratiques funéraires néolithiques avant 3500 av. J.-C. en France et dans les régions limitrophes: table ronde SPF, Saint-Germain-en-Laye, 15–17 juin 2001: actes,* Paris: Société Préhistorique Française.

Chapman, J. (1997), 'The impact of modern invasions and migrations on archaeological explanation', in J. Chapman and H. Hamerow (eds),

Migrations and Invasions in Archaeological Explanation, 11–20, Oxford: Archaeopress.

Chapman, J. and H. Hamerow (1997), 'On the move again: Migrations and invasions in archaeological explanation', in J. Chapman and H. Hamerow (eds), *Migrations and Invasions in Archaeological Explanation*, 1–10, Oxford: Archaeopress.

Chapple, R. M., R. McLaughlin and G. Warren (2022), '"... where they pass their unenterprising existence ...": Change over time in the Mesolithic of Ireland as shown in radiocarbon-dated activity', *Proceedings of the Royal Irish Academy: Archaeology, Culture, History, Literature*, 112C: 1–38.

Cheung, C., E. Herrscher, G. Andre, L. Bedault, L. Hachem, A. Binois-Roman, D. Simonin and A. Thomas (2021), 'The grandeur of death – Monuments, societies, and diets in Middle Neolithic Paris basin', *Journal of Anthropological Archaeology*, 63: 101332. https://doi.org/10.1016/j.jaa.2021.101332

Childbayeva, A. [+14 others] and W. Haak (2022), 'Population genetics and signatures of selection in Early Neolithic European farmers', *Molecular Biology and Evolution*, 39 (6): msac108. https://doi.org/10.1093/molbev/msac108

Childe, V. G. (1936), *Man Makes Himself*, London: Watts.

Choin, J. [+20 others] and L. Quintana-Murci (2021), 'Genomic insights into population history and biological adaptation in Oceania', *Nature*, 592: 583–9.

Cipolla, C. N. (2013), *Becoming Brothertown: Native American Ethnogenesis and Endurance in the Modern World*, Tucson: University of Arizona Press.

Ciugudean, H. (2011), 'Mounds and mountains: Burial rituals in Early Bronze Age Transylvania', in S. Berecki, R. E. Németh and B. Rezi (eds), *Bronze Age Rites and Rituals in the Carpathian Basin: Proceedings of the International Colloquium from Târgu Mureş, 8–10 October 2010*, 21–57, Târgu Mureş: Mega.

Cladders, M. and H. Stäuble (2003), 'Das 53. Jahrhundert v. Chr.: Aufbruch und Wandel', in J. Eckert, U. Eisenhauer and A. Zimmermann (eds), *Archäologische Perspektiven: Analysen und Interpretationen im Wandel. Festschrift für Jens Lüning zum 65. Geburtstag*, 491–503, Rahden: Marie Leidorf.

Clark, J. J. [+10 others] and J. A. Ware (2019), 'Resolving the migrant paradox: two pathways to coalescence in the late precontact US Southwest', *Journal of Anthropological Archaeology*, 53: 262–87.

Clarkson, F. (2021), 'Interpretesses: Native American women translators in colonial America', *Undergraduate Research Awards*, 57, https://digitalcommons.hollins.edu/researchawards/57 [last accessed 23.03.22].

Clastres, P. (1989 [1974]), *Society Against the State: Essays in Political Anthropology* (4th edn), New York: Zone Books.

Clastres, P. (1994 [1976]), *Archeology of Violence*, Cambridge, MA: MIT Press.

Clifford, J. (1988), *The Predicament of Culture: Twentieth-Century Ethnography, Literature, and Art*, Cambridge, MA: Harvard University Press.

Commendador, A. S., J. V. Dudgeon, B. P. Finney, B. T. Fuller and K. S. Esh (2013), 'A stable isotope (δ^{13}C and δ^{15}N) perspective on human diet on Rapa Nui (Easter Island) ca. AD 1400–1900', *American Journal of Physical Anthropology*, 152 (2): 173–85.

Comrie, B. (2008), 'Languages, genes, and prehistory, with special reference to Europe', in B. Laks (ed.), *Origin and Evolution of Languages: Approaches, Models, Paradigms*, 40–62, London: Equinox.

Conneller, C., N. Milner, B. Taylor and M. Taylor (2012), 'Substantial settlement in the European Early Mesolithic: new research at Star Carr', *Antiquity*, 86 (334): 1004–20.

Cordell, L. (1995), 'Tracing migration pathways from the receiving end', *Journal of Anthropological Archaeology*, 14 (2): 203–11.

Cramp, L. J. E., J. Jones, A. Sheridan, J. Smyth, H. Whelton, J. Mulville, N. Sharples and R. P. Evershed (2014), 'Immediate replacement of fishing with dairying by the earliest farmers of the northeast Atlantic archipelagos', *Proceedings of the Royal Society B: Biological Sciences*, 281 (1780): 20132372.

Crenshaw, K. (1991), 'Mapping the margins: Intersectionality, identity politics, and violence against women of color', *Stanford Law Review*, 43 (6): 1241–99.

Cresswell, T. (2006), *On the Move: Mobility in the Modern Western World*, London: Routledge.

Cresswell, T. (2010), 'Towards a politics of mobility', *Environment and Planning D: Society and Space*, 28 (1): 17–31.

Cresswell, T. (2014), 'Place', in R. Lee, N. Castree, R. Kitchin, V. Lawson, A. Paasi, C. Philo, S. Radcliffe, S. M. Roberts and C. Withers (eds), *The Sage Handbook of Human Geography*, 3–21, London: Sage.

Cresswell, T. and P. Merriman, eds (2011), *Geographies of Mobilities: Practices, Spaces, Subjects*, Farnham: Ashgate.

Cristiani, E., A. Pedrotti and S. Gialanella (2009), 'Tradition and innovation between the Mesolithic and Early Neolithic in the Adige valley (northeast

Italy): New data from a functional and residues analyses of trapezes from Gaban rockshelter', *Documenta Praehistorica*, 36: 191–205.

Crumley, C. (1995), 'Heterarchy and the analysis of complex societies', *Archaeological Papers of the American Anthropological Association*, 6 (1): 1–5.

Cummings, V. and C. Fowler (2023), 'Materialising descent: Lineage formation and transformation in Early Neolithic southern Britain', *Proceedings of the Prehistoric Society*, 89: 1–21.

Cummings, V. and J. Morris (2022), 'Neolithic explanations revisited: Modelling the arrival and spread of domesticated cattle into Neolithic Britain', *Environmental Archaeology*, 27 (1): 20–30.

Cummings, V., D. Hofmann, M. Bjørnevad-Ahlqvist and R. Iversen (2022), 'Muddying the waters: Reconsidering migration in the Neolithic of Britain, Ireland and Denmark', *Danish Journal of Archaeology*, 11: 1–25.

Cunliffe, B. (2018), *The Ancient Celts* (2nd edn), Oxford: Oxford University Press.

Currie, A. (2021), 'Stepping forwards by looking back: Underdetermination, epistemic scarcity and legacy data', *Perspectives on Science*, 29 (1): 104–32.

Czebreszuk, J. and M. Szmyt (2011), 'Identities, differentiation and interactions on the central European plain in the 3rd millennium BC', in S. Hansen and J. Müller (eds), *Sozialarchäologische Perspektiven: Gesellschaftlicher Wandel 5000–1500 v. Chr. zwischen Atlantik und Kaukasus*, 269–94, Darmstadt: Philipp von Zabern.

Damm, C. (2010), 'Ethnicity and collective identities in the Fennoscandian Stone Age', in Å. M. Larsson and L. Papmehl-Dufay (eds), *Uniting the Sea II: Stone Age Societies in the Baltic Sea Region*, 11–30, Uppsala: Uppsala University Press.

D'Amore, A. M., V. Murillo Gallegos and K. Zimányi (2016), 'Have faith in your vocabulary: The role of the interpreter in the conquest of power, language and ideology in the New Spain', *Linguistica Antverpiensia New Series*, 15: 36–50.

Dani, J. and G. Kulcsár (2021), 'Yamnaya interactions in the Carpathian basin', in V. Heyd, G. Kulcsár and B. Preda-Bălănică (eds), *Yamnaya Interactions: Proceedings of the international workshop held in Helsinki, 25–26 April 2019*, 329–59, Budapest: Archaeolingua.

Daniels, M. J. (2022), 'Movement as a constant? Envisioning a migration-centered worldview of human history', in M. J. Daniels (ed.), *Homo migrans: Modeling Mobility and Migration in Human History*, 1–28, New York: State University of New York Press.

Dark, K. R. (1994), *Civitas to Kingdom: British Political Continuity 300–800*, Leicester: Leicester University Press.

De Capitani, A. (2002), 'Gefässkeramik', in A. de Capitani, S. Deschler-Erb, U. Leuzinger, E. Marti-Grädel and J. Schibler (eds), *Die jungsteinzeitliche Seeufersiedlung Arbon-Bleiche 3. Funde*, 135–276, Frauenfeld: Departement für Erziehung und Kultur des Kantons Thurgau.

De Certeau, M. (1984), *The Practice of Everyday Life*, Berkeley: University of California Press.

Degasperi, N., E. Mottes, and M. Rottoli (2006), 'Recenti indagini nel sito neolitico de La Vela di Trento', in A. Pessina and P. Visentini (eds), *Preistoria dell' Italia settentrionale: Studi in ricordo di Bernardino Bagolini. Atti del Convegno Udine, 23–24 settembre 2005*, 145–70, Udine: Museo Friuliano di Storia Naturale.

Delâge, D. (2002), 'Madame Montour (Elisabeth ou Isabelle Couc), 1667–1752', *Recherches Amérindiennes au Québec*, 36 (1): 89–90.

De León, J. (2013), 'Undocumented migration, use wear, and the materiality of habitual suffering in the Sonoran Desert', *Journal of Material Culture*, 18 (4): 321–5.

Del Giudice, M. (2015), 'Attachment in middle childhood: An evolutionary-developmental perspective', *New Directions for Child and Adolescent Development*, 148: 15–30.

Demandt, A. (2014), *Der Fall Roms: Die Auflösung des römischen Reiches im Urteil der Nachwelt* (2nd edn), München: Beck.

Demandt, A. (2016a), 'Das Ende der alten Ordnung', *Frankfurter Allgemeine Zeitung*, 20.01.2016: 6. Available at: https://www.faz.net/-gq7-8clow

Demandt, A. (2016b), 'Der Untergang des Römischen Reichs: Das Ende der alten Ordnung. Stellungnahme Alexander Demandt, Fragen Reinhard Müller', *Frankfurter Allgemeine Zeitung* 20.01.2016.

Demoule, J.-P. (2023), *The Indo-Europeans: Archaeology, Language, Race, and the Search for the Origins of the West*, Oxford: Oxford University Press.

Derenne, E., V. Ard and M. Besse (2022), 'Potters' mobility contributed to the emergence of the Bell Beaker phenomenon in third millennium BCE alpine Switzerland: A diachronic technology study of domestic and funerary traditions', *Open Archaeology*, 8 (1): 925–55.

Diamond, J. M. (1997), *Guns, Germs and Steel: The Fates of Human Societies*, New York: W. W. Norton & Co.

Dieckmann, B. (1990), 'Zum Stand der archäologischen Untersuchungen in Hornstaad, in Siedlungsarchäologische Untersuchungen im Alpenvorland', *Bericht der Römisch-Germanischen Kommission*, 71 (1): 84–109.

Dieckmann, B., J. Köninger, U. Maier and R. Vogt (1997), 'Eine Stratigraphie des Mittelneolithikums mit Feuchtbodenerhaltung in Singen, Kreis Konstanz', *Archäologische Ausgrabungen in Baden-Württemberg*, 1996: 41–6.

Dieckmann, B., A. Harwath and J. Hoffstadt (2006), 'Hornstaad-Hörnle IA: Die Befunde einer jungsteinzeitlichen Pfahlbausiedlung am westlichen Bodensee', in Landesamt für Denkmalpflege (ed.), *Siedlungsarchäologie im Alpenvorland IX*, 8–275, Stuttgart: Theiss.

Dieckmann, B. [+10 others] and B. Theune-Großkopf (2016), 'Eine kurze Dorfgeschichte: Hornstaad-Hörnle IA am Bodensee', in Archäologisches Landesmuseum Baden-Württemberg (eds), *4000 Jahre Pfahlbauten: Begleitband zur Großen Landesausstellung Baden-Württemberg 2016*, 80–92, Ostfildern: Jan Thorbecke.

Dieckmann, B., J. Hald, J. Hoffstadt and R. Vogt (2017), 'Eine neue mittelneolithische Siedlungsstelle am westlichen Bodensee bei Allensbach-Hegne, Gemarkung Reichenau', *Archäologische Ausgrabungen in Baden-Württemberg*, 2016: 70–3.

Doppler, T. (2013), *Archäozoologie als Zugang zur Sozialgeschichte in der Feuchtbodenarchäologie: Forschungsperspektiven am Fallbeispiel der neolithischen Seeufersiedlung Arbon Bleiche 3 (Schweiz)*, Basel: University of Basel. doi:10.5451/unibas-006089936

Doppler, T., B. Pollmann, S. Pichler, S., Jacomet, J. Schibler and B. Röder (2011), 'Bauern, Fischerinnen und Jäger: unterschiedliche Ressourcen- und Landschaftsnutzung in der neolithischen Siedlung Arbon Bleiche 3 (Thurgau, Schweiz)?', in J. Studer, M. David-Ebiali and M. Besse (eds), *Paysage . . . Landschaft . . . Paesaggio . . . L'impact des activités humaines sur l'environnement du Paléolithique à la période romaine*, 143–58, Lausanne: Cahiers d'Archéologie romande.

Doppler, T. [+10 others] and K. W. Alt (2012), 'Gesamtheitliche Betrachtungen zum endneolithischen Kollektivgrab von Spreitenbach-Moosweg – Eine integrative Synthese', in T. Doppler (ed.), *Spreitenbach-Moosweg (Aargau, Schweiz): ein Kollektivgrab um 2500 v. Chr.*, 287–333, Basel: Archäologie Schweiz.

Douglas, M. (1991), 'The idea of a home: A kind of space', *Social Research*, 58 (1): 287–307.

Dressler, W. (1965), 'Methodische Vorfragen bei der Bestimmung der "Urheimat"', *Die Sprache*, 11: 25–60.

Earle, T. (1997), *How Chiefs Come to Power: The Political Economy in Prehistory*, Redwood City: Stanford University Press.

Ebbesen, K. (2011), *Danmarks megalitgrave*, Copenhagen: Attika.

Ebersbach, R. (2010), 'Vom Entstehen und Vergehen – Überlegungen zur Dynamik von Feuchtbodenhäusern und -siedlungen', in I. Matuschik and C. Strahm (eds), *Vernetzungen: Aspekte siedlungsarchäologischer Forschung. Festschrift für Helmut Schlichtherle zum 60. Geburtstag*, 41–50, Freiburg i. B.: Lavori.

Ebersbach, R., T. Doppler, D. Hofmann and A. Whittle (2017), 'No time out: Scaling material diversity and change in the Alpine foreland Neolithic', *Journal of Anthropological Archaeology*, 45: 1–14.

Eger, C. (2005), 'Westgotische Gräberfelder auf der Iberischen Halbinsel als historische Quelle: Probleme der ethnischen Deutung', in B. Päffgen, E. Pohl and M. Schmauder (eds), *Cum grano salis: Beiträge zur europäischen Vor- und Frühgeschichte. Festschrift für Volker Bierbrauer zum 65. Geburtstag*, 165–81, Friedberg: Likias.

Eger, C. (2011), 'Kleidung und Grabausstattung barbarischer Eliten im 5. Jahrhundert. Gedanken zu Philipp von Rummels "habitus barbarus"', *Germania*, 89: 215–30.

Eger, C. (2020), 'The Visigothic kingdom – a kingdom without Visigoths? The debate on the ethnic interpretation of the Early Medieval cemeteries on the Iberian Peninsula', in S. Panzram and P. Pachá (eds), *The Visigothic Kingdom: The Negotiation of Power in Post-Roman Iberia*, 173–93, Amsterdam: Amsterdam University Press.

Eggert, M. (1978), 'Zum Kulturkonzept in der prähistorischen Archäologie', *Bonner Jahrbücher*, 178: 1–20.

Elliott, B., A. Little, G. Warren, A. Lucquin, E. Blinkhorn and O. E. Craig (2020), 'No pottery at the western periphery of Europe: Why was the Final Mesolithic of Britain and Ireland aceramic?', *Antiquity*, 94 (377): 1152–67.

English, N. B., J. L. Betancourt, J. S. Dean and J. Quade (2001), 'Strontium isotopes reveal distant sources of architectural timber in Chaco Canyon, New Mexico', *Proceedings of the National Academy of Sciences*, 98 (21): 11891–6.

Ensor, B. E. (2021), *The Not Very Patrilocal European Neolithic: Strontium, aDNA, and Archaeological Kinship Analyses*, Oxford: Archaeopress.

Erben, P. M. (2019), '"Wie ein Nimrod / Like a Nimrod": Babel, confusion, and coercive bilingualism in the eighteenth-century Mid-Atlantic', in B. Wiggin (ed.), *Babel of the Atlantic*, 41–74, Pennsylvania: Pennsylvania University Press.

Eriksen, P. and N. H. Andersen (2017), *Dolmens in Denmark: Architecture and function*, Højbjerg: Jutland Archaeological Society.

Espiritu, Y. L. (2013), 'Panethnicity', in S. J. Gold and S. J. Nawyn (eds), *The Routledge International Handbook of Migration Studies*, 239–49, London: Routledge.

Europol (2022), 'Facilitation of illegal immigration', available at: https://www.europol.europa.eu/crime-areas-and-statistics/crime-areas/facilitation-of-illegal-immigration

Evans, N. (2022), *Words of Wonder: Endangered Languages and What They Tell Us*, Oxford: Wiley-Blackwell.

Farnell, B. (2000), 'Getting out of the habitus: An alternative model of dynamically embodied social action', *Journal of the Royal Anthropological Institute*, 6 (3): 397–418.

Faull, K. (2019), 'Women, migration and Moravian mission: Negotiating Pennsylvania's colonial landscapes', in B. Wiggin (ed.), *Babel of the Atlantic*, 101–27, Pennsylvania: Pennsylvania University Press.

Faulstich Orellana, M., L. Dorner and L. Pulido (2003), 'Accessing assets: Immigrant youths' work as family translators or "para-phrasers"', *Social Problems*, 50 (4): 505–24.

Feeser, I., W. Dörfler, F.-R. Averdieck and J. Wiethold (2012), 'New insight into regional and local land-use and vegetation patterns in eastern Schleswig-Holstein during the Neolithic', in M. Hinz and J. Müller (eds), *Siedlung, Grabenwerk, Großsteingrab: Studien zu Gesellschaft, Wirtschaft und Umwelt der Trichterbechergruppen im nördlichen Mitteleuropa*, 159–90, Bonn: Rudolf Habelt.

Fehr, H. (2010), *Germanen und Romanen im Merowingerreich: Frühgeschichtliche Archäologie zwischen Wissenschaft und Zeitgeschehen. Reallexikon der Germanischen Altertumskunde, Ergänzungsband 68*, Berlin: De Gruyter.

Fenner, J. N., E. Herrscher, F. Valentin and J. Clark (2021), 'An isotopic analysis of Late Lapita and State Period diets in Tonga', *Archaeological and Anthropological Sciences*, 13: 22. https://doi.org/10.1007/s12520-020-01267-z

Fernández-Götz, M. (2013), 'Revisiting Iron Age ethnicity', *European Journal of Archaeology*, 16 (1): 116–36.

Field, J. S., E. Cochrane and D. Greenlee (2009), 'Dietary change in Fijian prehistory: Isotopic analyses of human and animal skeletal material', *Journal of Archaeological Science,* 36 (7): 1547–56.

Finney, B. (1991), 'Myth, experiment, and the reinvention of Polynesian voyaging', *American Anthropologist,* 93 (2): 383–404.

Fischer, A. (2002), 'Food for feasting? An evaluation of explanations of the Neolithisation of Denmark and southern Sweden', in A. Fischer and K. Kristiansen (eds), *The Neolithisation of Denmark: 150 Years of Debate,* 343–93, Sheffield: Collis Publications.

Fischer, A. and K. Kristiansen, eds (2002), *The Neolithisation of Denmark: 150 Years of Debate,* Sheffield: Collis Publications.

Fischer, A., J. Olsen, M. Richards, J. Heinemeier, Á Sveinbjörnsdóttir and P. Bennike (2007), 'Coast–inland mobility and diet in the Danish Mesolithic and Neolithic: Evidence from stable isotope values of humans and dogs', *Journal of Archaeological Science,* 34: 2125–50.

Fitzpatrick, S. M. and R. T. Callaghan (2013), 'Estimating trajectories of colonisation to the Mariana islands, western Pacific', *Antiquity,* 87 (337): 840–53.

Flexner, J. L. and E. Gonzalez-Tennant, eds (2018), 'Anarchy and archaeology: Forum', *Journal of Contemporary Archaeology,* 5 (2): 213–302.

Flexner, J. L., S. Bedford and F. Valentin (2019), 'Who was Polynesian? Who was Melanesian? Hybridity and ethnogenesis in the South Vanuatu Outliers', *Journal of Social Archaeology,* 19 (3): 403–26.

Fontijn, D. (2021), 'Power requires others: Institutional realities and the significance of individual power in late prehistoric Europe', in T. L. Thurston and M. Fernández-Götz (eds), *Power from Below in Premodern Societies: The Dynamics of Political Complexity in the Archaeological Record,* 90–105, Cambridge: Cambridge University Press.

Foucault, M. (1982), 'The subject and power', *Critical Inquiry,* 8 (4): 777–95.

Fowler, C., J. Harding and D. Hofmann, eds (2015), *The Oxford Handbook of Neolithic Europe,* Oxford: Oxford University Press.

Fowler, C. [+8 others] and D. Reich (2022), 'A high-resolution picture of kinship practices in an Early Neolithic tomb', *Nature,* 601: 584–7.

Fowles, S. (2005), 'Historical contingency and the prehistoric foundations of moiety organization among the eastern Pueblos', *Journal of Anthropological Research,* 61 (1): 25–52.

Fowles, S. and S. Eiselt (2019), 'Apache, Tiwa, and back again: Ethnic shifting in the American Southwest', in S. Duwe and R. W. Preucel (eds), *The*

Continuous Path: Pueblo Movement and the Archaeology of Becoming, 166–94, Tucson: University of Arizona Press.

Fox, J. J. and C. Sather, eds (1996), *Origins, Ancestry and Alliance: Explorations in Austronesian Ethnography*, Canberra: ANU Press.

Frieman, C. J. (2008), 'Islandscapes and islandness: the prehistoric Isle of Man in the Irish seascape', *Oxford Journal of Archaeology*, 27 (2): 135–51.

Frieman, C. J. (2012), *Innovation and Imitation: Stone Skeuomorphs of Metal from 4th–2nd Millennia* BC *Northwest Europe*, Oxford: Archaeopress.

Frieman, C. J. (2021), *An Archaeology of Innovation: Approaching Social and Technological Change in Human Society*, Manchester: Manchester University Press.

Frieman, C. J. (2023), 'Innovation, continuity and the punctuated temporality of archaeological narratives', in A. McGrath, L. Rademaker and J. Troy (eds), *Everywhen: Knowing the Past Through Language and Culture*, 8–31. Lincoln, NE: University of Nebraska Press.

Frieman, C. J. and D. Hofmann (2019), 'Present pasts in the archaeology of genetics, identity, and migration in Europe: A critical essay', *World Archaeology*, 51 (4): 528–45.

Frieman, C. J. and S. K. May (2020), 'Navigating contact: Tradition and innovation in Australian contact rock art', *International Journal of Historical Archaeology*, 24 (2): 342–66.

Frieman, C., A. Teather and C. Morgan (2019), 'Bodies in motion: Narratives and counter narratives of gendered mobility in European later prehistory', *Norwegian Archaeological Review*, 52: 148–69.

Frirdich, C. (2005), 'Struktur und Dynamik der bandkeramischen Landnahme', in J. Lüning, C. Frirdich and A. Zimmermann (eds), *Die Bandkeramik im 21. Jahrhundert: Symposium in der Abtei Brauweiler bei Köln vom 16.9.–19.9.2002*, 81–109, Rahden: Marie Leidorf.

Fu, Q. [+62 others] and D. Reich (2016), 'The genetic history of Ice Age Europe', *Nature*, 534: 200–5.

Fuchs, K., C. Rinne, C. Drummer, A. Immel, B. Krause-Kyora and A. Nebel (2019), 'Infectious diseases and Neolithic transformations: Evaluating biological and archaeological proxies in the German loess zone between 5500 and 2500 BCE', *The Holocene*, 29 (10): 1545–57.

Fukuyama, F. (2012), *The Origins of Political Order: From Prehuman Times to the French Revolution*, New York: Farrar Strauss & Giroux.

Furholt, M. (2008), 'Pottery, cultures, people? The European Baden material re-examined', *Antiquity*, 82 (317): 617–28.

Furholt, M. (2009), *Die nördlichen Badener Keramikstile im Kontext des mitteleuropäischen Spätneolithikums (3650–2900 v. Chr.)*, Bonn: Rudolf Habelt.

Furholt, M. (2014), 'Upending a "totality": Re-evaluating Corded Ware variability in Late Neolithic Europe', *Proceedings of the Prehistoric Society*, 80: 67–86.

Furholt, M. (2018), 'Massive migrations? The impact of recent aDNA studies on our view of third millennium Europe', *European Journal of Archaeology*, 21 (2): 159–91.

Furholt, M. (2019a), 'De-contaminating the aDNA – archaeology dialogue on mobility and migration: Discussing the culture-historical legacy', *Current Swedish Archaeology*, 27: 53–68.

Furholt, M. (2019b), 'Re-integrating archaeology: A contribution to aDNA studies and the migration discourse on the 3rd millennium BC in Europe', *Proceedings of the Prehistoric Society*, 85: 115–29.

Furholt, M. (2020), 'Social worlds and communities of practice: A polythetic culture model for 3rd millennium BC Europe in the light of current migration debates', *Préhistoires Méditerranéennes*, 8: https://doi. org/10.4000/pm.2383

Furholt, M. (2021), 'Mobility and social change: Understanding the European Neolithic period after the archaeogenetic revolution', *Journal of Archaeological Research*, 29: 481–53.

Furtwängler, A. [+18 others] and J. Krause (2020), 'Ancient genomes reveal social and genetic structure of Late Neolithic Switzerland', *Nature Communications*, 11: 1915. https://doi.org/10.1038/s41467-020-15560-x

Gailey, C. W. (2019), 'Adoption', in S. Bamford (ed.), *The Cambridge Handbook of Kinship*, 231–52, Cambridge: Cambridge University Press.

Garrow, D. and F. Sturt (2011), 'Grey waters bright with Neolithic argonauts? Maritime connections and the Mesolithic–Neolithic transition within the "western seaways" of Britain, c. 5000–3500 BC', *Antiquity*, 85 (327): 59–72.

Garrow, D. and F. Sturt (2017), 'The Mesolithic–Neolithic transition in the Channel Islands: maritime and terrestrial perspectives', *Oxford Journal of Archaeology*, 36 (1): 3–23.

Gebauer, A. B., L. V. Sørensen, M. Taube and D. K. P. Wielandt (2021), 'First metallurgy in northern Europe: An Early Neolithic crucible and a possible tuyère from Lønt, Denmark', *European Journal of Archaeology*, 24 (1): 27–47.

Gelabert, P. [+82 others] and D. Reich (2023), 'Social and genetic diversity among the first farmers of central Europe', *bioRxiv*, https://doi. org/10.1101/2023.07.07.548126

Gerdau, K. (2019), 'Mobilités préhistoriques en Europe du 6e au 3e millénaire avant notre ère: Apports des études sur l'ADN ancien et sur les isotopes stables', habilitation thesis, University of Strasbourg.

Gerling, C., E. Bánffy, J. Dani, K. Köhler, G. Kulcsár, A. W. G. Pike, V. Szeverényi and V. Heyd (2012), 'Immigration and transhumance in the Early Bronze Age Carpathian basin: The occupants of a *kurgan*', *Antiquity*, 86 (334): 1097–111.

Gero, J. (2007), 'Honoring ambiguity/problematizing certitude', *Journal of Archaeological Method and Theory*, 14: 311–27.

Geschwinde, M. and D. Raetzel-Fabian (2009), *EWBSL: Eine Fallstudie zu den jungneolithischen Erdwerken am Nordrand der Mittelgebirge*, Rahden: Marie Leidorf.

Gibson, C. (2021), 'Making journeys, blurring boundaries and celebrating transience: A movement towards archaeologies of in-between', in C. Gibson, K. Cleary and C. J. Frieman (eds), *Making Journeys: Archaeologies of Mobility*, 1–15, Oxford: Oxbow Books.

Gibson, C., K. Cleary and C. J. Frieman, eds (2021), *Making Journeys: Archaeologies of Mobility*, Oxford: Oxbow Books.

Giddens, A. (1984), *The Constitution of Society: Outline of the Theory of Structuration,* Cambridge: Polity Press.

Gidney, T. P. (2021), 'Bypassing the Dutch monopoly of relations with Japan: Vasily Golovnin's captivity (1811–1813)', *Terrae Incognitae*, 53 (2): 135–57.

Glick Schiller, N. and N. B. Salazar (2013), 'Regimes of mobility across the globe', *Journal of Ethnic and Migration Studies,* 39 (2): 183–200.

Glørstad, H. (2008), 'Celebrating materiality: The Antarctic lesson', in H. Glørstad and L. Hedeager (eds), *Six Essays on the Materiality of Society and Culture*, 173–211, Gothenburg: Bricoleur Press.

Gomolka-Fuchs, G., ed. (1999), *Die Sintana de Mureş-Černjachov-Kultur: Akten des internationalen Kolloquiums in Caputh vom 20. bis 24. Oktober 1995*, Bonn: Rudolf Habelt.

Gorgen, P. (2021), 'Mohawk and Dutch relations in the Mohawk valley: Alliance, diplomacy, and families from 1600 to the Two Row Treaty renewal campaign', in L. Lavin (ed.), *Dutch and Indigenous Communities in Seventeenth-Century Northeastern North America: What Archaeology, History, and Indigenous Oral Traditions Teach Us about Their Intercultural Relationships*, 105–28, Albany: State University of New York Press.

Gosling, A. L. and E. Matisoo-Smith (2018), 'The evolutionary history and human settlement of Australia and the Pacific', *Current Opinions in Genetics & Development*, 53: 53–9.

Graeber, D. and D. Wengrow (2021), *The Dawn of Everything: A New History of Humanity*, London: Allen Lane.

Greenblatt, S. J. (1991), *Marvelous Possessions: The Wonder of the New World*, Oxford: Clarendon.

Greenblatt, S. J. (1992), *Learning to Curse: Essays in Early Modern Culture*, London: Routledge.

Gretzinger, J. [+78 others] and S. Schiffels (2022), 'The Anglo-Saxon migration and the formation of the early English gene pool', *Nature*, 610: 112–19.

Griffiths, S. (2014), 'Points in time: The Mesolithic–Neolithic transition and the chronology of late rod microliths in Britain', *Oxford Journal of Archaeology*, 33 (3): 221–43.

Grisafi, L. (2020), 'Living in the blast zone: Sexual violence piped onto Native land by extractive industries', *Columbia Journal of Law and Social Problems*, 53 (4): 509–40.

Gron, K. J. and L. Sørensen (2018), 'Cultural and economic negotiation: A new perspective on the Neolithic transition of southern Scandinavia', *Antiquity*, 92 (364): 958–74.

Gron, K. J., P. Rowley-Conwy, E. Fernandez-Dominguez, D. R. Gröcke, J. Montgomery, G. M. Nowell and W. P. Patterson (2018), 'A meeting in the forest: hunters and farmers at the Coneybury "Anomaly", Wiltshire', *Proceedings of the Prehistoric Society*, 84: 111–44.

Gronenborn, D. (2001), 'Zum (möglichen) Nachweis von Sklaven/Unfreien in prähistorischen Gesellschaften Mitteleuropas', *Ethnographisch-Archäologische Zeitschrift*, 42: 1–42.

Gronenborn, D. (2016), 'Some thoughts on political differentiation in Early to Young Neolithic societies in western and central Europe', in H. Meller, H. P. Hahn, R. Jung and R. Risch (eds), *Rich and Poor – Competing for Resources in Prehistoric Societies*, 61–75, Halle: Landesmuseum für Vorgeschichte.

Groß, D. [+10 others] and D. Wilken (2019), 'Adaptations and transformations of hunter-gatherers in forest environments: New archaeological and anthropological insights', *The Holocene*, 29 (10): 1531–44.

Gross, E. (2017), 'Cultural and chronological attribution of pottery on the move: From rigid time-space schemata towards flexible microarchaeological "messworks"', in C. Heitz and R. Stapfer (eds), *Mobility and Pottery Production: Archaeological and Anthropological Perspectives*, 169–86, Leiden: Sidestone Press.

Gross-Klee, E. and S. Hochuli (2002), 'Die jungsteinzeitliche Doppelaxt von Cham-Eslen: Gesamtbericht über einen einzigartigen Fund aus dem Zugersee', *Tugium*, 18: 69–101.

Haak, W. [+16 others] and the Genographic Consortium (2010), 'Ancient DNA from European Early Neolithic farmers reveals their Near Eastern affinities', *PLoS Biology*, 8: e1000536.

Haak, W. [+37 others] and D. Reich (2015), 'Massive migration from the steppe was a source for Indo-European languages in Europe', *Nature*, 522: 207–11.

Haak, W. [+10 others] and K. Kristiansen (2023), 'The Corded Ware complex in Europe in light of current archaeogenetic and environmental evidence', in E. Willerslev, G. Kroonen and K. Kristiansen (eds), *The Indo-European Puzzle Revisited: Integrating Archaeology, Genetics, and Linguistics*, 63–80, Cambridge: Cambridge University Press.

Hachem, L. (2018), 'Animals in LBK society: Identity and gender markers', *Journal of Archaeological Science: Reports*, 20: 910–21.

Hafner, A. and P. Suter (2000), *-3400. Die Entwicklung der Bauerngesellschaften im 4. Jahrtausend v. Chr. am Bielersee aufgrund der Rettungsgrabungen von Nidau und Sutz-Lattrigen*, Bern: Berner Lehrmittel- und Medienverlag.

Hafner, A. and P. Suter (2003), 'Das Neolithikum in der Schweiz', *Journal of Neolithic Archaeology*, 5: https://doi.org/10.12766/jna.2003.4

Hafner, A., P. Pétrequin and H. Schlichtherle (2016), 'Ufer- und Moorsiedlungen: Chronologie, kulturelle Vielfalt und Siedlungsformen', in Archäologisches Landesmuseum Baden-Württemberg (eds), *4000 Jahre Pfahlbauten: Begleitband zur Großen Landesausstellung Baden-Württemberg 2016*, 59–64, Ostfildern: Jan Thorbecke.

Hakenbeck, S. (2019), 'Genetics, archaeology and the far right: An unholy trinity', *World Archaeology*, 51 (4): 517–27.

Halbmayer, E. (2004) '"The one who feeds has the rights": Adoption and fostering of kin, affines and enemies among the Yukpa and other Carib-speaking Indians of lowland South America', in F. Bowie (ed.), *Cross-cultural Approaches to Adoption*, 145–64, London: Routledge.

Hald, J., M. Merkl and J. Wahl (2016), 'Hockergräber und rätselhafte Brandreste: Bestattungssitten am Ende der Steinzeit im Hegau', in Archäologisches Landesmuseum Baden-Württemberg (eds), *4000 Jahre Pfahlbauten: Begleitband zur Großen Landesausstellung Baden-Württemberg 2016*, 202–5, Ostfildern: Jan Thorbecke.

Hald, J., E. Marinova and A. Weide (2020), 'Seeblick garantiert: Eine Ackerbausiedlung am westlichen Bodensee aus dem 5. Jahrtausend v. Chr.', *Denkmalpflege in Baden-Württemberg,* 49: 240–4.

Hall, S. (1990), 'Cultural identity and diaspora', in J. Rutherford (ed.), *Identity: Community, Culture, Difference,* 222–37, London: Lawrence and Wishart.

Hallgren, F. (2008), *Identitet i praktik: Lokala, regionala och överregionala sociala sammanhang inom nordlig trattbägarkultur,* Uppsala: Uppsala University.

Halsall, G. (2008), *Barbarian Migrations and the Roman West, 376–568,* Cambridge: Cambridge University Press.

Hamilakis, Y. (2018a), 'Preface', in Y. Hamilakis (ed.), *The New Nomadic Age: Archaeologies of Forced and Undocumented Migration,* xiii–xiv, London: Equinox.

Hamilakis, Y. (2018b), 'Introduction: Archaeologies of forced and undocumented migration', in Y. Hamilakis (ed.), *The New Nomadic Age: Archaeologies of Forced and Undocumented Migration,* 1–19, London: Equinox.

Hansen, R. and D. King (2001), 'Eugenic ideas, political interests, and policy variance: Immigration and sterilization policy in Britain and the U.S.', *World Politics,* 53 (2): 237–63.

Harb, C., N. Bleicher, E. Jochum Zimmermann, A. Kienholz, B. Ruckstuhl and M. Weber (2017), 'Mensch und Gesellschaft', in N. Bleicher and C. Harb (eds), *Zürich-Parkhaus Opéra: Eine neolithische Feuchtbodenfundstelle. Naturwissenschaftliche Analysen und Synthese,* 246–62, Zürich: Kantonsarchäologie Zürich.

Härke, H. (1997), 'Wanderungsthematik, Archäologen und politisches Umfeld', *Archäologische Informationen,* 20: 61–71.

Härke, H. (1998), 'Archaeologists and migrations: A problem of attitude?', *Current Anthropology,* 39 (1): 19–45.

Härke, H. (2003), 'Population replacement or acculturation? An archaeological perspective on population and migration in Post-Roman Britain', in H. L. C. Tristram (ed.), *The Celtic Englishes III, Anglistische Forschungen 324,* 13–28, Heidelberg: Winter.

Härke, H. (2011), 'Anglo-Saxon immigration and ethnogenesis', *Medieval Archaeology,* 55 (1): 1–28.

Harris, O. J. T. (2014), '(Re)assembling communities', *Journal of Archaeological Method and Theory,* 21 (1): 76–97.

Harrison, R., S. Appelgren and A. Bohlin (2018), 'Commentary: Belonging and belongings: On migrant and nomadic heritages *in* and *for* the Anthropocene', in Y. Hamilakis (ed.), *The New Nomadic Age: Archaeologies of Forced and Undocumented Migration*, 209–20, London: Equinox.

Harrod, R. P. (2012), 'Centers of control: Revealing elites among the Ancestral Pueblo during the "Chaco phenomenon"', *International Journal of Paleopathology*, 2 (2–3): 123–35.

Hayden, B. (2001), 'Richman, poorman, beggarman, chief: The dynamics of social inequality', in G. M. Feinman and T. D. Price (eds), *Archaeology at the Millennium*, 231–72, Boston: Springer.

Hayden, B. (2014), *The Power of Feasts: From Prehistory to the Present*, Cambridge: Cambridge University Press.

Heather, P. (1998), *The Goths*, Oxford: Blackwell.

Heather, P. (2005), *The Fall of the Roman Empire*, London: Macmillan.

Hedges, R. E. M. [+8 others] and A. Whittle (2013), 'The supra-regional perspective', in P. Bickle and A. Whittle (eds), *The First Farmers of Central Europe: Diversity in LBK Lifeways*, 343–84, Oxford: Oxbow Books.

Hegmon, M., J. Freeman, K. W. Kintigh, M. C. Nelson, S. Oas, M. A. Peeples and A. Torvinen (2016), 'Marking and making differences: Representational diversity in the U.S. Southwest', *American Antiquity*, 81 (2): 253–72.

Heggarty, P. [+ 31 others] and R. D. Gray (2023), 'Language trees with sampled ancestors support a hybrid model for the origin of Indo-European languages', *Science*, 381: eabg0818. doi:10.1126/science.abg0818

Heitz, C. (2017), 'Making things, being mobile: Pottery as intertwined histories of humans and materials', in C. Heitz and R. Stapfer (eds), *Mobility and Pottery Production: Archaeological and Anthropological Perspectives*, 257–91, Leiden: Sidestone Press.

Heitz, C., M. Hinz, J. Laab and A. Hafner (2021), 'Mobility as resilience capacity in northern Alpine Neolithic settlement communities', *Archaeological Review from Cambridge*, 36: 75–105.

Herrscher, E., J. N. Fenner, F. Valentin, G. Clark, C. Reepmeyer, L. Bouffandeau and G. André (2018), 'Multi-isotopic analysis of first Polynesian diet (Talasiu, Tongatapu, Kingdom of Tonga)', *Journal of Archaeological Science: Reports*, 18: 308–17.

Hertz, R. (1960 [1907]), *Death and the Right Hand*, Glencoe: The Free Press.

Hessenrecht (2019), 'VG Gießen 4. Kammer, Wahlplakat versus Ordnungsbehörde', available at: https://www.rv.hessenrecht.hessen.de/bshe/document/LARE190036038

Heumüller, M. (2009), *Der Schmuck der jungneolithischen Seeufersiedlung Hornstaad-Hörnle IA im Rahmen des mitteleuropäischen Mittel- und Jungneolithikums: Siedlungsarchäologie im Alpenvorland X*, Stuttgart: Theiss.

Heyd, V. (2011), 'Yamnaya groups and tumuli west of the Black Sea', in E. Borgna and S. Müller Celka (eds), *Ancestral Landscapes: Burial Mounds in the Copper and Bronze Ages (Central and Eastern Europe – Balkans – Adriatic – Aegean, 4th–2nd Millennium BC)*, 535–56, Lyon: Persée.

Higham, N. (1992), *Rome, Britain and the Anglo-Saxons*, London: Seaby.

Hill, B. J., J. J. Clark, W. H. Doelle and P. D. Lyons (2004), 'Prehistoric demography in the Southwest: Migration, coalescence and Hohokam population decline', *American Antiquity*, 69 (4): 689–716.

Hills, C. (2003), *Origins of the English*, London: Duckworth.

Hills, C. (2009), 'Anglo-Saxon DNA?', in D. Sayer and H. Williams (eds), *Mortuary Practices and Social Identities in the Middle Ages: Essays in Burial Archaeology in Honour of Heinrich Härke*, 123–40, Exeter: University of Exeter Press.

Hills, C. (2011), 'Overview: Anglo-Saxon identity', in H. H. Hamerow, D. A. Hinton and S. Crawford (eds), *The Oxford Handbook of Anglo-Saxon Archaeology*, 30–45, Oxford: Oxford University Press.

Hills, C. (2015), 'The Anglo-Saxon migration: An archaeological case study of disruption', in B. J. Baker and T. Tsuda (eds), *Migrations and Disruptions: Toward a Unifying Theory of Ancient and Contemporary Migrations*, 33–51, Gainesville: University Press of Florida.

Hirsch, A. D. (2000), '"The celebrated Madame Montour": "Interpretress" across early American frontiers', *Explorations in Early American Culture*, 4: 81–112.

Hodder, I. (1982), *Symbols in Action: Ethnoarchaeological Studies of Material Culture*, Cambridge: Cambridge University Press.

Hodges, R. (1989), *The Anglo-Saxon Achievement: Archaeology & the Beginnings of English Society*, London: Duckworth.

Hofmann, D. (2013), 'Living by the lake: Domestic architecture in the Alpine foreland', in D. Hofmann and J. Smyth (eds), *Tracking the Neolithic House in Europe: Sedentism, Architecture and Practice*, 197–227, New York: Springer.

Hofmann, D. (2015), 'What have genetics ever done for us? The implications of aDNA data for interpreting identity in Early Neolithic central Europe', *European Journal of Archaeology*, 18 (3): 454–76.

Hofmann, D. (2016), 'Keep on walking: The role of migration in Linearbandkeramik life', *Documenta Praehistorica*, 43: 235–51.

Hofmann, D. (2020), 'Not going anywhere? Migration as a social practice in the Early Neolithic Linearbandkeramik', *Quaternary International,* 560/1: 228–39.

Hofmann, D. (2022), 'Structured deposition in the Münchshöfen culture – A move towards social inequality?', in M. Grygiel and P. Obst (eds), *Walking Among Ancient Trees: Festschrift for Peter Bogucki and Ryszard Grygiel,* 223–33, Łódź: Museum of Archaeology and Ethnography.

Hofmann, D. and P. Bickle (submitted), 'Gender relations, patrilocality and relatedness at the burial ground of Nitra, Slovakia', in S. Souvatzi and B. Ensor (eds), *Prehistoric Kinship: Contemporary Perspectives in Archaeology and Bioarchaeology,* Cambridge: Cambridge University Press.

Hofmann, D. and L. Husty (2019), 'Enclosures, structured deposits and selective innovations: Riedling and the role of the south Bavarian Münchshöfen culture in the new networks of the Late Neolithic', in J. Müller, M. Hinz and M. Wunderlich (eds), *Megaliths, Societies, Landscapes: Early Monumentality and Social Differentiation in Neolithic Europe. Proceedings of the International Conference, Volume 3,* 939–56, Bonn: Rudolf Habelt.

Hofmann, D., R. Ebersbach, T. Doppler and A. Whittle (2016), 'The life and times of the house: multi-scalar perspectives on settlement from the Neolithic of the north Alpine foreland', *European Journal of Archaeology,* 19 (4): 596–630.

Hofmann, D. [+9 others] and C. J. Frieman (2021), 'Forum: Populism, identity politics, and the archaeology of Europe', *European Journal of Archaeology,* 24 (4): 519–55.

Högberg, A. and Å. Berggren (2023), 'Human-material relationships around 4000 BCE: Continuity and change in south Scandinavian flint tool production technologies', *Journal of Neolithic Archaeology,* 24: 99–129.

Honegger, M. (2005), 'Les villages littoraux du Néolithique: Égalité et autarcie ou complémentarité et mise en réseau?', in P. Della Casa and M. Trachsel (eds), *WES '04: Wetland Economies and Societies. Proceedings of the international conference Zurich, 10–13 March 2004,* 185–94, Zurich: Chronos.

Honegger, M. (2007), 'Le site de Marin-Les Piécettes (Neuchâtel, Suisse) et la question des sanctuaires néolithiques: Potentiel et limite de l'approche archéologique', in M. Besse (ed.), *Sociétés néolithiques: Des faits archéologiques aux fonctionnements socio-économiques. Actes du 27e colloque interrégional sur le Néolithique (Neuchâtel, 1 et 2 octobre 2005),* 175–83, Lausanne: Cahiers d'Archéologie romande.

hooks, b. (1982), *ain't i a woman: black women and feminism*, London: Pluto Press.

Horsburgh, K. A. and M. D. McCoy (2017), 'Dispersal, isolation, and interaction in the islands of Polynesia: A critical review of archaeological and genetic evidence', *Diversity*, 9 (3): 1–21. https://doi.org/10.3390/d9030037

Horsburgh, K. A., A. L. Gosling, E. E. Cochrane, P. V. Kirch, J. A. Swift and M. D. McCoy (2022), 'Origin of Polynesian pigs revealed by mitochondrial whole genome ancient DNA', *Animals*, 12 (18): 2469.

Hrnčíř, V., V. Vondrovský and P. Květina (2020), 'Post-marital residence patterns in LBK: Comparison of different models', *Journal of Anthropological Archaeology*, 59: 101190.

Hu, D. (2013), 'Approaches to the archaeology of ethnogenesis: Past and emergent perspectives', *Journal of Archaeological Research*, 21 (4): 371–402.

Hübner, E. (2005), *Jungneolithische Gräber auf der jütischen Halbinsel: Typologische und chronologische Studien zur Einzelgrabkultur*, Copenhagen: Det kongelige oldskriftselskab.

Ince, A. and G. Barrera de la Torre (2016), 'For post-statist geographies', *Political Geography*, 55: 10–19.

Ingersoll, K. B., D. W. Ingersoll Jr. and A. Bove (2018), 'Healing a culture's reputation: Challenging the cultural labelling and libeling of the Rapanui', in S. H. Cardinali, K. B. Ingersoll, D. W. Ingersoll Jr. and C. M. Stevenson (eds), *Cultural and Environmental Change on Rapa Nui*, 187–202, London: Routledge.

Ingold, T. (2000), 'From trust to domination: An alternative history of human–animal relations', in T. Ingold (ed.), *The Perception of the Environment: Essays in Livelihood, Dwelling and Skill*, 61–76, London: Routledge.

Ingold, T. (2007), *Lines: A Brief History*, London: Routledge.

Ingold, T. (2011), *Redrawing Anthropology: Materials, Movements, Lines. Anthropological Studies of Creativity and Perception*, Farnham: Ashgate.

Ioannidis, A. G. [+29 others] and A. Moreno-Estrada (2020), 'Native American gene flow into Polynesia predating Easter Island settlement', *Nature*, 583: 572–7.

IOM (2016), *Global Migration Trends 2015: Factsheet*, Berlin: International Organization for Migration. http://publications.iom.int/books/global-migration-trendsfactsheet-2015 (accessed: 11.11.2022).

IOM (2021), *World Migration Report 2022*, Geneva: International Organization for Migration. https://publications.iom.int/system/files/pdf/WMR-2022.pdf (accessed June 24, 2022).

Ion, A. (2017), 'How interdisciplinary is *interdisciplinarity*? Revisiting the impact of aDNA research for the archaeology of human remains', *Current Swedish Archaeology*, 25: 177–98.

Ion, A. (2018), 'A taphonomy of a dark Anthropocene: A response to Þóra Pétursdóttir's OOO-inspired "Archaeology and anthropocene"', *Archaeological Dialogues*, 25 (2): 191–203.

Ion, A. (2019), 'Who are we as historical beings? Shaping identities in light of the archaeogenetics "revolution"', *Current Swedish Archaeology*, 27: 11–36.

Irwin, G. J. (1980), 'The prehistory of Oceania: Colonization and cultural change', in A. Sherratt (ed.), *The Cambridge Encyclopedia of Archaeology*, 324–32, Cambridge: Cambridge University Press.

Irwin, G. J. (1992), *The Prehistoric Exploration and Colonisation of the Pacific*, Cambridge: Cambridge University Press.

Isayev, E. (2022), 'The in/visibility of migration', in M. J. Daniels (ed.), *Homo migrans: Modeling Mobility and Migration in Human History*, 133–46, New York: State University of New York Press.

Iversen, R. (2019), 'On the emergence of Corded Ware societies in northern Europe: Reconsidering the migration hypothesis', in B. A. Olsen, T. Olander and K. Kristiansen (eds), *Tracing the Indo-Europeans: New Evidence from Archaeology and Historical Linguistics*, 73–95, Oxford: Oxbow Books.

Iversen, R. and G. Kroonen (2017), 'Talking Neolithic: Linguistic and archaeological perspectives on how Indo-European was implemented in southern Scandinavia', *American Journal of Archaeology*, 121 (4): 511–25.

Jacomet, S. and P. Vandorpe (2022), 'The search for a needle in a haystack – New studies on plant use during the Mesolithic in southwest central Europe', *Journal of Archaeological Science: Reports*, 41: 103308.

Jakucs, J. [+9 others] and A. Whittle (2016), 'Between the Vinča and Linearbandkeramik worlds: The diversity of practices and identities in the 54th–53rd centuries cal BC in southwest Hungary and beyond', *Journal of World Prehistory*, 29: 267–336.

Jarnut, J. (1982), *Geschichte der Langobarden*, Stuttgart: Kohlhammer.

Jensen, T. Z. T. [+21 others] and H. Schroeder (2019), 'A 5700 year-old human genome and oral microbiome from chewed birch pitch', *Nature Communications*, 10 (1): 5520.

Jeunesse, C. (2020), 'Les influences steppiques sur l'Europe occidentale: une première vague antérieure à l'impact Yamnaja?', *Rivista di Scienze Preistoriche*, LXX (S1): 161–80.

Johannsen, N. N. (2012), 'Archaeology and the inanimate agency proposition: A critique and a suggestion', in N. N. Johannsen, M. Jessen and H. J. Jensen (eds), *Excavating the Mind: Cross-Sections Through Culture, Cognition and Materiality*, 305–47, Aarhus: Aarhus University Press.

Johannsen, N. N. (2023), 'Niche construction: Hard-working settlers and a neglected principle in understanding the Early Neolithic of southern Scandinavia', in D. Groß and M. Rothstein (eds), *Changing Identity in a Changing World: Current Studies on the Stone Age around 4000 BCE*, 43–52, Leiden: Sidestone Press.

Johannsen, N. N, and S. T. Laursen (2010), 'Routes and wheeled transport in late 4th–early 3rd millennium funerary customs of the Jutland peninsula: Regional evidence and European context', *Praehistorische Zeitschrift*, 85: 15–58.

Johannsen, N. N., G. Larson, D. J. Meltzer and M. Vander Linden (2017), 'A composite window into human history', *Science*, 356 (6343): 1118–20.

Johansen, K. L. (2006), 'Settlement and land use at the Mesolithic–Neolithic transition in southern Scandinavia', *Journal of Danish Archaeology*, 14: 201–23.

Johnston, R. (2020), *Bronze Age Worlds: A Social Prehistory of Britain and Ireland*, London: Routledge.

Jones, E. D. (2019), 'Ancient genetics to ancient genomics: Celebrity and credibility in data-driven practice', *Biology and Philosophy*, 34: 1–35.

Jones, E. D. and E. Bösl (2021), 'Ancient human DNA: A history of hype (then and now)', *Journal of Social Archaeology*, 21 (2): 236–55.

Jones, S. (1997), *The Archaeology of Ethnicity: Constructing Identities in the Past and Present*, London: Routledge.

Kahn, J. G. (2018), 'Colonization, settlement, and process in central eastern Polynesia', in E. E. Cochrane and T. L. Hunt (eds), *The Oxford Handbook of Prehistoric Oceania*, 353–74, Oxford: Oxford University Press.

Kaiser, E. (2016), 'Migrationen von Ost nach West: Die Archäologie von Wanderungsbewegungen im 3. Jahrtausend v. Chr.', *Mitteilungen der Berliner Gesellschaft für Anthropologie, Ethnologie und Urgeschichte*, 37: 31–43.

Kaiser, E. (2021), 'Population dynamics in the third millennium BC – The interpretation of archaeological and palaeogenetic information', in V. Heyd, G. Kulcsár and B. Preda-Bălănică (eds), *Yamnaya interactions: Proceedings of the international workshop held in Helsinki, 25–26 April 2019*, 83–99, Budapest: Archaeolingua.

Kaiser, E. and K. Winger (2015), 'Pit graves in Bulgaria and the Yamnaya culture', *Praehistorische Zeitschrift*, 90: 114–40.

Kameʻeleihiwa, L. (1986), 'Land and the promise of capitalism', PhD dissertation, University of Hawaii.

Karmin, M. [+13 others] and M. P. Cox (2022), 'Episodes of diversification and isolation in Island Southeast Asian and Near Oceanian male lineages', *Molecular Biology and Evolution*, 39 (3): msac045, https://doi.org/10.1093/molbev/msac045

Karttunen, F. (1994), *Between Worlds: Interpreters, Guides, and Survivors*, New Brunswick: Rutgers University Press.

Kassabaum, M. (2019), 'A method for conceptualizing and classifying feasting: Interpreting communal consumption in the archaeological record', *American Antiquity*, 84 (4): 610–31.

Kazanski, M. (1989), 'La diffusion de la mode danubienne en Gaule (fin du IVe siècle–début du VIe siècle): essai d'interprétation historique', *Antiquités Nationales*, 21: 59–73.

Kelly, R.C. (1985), *The Nuer Conquest: The Structure and Development of an Expansionist System*, Ann Arbor: The University of Michigan Press.

Kennett, D. J. and B. Winterhalder (2008), 'Demographic expansion, despotism and the colonisation of east and south Polynesia', in G. Clark, F. Leach and S. O'Connor (eds), *Islands of Inquiry: Colonisation, Seafaring and the Archaeology of Maritime Landscapes*, 87–96, Canberra: ANU EPress.

Khelifa, A. (2017), 'Pocahontas and La Malinche: Mirror images and antithetical archetypes', *University of Saskatchewan Undergraduate Research Journal*, 3: 1–10.

Kiddey, R. (2023), 'We are displaced, but we are more than that: Using anarchist principles to materialize capitalism's cracks at sites of contemporary forced displacement in Europe', *International Journal of Historical Archaeology*, online first. https://doi.org/10.1007/s10761-023-00696-5

Kirch, P. V. (1982), 'The impact of the prehistoric Polynesians on the Hawaiian ecosystem', *Pacific Science*, 36 (3): 1–14.

Kirch, P. V. (2010), 'Peopling of the Pacific: A holistic anthropological perspective', *Annual Review of Anthropology*, 39: 131–48.

Kirch, P. V. (2011), 'When did Polynesians settle Hawai'i? A review of 150 years of scholarly inquiry and a tentative answer', *Hawaiian Archaeology*, 12: 123–6.

Kirch, P. V. (2017), *On the Road of the Winds: An Archaeological History of the Pacific Islands Before European Contact*, Berkeley: University of California Press.

Kirch, P. V., E. Conte, W. Sharp and C. Nickelsen (2010), 'The Onemea site (Taravai Island, Mangareva) and the human colonization of southeastern Polynesia', *Archaeology in Oceania*, 45 (2): 66–79.

Kirschneck, E. (2021), 'The phenomena La Hoguette and Limburg – Technological aspects', *Open Archaeology*, 7 (1): 1295–344. https://doi.org/10.1515/opar-2020-0195

Klassen, L. (2001), *Frühes Kupfer im Norden*, Højbjerg: Jutland Archaeological Society.

Klassen, L. (2004), *Jade und Kupfer: Untersuchungen zum Neolithisierungsprozess im westlichen Ostseeraum unter besonderer Berücksichtigung der Kulturentwicklung Europas 5500–3500 BC*, Aarhus: Aarhus University Press.

Klassen, L. (2010), 'Karpaten oder Alpen? Zur Herkunft der Kupferscheibe aus Hornstaad (Lkr. Konstanz)', *Archäologisches Korrespondenzblatt*, 40 (1): 29–48.

Knipper, C. (2011), *Die räumliche Organisation der linearbandkeramischen Rinderhaltung: naturwissenschaftliche und archäologische Untersuchungen*, Oxford: Archaeopress.

Knipper, C., M. Fragata, M. Brauns and K. W. Alt (2012), 'Isotopenanalysen an den menschlichen Skeletten aus dem endneolithischen Kollektivgrab von Spreitenbach: Studien zur Ernährung und Mobilität', in T. Doppler (ed.), *Spreitenbach-Moosweg (Aargau, Schweiz): ein Kollektivgrab um 2500 v. Chr.*, 188–219, Basel: Archäologie Schweiz.

Knipper, C. [+10 others] and P. W. Stockhammer (2017), 'Female exogamy and gene pool diversification at the transition from the Final Neolithic to the Early Bronze Age in central Europe', *Proceedings of the National Academy of Sciences*, 114 (38): 10083–8.

Koch, E. (1998), *Neolithic Bog Pots from Zealand, Møn, Lolland and Falster*, Copenhagen: The Royal Society of Northern Antiquaries.

Kopytoff, I. (1987), 'The internal African frontier: The making of African political culture', in I. Kopytoff (ed.), *The African Frontier: The Reproduction of Traditional African societies*, 3–84, Bloomington: Indiana University Press.

Kristiansen, K. (2014), 'Towards a new paradigm: The third science revolution and its possible consequences in archaeology', *Current Swedish Archaeology*, 22: 11–34.

Kristiansen, K. (2022), *Archaeology and the Genetic Revolution in European Prehistory*, Cambridge: Cambridge University Press.

Kristiansen, K. and T. Earle (2022), 'Modelling modes of production: European 3rd and 2nd millennium BC economies', in M. Frangipane, M. Poettinger and B. Schefold (eds), *Ancient Economies in Comparative Perspective. Material Life, Institutions and Economic Thought*, 131–63, New York: Springer Nature.

Kristiansen, K. [+10 others] and E. Willerslev (2017), 'Re-theorising mobility and the formation of culture and language among the Corded Ware culture in Europe', *Antiquity*, 91 (356): 334–47.

Kroeber, A. L. (1960), 'Statistics, Indo-European and taxonomy', *Language*, 36 (1): 1–21.

Kroon, E. J., D. J. Huisman, Q. P. J. Bourgeois, D. J. G. Braekmans and H. Fokkens (2019), 'The introduction of Corded Ware culture at a local level: An exploratory study of cultural change during the Late Neolithic of the Dutch west coast through ceramic technology', *Journal of Archaeological Science: Reports*, 26: 101873.

Kroonen, G. (2012), 'Non-Indo-European root nouns in Germanic: evidence in support of the agricultural substrate hypothesis', in R. Grünthal and P. Kallio (eds), *A Linguistic Map of Prehistoric Northern Europe*, 239–60, Helsinki: Société Finno-Ougrienne.

Kulikowski, M. (2002), 'Nation versus army: A necessary contrast?', in A. Gillet (ed.), *On Barbarian Identity: Critical Approaches to Ethnicity in the Early Middle Ages. Studies in the Early Middle Ages 4*, 69–84, Turnhout: Brepols.

Labadi, S. (2018), *Museums, Immigrants and Social Justice*, London: Routledge.

Laks, B. (2008), 'Comparativism: from genealogy to genetics', in B. Laks (ed.), *Origin and Evolution of Languages: Approaches, Models, Paradigms*, 157–91, London: Equinox.

Lancy, D. F. and M. A. Grove (2011), 'Getting noticed: Middle childhood in cross-cultural perspective', *Human Nature*, 22 (3): 281–302.

Lao, O., E. Altena, C. Becker, S. Brauer, T. Kraaijenbrink, M. van Oven, P. Nürnberg, P. de Knijff and M. Kayser (2013), 'Clinal distribution of human genomic diversity across the Netherlands despite archaeological evidence for genetic discontinuities in Dutch population history', *Investigative Genetics*, 4 (1): 9. https://doi.org/10.1186/2041-2223-4-9

Larson, G. [+30 others] and K. Dobney (2007), 'Phylogeny and ancient DNA of *Sus* provides insights into Neolithic expansion in Island Southeast Asia and Oceania', *Proceedings of the National Academy of Sciences*, 104 (12): 4834e4839.

Larsson, Å. M. (2009), *Breaking and Making Bodies and Pots: Material and Ritual Practices in Sweden in the Third Millennium* BC, Uppsala: Uppsala University.

Leary, J., ed. (2014), *Past Mobilities: Archaeological Approaches to Movement and Mobility*, London: Routledge.

Lechterbeck, J., T. Kerig, A. Kleinmann, M. Sillmann, L. Wick and M. Rösch (2014), 'How was Bell Beaker economy related to Corded Ware and Early Bronze Age lifestyles? Archaeological, botanical and palynological evidence from the Hegau, western Lake Constance region', *Environmental Archaeology*, 19 (2): 95–113.

Lefebvre, H. (1974), 'La production de l'espace', *Homme Société*, 31: 15–32.

Lefebvre, H. (1992), *Eléments de rythmanalyse: introduction à la connaissance des rythmes*, Paris: Edition Syllepse.

Lefranc, P., A. Denaire and C. Jeunesse (2017), 'Human remains of the 4th millennium BC in the south of the Upper Rhine valley', in H. Meller and S. Friederich (eds), *Salzmünde – Regel oder Ausnahme? Internationale Tagung Halle*, 521–31, Halle: Landesmuseum für Vorgeschichte.

Lekson, S. H. and C. Cameron (1995), 'The abandonment of Chaco Canyon, the Mesa Verde migrations, and the reorganization of the Pueblo world', *Journal of Anthropological Archaeology*, 14 (2): 184–202.

Lengvarsky, A. (2009), 'Women and intercultural cooperation: Moravian, Delaware, Mahikan women and the negotiating space, 1741–1763', MA thesis, Ohio State University. Available at https://etd.ohiolink.edu/ apexprod/rws_olink/r/1501/10?p10_etd_subid=69109&clear=10 [last accessed 24.03.22].

Leppard, T. (2014), 'Mobility and migration in the Early Neolithic of the Mediterranean: Questions of motivation and mechanism', *World Archaeology*, 46 (4): 484–501.

Leppard, T. (2016), 'Between deterministic and random process in prehistoric Pacific island abandonment', *Journal of Pacific Archaeology*, 7 (2): 20–5.

Leppard, T. (2021), 'Process and dynamics of Mediterranean Neolithization (7000–5500 BC)', *Journal of Archaeological Research*, 30 (2): 231–83.

Le Roy, M. (2015), 'Les enfants au Néolithique: Du contexte funéraire à l'interprétation socioculturelle en France de 5700 à 2100 ans av. J.-C', unpublished PhD thesis, Université de Bordeaux.

Le Roy, M., M. Rivollat, F. Mendisco, M.-H. Pemonge, C. Coutelier, C. Couture, A.-M. Tillier, S. Rottier and M.-F. Deguilloux (2016), 'Distinct ancestries for similar funerary practices? A GIS analysis comparing funerary, osteological and aDNA data from the Middle Neolithic necropolis Gurgy "Les Noisats", Yonne, France', *Journal of Archaeological Science*, 73: 45–54.

Leuzinger, U. [+17 others] and H. Brem (2021), '"Hügeli" im Bodensee – rätselhafte Steinschüttungen in der Flachwasserzone zwischen Romanshorn und Altnau, Kanton Thurgau (Schweiz)', *Jahrbuch Archäologie Schweiz*, 104: 101–16.

Levine, M. A. (2020), 'The fabric of empire in a native world: An analysis of trade cloth recovered from eighteenth-century Otstonwakin', *American Antiquity*, 85 (1): 51–71.

Lipson, M. [+55 others] and D. Reich (2017), 'Parallel palaeogenomic transects reveal complex genetic history of early European farmers', *Nature*, 551: 368–72.

Lipson, M. [+28 others] and D. Reich (2018), 'Population turnover in Remote Oceania shortly after initial settlement', *Current Biology*, 28 (7): 1157–65.

Lipson, M. [+11 others] and D. Reich (2020), 'Three phases of ancient migration shaped the ancestry of human populations in Vanuatu', *Current Biology*, 30 (24): 4846–56.

Liu, Y.-C. [+38 others] and D. Reich (2022), 'Ancient DNA reveals five streams of migration into Micronesia and matrilocality in early Pacific seafarers', *Science*, 377 (6601): 72–9.

Lösch, S., I. Siebke, A. Furtwängler, N. Steuri, A. Hafner, S. Szidat and J. Krause (2020), 'Bioarchäologische Untersuchungen der Knochen aus dem Dolmen von Oberbipp, Steingasse', *Archäologie Bern*, 2020: 202–30.

Lucassen, J. and L. Lucassen (2013), 'European migration history', in S. J. Gold and S. J. Nawyn (eds), *The Routledge International Handbook of Migration Studies*, 52–63, London: Routledge.

Lund, J., M. Furholt and K. I. Austvoll (2022), 'Reassessing power in the archaeological discourse: How collective, cooperative and affective perspectives may impact our understanding of social relations and organization in prehistory', *Archaeological Dialogues*, 29 (1): 33–50.

Magny, M., O. Peyron, C. Bégeot and J. Guiot (2005a), 'Quantitative reconstruction of mid-Holocene climatic variations in the northern Alpine foreland based on Lake Morat (Swiss Plateau) and Lake Annency (French Pre-Alps) data', *Boreas*, 34 (4): 434–44.

Magny, M., C. Bégeot, O. Peyron, I. Richoz, A. Marguet and Y. Billaud (2005b), 'Habitats littoraux et histoire des premières communautés agricoles au Néolithique et à l'Âge du Bronze: une mise en perspective paléoclimatique', in P. della Casa and M. Trachsel (eds), *WES'04 – Wetland economies and societies: Proceedings of the international conference in Zurich, 10–13 March 2004*, 133–42, Zurich: Chronos.

Magomedov, B.V. (2004), 'Körpergräber in der Černjachov-Sîntana de Mureş-Kultur', *Eurasia Antiqua*, 10: 281–331.

Maier, R., P. Flegontov, O. Flegontova, U. Isildak, P. Changmai and D. Reich (2023), 'On the limits of fitting complex models of population history to *f*-statistics', *eLife*, 12: e85492. https://doi.org/10.7554/eLife.85492

Malkii, L. (1992), 'National Geographic: The rooting of peoples and the territorialization of national identity among scholars and refugees', *Cultural Anthropology*, 7 (1): 24–44.

Mallory, J. P. (1989), *In Search of the Indo-Europeans: Language, Archaeology and Myth*, London: Thames and Hudson.

Mallory, J. P. and D. Q. Adams (2006), *The Oxford Introduction to Proto-Indo-European and the Proto-Indo-European World*, Oxford: Oxford University Press.

Manen, C. and F. Convertini (2009), 'La céramique du Néolithique ancien', in J.-L. Voruz (ed.), *La grotte du Gardon (Ain): Volume 1, Le site et la séquence néolithique des couches 60 à 47*, 255–66, Toulouse: Ecole des Hautes Etudes en Sciences Sociales.

Maréchal, D., A.-M. Pétrequin, P. Pétrequin and R.-M. Arbogast (1998), 'Les parures du Néolithique final à Chalain et Clairvaux', *Gallia Préhistoire*, 40: 141–203.

Mathieson, I. [+36 others] and D. Reich (2015), 'Genome-wide patterns of selection in 230 ancient Eurasians', *Nature*, 528: 499–503.

Mathieson, I. [+115 others] and D. Reich (2018), 'The genomic history of southeastern Europe', *Nature*, 555: 197–203.

Matisoo-Smith, E. (2015), 'Ancient DNA and the settlement of the Pacific: A review', *Journal of Human Evolution*, 79: 93–104.

Mattioli, A. (2017), *Verlorene Welten: Eine Geschichte der Indianer Nordamerikas 1700–1910*, Stuttgart: Klett Cotta.

Mauvilly, M., C. Jeunesse and T. Doppler (2008), 'Ein Tonstempel aus der spätmesolithischen Fundstelle von Arconciel/La Souche (Kanton Freiburg, Schweiz)', *Quartär*, 55: 151–7.

May, S. K., L. Taylor, C. J. Frieman, P. S. C. Taçon, D. Wesley, T. Jones, J. Goldhahn and C. Mungulda (2020), 'Survival, social cohesion and rock art: The painted hands of Western Arnhem Land, Australia', *Cambridge Archaeological Journal*, 30 (3): 491–510.

McConvell, P. and F. Meakins (2005), 'Gurindji Kriol: A mixed language emerges from code-switching', *Australian Journal of Linguistics*, 25 (1): 9–30.

McFadden, C., R. Walter, H. Buckley and M. F. Oxenham (2021), 'Temporal trends in the colonisation of the Pacific: Palaeodemographic insights', *Journal of World Prehistory*, 34: 47–73.

McGlade, J. and S. E. van der Leeuw (1997), 'Introduction: Archaeology and non-linear dynamics – new approaches to long-term change', in S. E. van der Leeuw and J. McGlade (eds), *Time, Process and Structured Transformation in Archaeology*, 1–31, London: Routledge.

McGuire, R. H. and D. J. Saitta (1996), 'Although they have petty captains, they obey them badly: The dialectics of Prehispanic western Pueblo social organization', *American Antiquity*, 61 (2): 197–216.

Mehrer, M. W. (2000), 'Heterarchy and hierarchy: The community plan as institution in Cahokia's polity', in M.-A. Canuto and J. Yaeger (eds), *Archaeology of Communities: A New World Perspective*, 44–57, London: Routledge.

Meier, M. (2019), *Geschichte der Völkerwanderung: Europa, Asien und Afrika vom 3. bis zum 8. Jahrhundert n. Chr.*, München: Beck.

Meixner, D. (2009), 'Ausnahme oder Regel – Zum Phänomen der Münchshöfener Bestattungen', in K. Schmotz (ed.), V*orträge des 27. Niederbayerischen Archäologentages*, 91–144, Rahden: Marie Leidorf.

MeLa project. (2015), *MeLa project: European Museums in an Age of Migrations. Final brochure.* Available at https://www.mela-project.polimi.it/publications/1266.htm [accessed June 2023].

Meller, H. and S. Friederich, eds (2014), *Salzmünde-Schiepzig – ein Ort, zwei Kulturen: Ausgrabungen an der Westumfahrung Halle (A 143) Teil 1. Archäologie in Sachsen-Anhalt, Sonderband 21/I*, Halle: Landesmuseum für Vorgeschichte.

Menotti, F. (2004), 'Displacement, readaptation and cultural continuity: A lake-dwelling perspective', in F. Menotti (ed.), *Living on the Lake in Prehistoric Europe: 150 Years of Lake-Dwelling Research*, 207–17, London: Routledge.

Merrell, J. H. (1998), 'Shamokin, "the very seat of the Prince of Darkness": Unsettling the early American frontier', in A. R. L. Cayton and F. J. Teute (eds), *Contact Points: American Frontiers from the Mohawk Valley to the Mississippi, 1750–1830*, 16–59, Chapel Hill: University of North Carolina Press.

Merrell, J. H. (1999), *Into the American Woods: Negotiators on the Pennsylvania Frontier*, New York: W. W. Norton.

Metcalf, P. (2010), *The Life of the Longhouse: An Archaeology of Ethnicity*, Cambridge: Cambridge University Press.

Meyer, C., S. Karimnia, C. Knipper, M. Stecher, G. Brandt, B. Schlenker, F. Ramsthaler and K.W. Alt (2013), 'Eine komplexe Mehrfachbestattung der Salzmünder Kultur', in H. Meller (ed.), *3300 BC: Mysteriöse Steinzeittote und ihre Welt*, 290–9, Halle: Landesmuseum für Vorgeschichte.

Meyer, M. and D. Raetzel-Fabian (2006), 'Neolithische Grabenwerke in Mitteleuropa: Ein Überblick', *Journal of Neolithic Archaeology*, 8. https://doi.org/10.12766/jna.2006.20

Midgley, M. S. (1992), *TRB Culture: The First Farmers of the North European Plain*, Edinburgh: Edinburgh University Press.

Midgley, M. S. (2005), *The Monumental Cemeteries of Prehistoric Europe*, Stroud: Tempus.

Mikaere, A. (2005), *Cultural Invasion Continued: The Ongoing Colonisation of Tikanga Maori*, Hamilton: University of Waikato.

Milisauskas, S. (2002), *European Prehistory: A Survey*, New York: Springer.

Mills, B. J. (2007), 'Multicrafting, migration, and identity in the American Southwest', in I. Shimada (ed.), *Craft Production in Complex Societies: Multicraft and Producer Perspectives*, 25–43, Salt Lake City: University of Utah Press.

Mills, B. J. (2011), 'Themes and models for understanding migration in the Southwest', in M. C. Nelson and C. Strawhacker (eds), *Movement, Connectivity, and Landscape Change in the Ancient Southwest*, 347–61, Boulder: University Press of Colorado.

Mills, B. J. (2023), 'From frontier to centre place: The dynamic trajectory of the Chaco world', *Journal of Urban Archaeology*, 7: 215–52.

Mills, B. J. [+8 others] and R. L. Breiger (2013), 'The dynamics of social networks in the late Prehispanic US Southwest', in C. Knappett (ed.), *Network Analysis in Archaeology: New Approaches to Regional Interaction*, 181–202, Oxford: Oxford University Press.

Mills, B. J., M. A. Peeples, L. D. Aragon, B. A. Bellorado, J. J. Clark, E. Gioni and T. C. Windes (2018), 'Evaluating Chaco migration scenarios using dynamic social network analysis', *Antiquity*, 92 (364): 922–39.

Mittnik, A. [+22 others] and J. Krause (2019), 'Kinship-based social inequality in Bronze Age Europe', *Science*, 366 (6466): 731–4.

Moinat, P. and W. Stöckli (1995), 'Glaube und Grabriten', in W. Stöckli, U. Niffeler and E. Gross-Klee (eds), *Die Schweiz vom Paläolithikum bis zum frühen Mittelalter. Band II Neolithikum*, 231–57, Basel: Verlag Schweizerische Gesellschaft für Ur- und Frühgeschichte.

Moinat, P., C. Falquet and M. Wittig (2007), 'Une inhumation d'enfant à Onnens-Praz Berthoud (Vaud, Suisse)', in P. Moinat and P. Chambon (eds), *Les cistes de Chamblandes et la place des coffres dans les pratiques funéraires du Néolithique moyen occidental: Actes du colloque de Lausanne, 12 et 13 mai 2006*, 233–9, Lausanne: Cahiers d'Archéologie romande.

Mufwene, S.S. (2001), *The Ecology of Language Evolution*, Cambridge: Cambridge University Press.

Müller, J. (2023), *Separation, Hybridisation, and Networks: Globular Amphora Sedentary Pastoralists ca. 3200–2700 bce*, Leiden: Sidestone Press.

Müller, J. and A. Diachenko (2019), 'Tracing long-term demographic changes: The issue of spatial scales', *PLoS ONE*, 14 (1): e0208739.

Münster, A. [+16 others] and K. W. Alt (2018), '4000 years of human dietary evolution in central Germany, from the first farmers to the first elites', *PLoS ONE*, 13: e0194862.

Murphy, L. E. (1998), 'To live among us: Accommodation, gender, and conflict in the western Great Lakes region, 1760–1832', in A. R. L. Cayton and F. J. Teute (eds), *Contact Points: American Frontiers from the Mohawk Valley to the Mississippi, 1750–1830*, 270–303, Chapel Hill: University of North Carolina Press.

Naranjo, T. (1995), 'Thoughts on migration by Santa Clara Pueblo', *Journal of Anthropological Archaeology*, 14: 247–50.

Nash, C. (2002), 'Genealogical identities', *Environment and Planning D: Society and Space*, 20 (1): 27–52.

Nash, C. (2005), 'Geographies of relatedness', *Transactions of the Institute of British Geographers*, 30 (4): 449–62.

Nash, C. (2012), 'Gendered geographies of genetic variation: Sex, power and mobility in human population genetics', *Gender, Place & Culture: a Journal of Feminist Geography*, 19 (4): 409–28.

Needham, S. (2009), 'Encompassing the sea: "maritories" and Bronze Age maritime interactions', in P. Clark (ed.), *Bronze Age Connections: Cultural Contact in Prehistoric Europe*, 12–37, Oxford: Oxbow Books.

Neil, S., J. Evans, J. Montgomery and C. Scarre (2020), 'Isotopic evidence for human movement into central England during the Early Neolithic', *European Journal of Archaeology*, 23 (4): 512–29.

Nelson, E. S. and S. L. Chatfield (2022), 'A conversation in time: A new concept for creating Stream Graphs for qualitative data visualization', *The Qualitative Report*, 27 (11): 2605–22.

Nickel, C. (1997), 'Menschliche Skelettreste aus Michelsberger Fundzusammenhängen: Zur Interpretation einer Fundgattung', *Bericht der Römisch-Germanischen Kommission*, 78: 29–196.

Nielsen, E. (1997), 'Fällanden ZH-Usserriet. Zum Übergangsbereich Spätmesolithikum – Frühneolithikum in der Schweiz', *Jahrbuch der Schweizerischen Gesellschaft für Ur- und Frühgeschichte*, 80: 57–84.

Nielsen, E. (2004), 'The seventh and sixth millennia transition in Switzerland', in E. Walker, F. Wenban-Smith and F. Healy (eds), *Lithics in Action: Papers from the Conference 'Lithic Studies in the Year 2000'*, 185–96. Oxford: Oxbow Books.

Nielsen, P. O. and F. O. S. Nielsen (2020), *First Farmers on the Island of Bornholm*, Copenhagen: The Royal Society of Northern Antiquaries.

Nielsen, S. K. and N. N. Johannsen (2023), 'Mortuary palisades, single graves and cultural admixture: The establishment of Corded Ware culture on the Jutland Peninsula', *Praehistorische Zeitschrift*, 23: https://doi.org/10.1515/pz-2023-2022

Nikitin, A. G. [+9 others] and D. Reich (2019), 'Interactions between earliest *Linearbandkeramik* farmers and central European hunter gatherers at the dawn of European Neolithization', *Scientific Reports*, 9: 19544. https://doi.org/10.1038/s41598-019-56029-2

Notermans, C. (2004), 'Fosterage and the politics of marriage and kinship in east Cameroon', in F. Bowie (ed.), *Cross-cultural Approaches to Adoption*, 48–63, London: Routledge.

Nyland, A. J., D. Hofmann and R. Iversen (2023), 'The blurry third millennium: "Neolithisation" in a Norwegian context', *Open Archaeology*, 9(1): 20220287. https://doi.org/10.1515/opar-2022-0287

Odling-Smee, F. J., K. N. Laland and M. W. Feldman (2003), *Niche Construction: The Neglected Process in Evolution*, Princeton: Princeton University Press.

O'Gorman, J. A. and D. Conner (2023), 'Making community: Implications of hybridity and coalescence at Morton Village', *American Antiquity*, 88 (1): 79–98.

Okrent, D. (2019), *The Guarded Gate: Bigotry, Eugenics, and the Law That Kept Two Generations of Jews, Italians, and Other European Immigrants Out of America*, New York: Scribner.

Olsen, B. (2003), 'Material culture after text: Re-membering things', *Norwegian Archaeological Review*, 36: 87–104.

Olsen, B. and Z. Kobyliński (1991), 'Ethnicity in anthropological and archaeological research: A Norwegian–Polish perspective', *Archaeologia Polona*, 29 (4): 5–27.

Omrak, A. [+8 others] and A. Götherström (2016), 'Genomic evidence establishes Anatolia as the source of the European Neolithic gene pool', *Current Biology*, 26 (2): 270–5.

O'Shannessy, C. (2019), 'Why do children lead contact-induced language change in some contexts but not others?', in E. Doron, M. Rappaport Hovav, Y. Reshef and M. Taube (eds), *Language Contact, Continuity and Change in the Genesis of Modern Hebrew*, 321–35, Amsterdam: John Benjamins Publishing Company.

O'Shannessy, C. (2021), 'How ordinary child language acquisition processes can lead to the unusual outcome of a mixed language', *International Journal of Bilingualism*, 25 (2): 458–80.

Palmberger, M. and J. Tošić, eds (2016), *Memories on the Move: Experiencing Mobility, Rethinking the Past. Migration, Diasporas and Citizenship*, London: Palgrave Macmillan.

Parkes, P. (2006), 'Celtic fosterage: Adoptive kinship and clientage in northwest Europe', *Comparative Studies in Society and History*, 48 (2): 359–95.

Patterson, N. [+227 others] and D. Reich (2022), 'Large-scale migration into Britain during the Middle to Late Bronze Age', *Nature*, 601: 588–94.

Pattison, J. E. (2008), 'Is it necessary to assume an apartheid-like social structure in Early Anglo-Saxon England?', *Proceedings of the Royal Society B*, 275: 2423–9.

Pauketat, T. (2000), 'Politicization and community in the Pre-Columbian Mississippi Valley', in M.-A. Canuto and J. Yaeger (eds), *Archaeology of Communities: A New World Perspective*, 16–43, London: Routledge.

Pearce, C. E. M. and F. M. Pearce (2010), *Oceanic Migration: Paths, Sequence, Timing and Range of Prehistoric Migration in the Pacific and Indian Oceans*, New York: Springer.

Pechtl, J. (2011), 'Am Rande des Machbaren: zwei gescheiterte linienbandkeramische Kolonisationswellen im Lechtal', in T. Doppler, B. Ramminger and D. Schimmelpfennig (eds), *Grenzen und Grenzräume? Beispiele aus Neolithikum und Bronzezeit*, 37–51, Kerpen-Loogh: Welt und Erde.

Pechtl, J. (2020), 'Constant change of LBK settlement in the Upper Danube region', *Quaternary International*, 560/1: 240–7.

Penske, S. [+27 others] and W. Haak (2023), 'Early contact between late farming and pastoralist societies in southeastern Europe', *Nature*, 620 (7974): 358–65.

Pereltsvaig, A. and M. W. Lewis (2015), *The Indo-European Controversy: Facts and Fallacies in Historical Linguistics*, Cambridge: Cambridge University Press.

Perrin, T. (2009), 'New perspectives on the Mesolithic/Neolithic transition in northern Italy', in S. McCartan, R. Schulting, G. Warren and P. Woodman (eds), *Mesolithic Horizons Volume II*, 514–20, Oxford: Oxbow Books.

Persson, P. (1999), *Neolitikums början: undersökningar kring jordbrukets introduktion i Nordeuropa*, Gothenburg: University of Gothenburg.

Perutka, A., F. Schreil, D. Hofmann, M. Szilágyi, J. Ewersen, L. Husty, C. Sarkady and G. Grupe (2021), 'Conspicuous burials in a Neolithic enclosure at Riedling (Bavaria, Germany) – A selection of individuals?', *Journal of Archaeological Science: Reports*, 39: 103154.

Petersen, P. V. (1999), *Flint fra Danmarks oldtid*, Copenhagen: Høst & Søn.

Petrasch, J. (2020), 'Settlements, migration and the break of tradition: The settlement patterns of the earliest Bandkeramik and the LBK and the formation of a Neolithic lifestyle in western central Europe', *Quaternary International*, 560/1: 248–58.

Pétrequin, P., R. Martineau, P. Nowicki, E. Gauthier and C. Schaal (2009), 'La poterie Hoguette de Choisey (Jura), les Champins: Observations techniques et insertion régionale', *Bulletin de la Société Préhistorique Française*, 106: 491–515.

Pinker, S. (2011), *The Better Angels of Our Nature: Why Violence Has Declined*, New York: Penguin Books.

Pioffet, H. C. S. (2014), 'Sociétés et identités du premier Néolithique de Grande-Bretagne et d'Irlande dans leur contexte ouest européen: caractérisation et analyses comparatives des productions céramiques entre Manche, Mer d'Irlande et Mer du Nord', PhD thesis, University of Durham.

Pohl, W. (1998), 'Gentilismus', in H. Beck, H. Steuer and D. Timpe (eds), *Reallexikon der Germanischen Altertumskunde 11*, 91–101, Berlin: de Gruyter.

Pohl, W. (2002a), *Die Völkerwanderung: Eroberung und Integration*, Stuttgart: Kohlhammer.

Pohl, W. (2002b), 'Ethnicity, theory, and tradition: A response', in A. Gillet (ed.), *On Barbarian Identity: Critical Approaches to Ethnicity in the Early Middle Ages*, 221–39, Turnhout: Brepols.

Pohl, W. (2005), 'Geschichte und Identität im Langobardenreich', in W. Pohl and P. Erhart (eds), *Die Langobarden: Herrschaft und Identität*, 555–66, Wien: Österreichische Akademie der Wissenschaften.

Pohl, W. and P. Erhart, eds (2005), *Die Langobarden: Herrschaft und Identität*, Wien: Österreichische Akademie der Wissenschaften.

Pope, R. (2022), 'Re-approaching Celts: Origins, society, and social change', *Journal of Archaeological Research*, 30: 1–67.

Posth, C. [+27 others] and A. Powell (2018), 'Language continuity despite population replacement in Remote Oceania', *Nature Ecology and Evolution*, 2: 731–40.

Preda-Bălănică, B. (2021), 'Still making waves: Marija Gimbutas in current archaeological debates', in V. Heyd, G. Kulcsár and B. Preda-Bălănică (eds), *Yamnaya interactions: Proceedings of the international workshop held in Helsinki, 25–26 April 2019*, 137–70, Budapest: Archaeolingua.

Preda-Bălănică, B. and Y. Diekmann (2023), 'Ancestry and identity in the Balkans and the Carpathian basin between the 5th and 3rd millennia cal BC', in A. Whittle, J. Pollard and S. Greaney (eds), *Ancient DNA and the European Neolithic: Relations and Descent*, 107–22, Oxford: Oxbow Books.

Prescott, C. (2019), 'Changing demographics and cultural heritage in northern Europe: Transforming narratives and identifying obstacles – a case study from Oslo, Norway', in C. Holtorf, A. Pantazatos and G. Scarre (eds), *Cultural Heritage, Ethics and Contemporary Migrations*, 52–69, London: Routledge.

Prien, R. (2005), *Archäologie und Migration: Vergleichende Studien zur archäologischen Nachweisbarkeit von Wanderungsbewegungen*, Bonn: Rudolf Habelt.

Pugach, I., A. Hübner, H.-C. Hung, M-T. Carson and M. Stoneking (2021), 'Ancient DNA from Guam and the peopling of the Pacific', *Proceedings of the National Academy of Sciences*, 118 (1): e2022112118.

Rasmussen, P. (2005), 'Mid- to late-Holocene land-use change and lake development at Dallund Sø, Denmark: Vegetation and land-use history inferred from pollen data', *The Holocene*, 15 (8): 1116–29.

Renfrew, C. (1973), *Before Civilization: The Radiocarbon Revolution and Prehistoric Europe*, London: Jonathan Cape.

Renfrew, C. (1987), *Archaeology and Language: The Puzzle of Indo-European Origins*, London: Cape.

Ribeiro, A. (2019), 'Science, data, and case-studies under the third science revolution: Some theoretical considerations', *Current Swedish Archaeology*, 27: 115–32.

Richards, C. (2008), 'The substance of Polynesian voyaging', *World Archaeology*, 40 (2): 206–23.

Richwine, L. (2022), 'Comity at the crossroads: How friendships between Moravian and Native women sustained the Moravian mission at Shamokin, 1745–1755', *Pennsylvania History: A Journal of Mid-Atlantic Studies*, 89 (1): 74–101.

Rigert, E., I. Ebneter, R. Ebersbach, Ö. Akeret and U. Leuzinger (2005), 'Die Epi-Rössener Siedlung von Sevelen SG-Pfäfersbüel', *Jahrbuch der Schweizer Gesellschaft für Ur- und Frühgeschichte*, 88: 41–86.

Rimantienė, R. (1989), *Nida: senųjų baltų gyvenvietė*, Vilnius: Mokslas.

Ringe, D. and T. Warnow (2008), 'Linguistic history and computational cladistics', in B. Laks (ed.), *Origin and Evolution of Languages: Approaches, Models, Paradigms*, 257–71, London: Equinox.

Rivollat, M., H. Réveillas, F. Mendisco, M.-H. Pemonge, P. Justeau, C. Couture, P. Lefranc, C. Féliu and M.-F. Deguilloux (2016), 'Ancient mitochondrial DNA from the Middle Neolithic necropolis of Obernai extends the genetic influence of the LBK to west of the Rhine', *American Journal of Physical Anthropology*, 161 (3): 522–9.

Rivollat, M. [+20 others] and W. Haak (2020), 'Ancient genome-wide DNA from France highlights the complexity of interactions between Mesolithic hunter-gatherers and Neolithic farmers', *Science Advances*, 6 (22): eaaz5344. https://doi.org/10.1126/sciadv.aaz5344

Rivollat, M. [+19 others] and W. Haak (2023), 'Extensive pedigrees reveal the social organization of a Neolithic community', *Nature*, 620: 600–6. https://doi.org/10.1038/s41586-023-06350-8

Robb, J. (1991), 'Random causes with directed effects: The Indo-European language spread and the stochastic loss of lineages', *Antiquity*, 65 (247): 287–91.

Robb, J. (1993), 'A social prehistory of European languages', *Antiquity*, 67 (257): 747–60.

Robb, J. (2007), *The Early Mediterranean Village: Agency, Material Culture, and Social Change in Neolithic Italy*, Cambridge: Cambridge University Press.

Robb, J. (2014), 'The future Neolithic: a new research agenda', in A. Whittle and P. Bickle (eds), *Early Farmers: The View from Archaeology and Science*, 21–8, Oxford: Oxford University Press.

Robb, J. and P. Miracle (2007), 'Beyond "migration" versus "acculturation": New models for the spread of agriculture', in A. Whittle and V. Cummings (eds), *Going Over: The Mesolithic–Neolithic Transition in North-west Europe*, 99–115, Oxford: Oxford University Press.

Robb, J. and T. Pauketat (2013), 'From moments to millennia: Theorizing scale and change in human history', in J. Robb and T. Pauketat (eds), *Big Histories, Human Lives: Tackling Problems of Scale in Archaeology*, 3–33, Santa Fe: SAR Press.

Roddick, A. P. and A. B. Stahl, eds (2016), *Knowledge in Motion: Constellations of Learning Across Time and Place*, Tucson: University of Arizona Press.

Roesch-Rhomberg, I. (2004), 'Korean institutionalized adoption', in F. Bowie (ed.), *Cross-cultural Approaches to Adoption*, 81–96, London: Routledge.

Rogers, L. O. (2020), '"I'm kind of a feminist": Using master narratives to analyze gender identity in middle childhood', *Child Development*, 91 (1): 179–96.

Rogers, T. A., J. S. Crary, A. Ward and S. Germick (2021), 'Reevaluating Kayenta migration scenarios: A revision of the Goat Hill phase in the San Carlos Safford area of southeastern Arizona', *Journal of Arizona Archaeology*, 8: 123–56.

Rösch, M. (2005), 'Spätneolithische und bronzezeitliche Landnutzung am westlichen Bodensee – Versuch einer Annäherung anhand archäologischer und experimenteller Daten', in P. della Casa and M. Trachsel (eds), *WES'04 – Wetland economies and societies: Proceedings of the international conference in Zurich, 10–13 March 2004*, 105–19, Zurich: Chronos.

Rosenberg, M. and T. Rocek (2019), 'Socio-political organization in the aceramic Neolithic of southwestern Asia: The complex evolution of socio-political complexity', *Journal of Anthropological Archaeology*, 54: 17–30.

Rottier, S., C. Mordant, P. Chambon and C. Thévenet (2005), 'Découverte de plus d'une centaine de sépultures du Néolithique moyen à Gurgy, les Noisats (Yonne)', *Bulletin de la Société Préhistorique Française*, 102: 641–5.

Roullier, C., L. Benoit, D. B. McKey and V. Lebot (2012), 'Historical collections reveal patterns of diffusion of sweet potato in Oceania obscured by modern plant movements and recombination', *Proceedings of the National Academy of Sciences*, 110 (6): 2205–10.

Rountree, H. (2005), *Pocahontas, Powhatan, and Opechancanough: Three Indian Lives Changed by Jamestown*, Charlottesville: University of Virginia Press.

Rouse, I. (1986), *Migrations in Prehistory: Inferring Population Movement from Cultural Remains*, New Haven: Yale University Press.

Rowley-Conwy, P., K. J. Gron, R. R. Bishop, J. Dunne, R. Evershed, C. Longford, R. Schulting and E. Treasure (2020), 'The earliest farming in Britain: Towards a new synthesis', in P. Rowley-Conwy, K.J. Gron and L. Sørensen (eds), *Farmers at the Frontier*, 401–24, Oxford: Oxbow Books.

Ruiz Rosendo, L. and C. Persaud (2016), 'Interpreting in conflict zones throughout history', *Linguistica Antverpiensia New Series*, 15: 1–35.

Rutherford, A. (2016), *A Brief History of Everyone Who Ever Lived: The Stories in Our Genes*, London: Weidenfeld & Nicolson.

Sahlins, M. (1974), *Stone Age Economics*, London: Routledge.

Sahlins, M. (1985), *Islands of History*, Chicago: University of Chicago Press.

Sasse, B. (1997), 'Die Westgoten in Südfrankreich und Spanien: Zum Problem der archäologischen Identifikation einer wandernden "gens"', *Archäologische Informationen*, 20 (1): 29–48.

Scharl, S. (2004), *Die Neolithisierung Europas: Ausgewählte Modelle und Hypothesen*, Rahden: Marie Leidorf.

Schier, W. (2017), 'Die Tertiäre Neolithisierung – Fakt oder Fiktion?', in J. Lechterbeck and E. Fischer (eds), *Kontrapunkte: Festschrift für Manfred Rösch*, 129–45, Bonn: Rudolf Habelt.

Schiffels, S. [+11 others] and R. Durbin (2016), 'Iron Age and Anglo-Saxon genomes from east England reveal British migration history', *Nature Communications*, 7: 10408. https://doi.org/10.1038/ncomms10408

Schiller, F. (1790), *Allgemeine Sammlung historischer Memoires vom zwölften Jahrhundert bis auf die neuesten Zeiten 1,1*, Jena: Mauke.

Schlenker, B., M. Stecher, K. W. Alt and S. Friederich (2017), 'Bestattungsformen der Salzmünder Kultur am eponymen Fundort Salzmünde', in H. Meller and S. Friederich (eds), *Salzmünde – Regel oder Ausnahme? Internationale Tagung vom 18. bis 20. Oktober 2012 in Halle (Saale)*, 33–51, Halle: Landesmuseum für Vorgeschichte.

Schlichtherle, H. (2004), 'Große Häuser, kleine Häuser: Archäologische Befunde zum Siedlungswandel am neolithischen Federsee', in J. Köninger and H. Schlichtherle (eds), *Ökonomischer und ökologischer Wandel am vorgeschichtlichen Federsee: Archäologische und naturwissenschaftliche Untersuchungen*, 13–56, Hemmenhofen: Landesdenkmalamt Baden-Württemberg.

Schlichtherle, H. (2010), 'Kultbilder in den Pfahlbauten des Bodensees', in Badisches Landesmuseum (ed.), *Jungsteinzeit im Umbruch. Die*

'*Michelsberger Kultur' und Mitteleuropa vor 6,000 Jahren*, 256–77, Karlsruhe: Badisches Landesmuseum.

Schlichtherle, H. (2011), 'Die Ausgrabungen in der endneolithischen Moorsiedlung Bad Buchau-Torwiesen II. Eine Einführung in Befunde und Fundverteilungen', in H. Schlichtherle, R. Vogt, U. Maier, C. Herbig, E. Schmidt, K. Ismail-Meyer, M. Kühn, L. Wick and A. Dufraisse (eds), *Die endneolithische Moorsiedlung Bad-Buchau-Torwiesen II am Federsee. Band 1: Naturwissenschaftliche Untersuchungen*, 11–28, Hemmenhofen: Landesamt für Denkmalpflege.

Schlichtherle, H., N. Bleicher, A. Dufraisse, P. Kieselbach, U. Maier, E. Schmidt, E. Stephan and R. Vogt (2010), 'Bad Buchau-Torwiesen II: Baustrukturen und Siedlungsabfälle als Indizien der Sozialstruktur und Wirtschaftsweise einer endneolithischen Siedlung', in E. Claßen, T. Doppler and B. Ramminger (eds), *Familie – Verwandtschaft – Sozialstrukturen: Sozialarchäologische Forschungen zu neolithischen Befunden*, 157–78, Kerpen-Loogh: Welt und Erde.

Schmitt, R. (2000), 'Indogermanische Altertumskunde, I. Sprachliches', *Reallexikon der Germanischen Altertumskunde*, 15: 384–402.

Schneider, T. D. and L. M. Panich, eds (2022), *Archaeologies of Indigenous Presence*, Gainesville: University Press of Florida.

Schofield, J. (2018) '"Heritage on exile": Reflecting on the roles and responsibilities of heritage organizations towards those affected by forced migration', in Y. Hamilakis (ed.), *The New Nomadic Age: Archaeologies of Forced and Undocumented Migration*, 184–91, London: Equinox.

Schröter, R. (2009), *Die Ausgrabungen des Urgeschichtlichen Forschungsinstituts der Universität Tübingen (UFI) in Aichbühl und Riedschachen (1919–1930). Berichte zu Ufer- und Moorsiedlungen Südwestdeutschlands IV*, Stuttgart: Theiss.

Schulting, R. (2013), 'War without warriors? The nature of interpersonal conflict before the emergence of formalized warrior elites', in S. Ralph (ed.), *The Archaeology of Violence: Interdisciplinary Approaches*, 19–36, Albany: SUNY Press.

Schultrich, S. (2022), 'Kriegerideal und Netzwerke: Die Doppeläxte West- und Mitteleuropas im Kontext der jung- bis endneolithischen Kulturentwicklung', PhD dissertation, Christian-Albrechts University Kiel. Available at: https://macau.uni-kiel.de/receive/macau_mods_00002793

Schunke, T., C. Knipper and L. Renner (2013), 'Bestattet im Graben – die Umbettung eines Kollektivgrabes der Bernburger Kultur', in H. Meller (ed.), *3300 BC: Mysteriöse Steinzeittote und ihre Welt*, 324–31, Halle: Landesmuseum für Vorgeschichte.

Schuster, C.E. (2023), 'Gender, capitalism, and the erotics of finance', in M. Fotta, C. McCallum and S. Posocco (eds), *Cambridge Handbook for the Anthropology of Gender and Sexuality*, 425–54, Cambridge: Cambridge University Press.

Scott, J. C. (1985), *Weapons of the Weak: Everyday Forms of Peasant Resistance*, New Haven: Yale University Press.

Seebold, E. (2000), 'Indogermanische Sprache und Sprachfamilien', *Reallexikon der Germanischen Altertumskunde*, 15: 408–13.

Seidel, U. (2012), 'Wechselnde Überlieferungsdichten von Fundstellen an der Wende vom 5.–4. Jahrtausend v. Chr. am Beispiel der Michelsberger Besiedelung im nördlichen Baden-Württemberg', in R. Gleser and V. Becker (eds), *Mitteleuropa im 5. Jt. v. Chr. Beiträge zur internationalen Konferenz in Münster 2010*, 291–308, Berlin: Lit Verlag.

Seidel, U. (2017), 'Evidence for mobility in the settlement system of the Michelsberg culture in south Germany', in S. Scharl and B. Gehlen (eds), *Mobility in Prehistoric Sedentary Societies*, 145–62, Rahden: Marie Leidorf.

Seifert, M. (2012), 'Zizers GR-Friedau – mittelneolithische Siedlung mit Hinkelsteinkeramik im Bündner Alpenrheintal (Schweiz)', in A. Boschetti-Maradi, A. de Capitani, S. Hochuli and U. Niffeler (eds), *Form, Zeit und Raum. Grundlagen für eine Geschichte aus dem Boden: Festschrift für Werner E. Stöckli zu seinem 65. Geburtstag*, 79–94, Basel: Archäologie Schweiz.

Sewell, W.H. (2005), *Logics of History: Social Theory and Social Transformation*, Chicago: University of Chicago Press.

Shah, S. (2020), *The Next Great Migration: The Story of Movement on a Changing Planet*, London: Bloomsbury.

Shanks, M. and C. Tilley (1987), *Social Theory and Archaeology*, Albuquerque: University of New Mexico Press.

Sharp, A. (1956), *Ancient Voyagers in the Pacific*, Wellington: Polynesian Society.

Shaw, B. [+17 others] and Brooker and Panaeti Island Communities, Papua New Guinea (2022), 'Frontier Lapita interaction with resident Papuan populations set the stage for initial peopling of the Pacific', *Nature Ecology and Evolution*, 6: 802–12.

Sheller, M. (2016), 'Mobility, freedom and public space', in S. Bergmann and T. Sager (eds), *The Ethics of Mobilities: Rethinking Place, Exclusion, Freedom and Environment*, 25–38, London: Routledge.

Sheller, M. and J. Urry (2006), 'The new mobilities paradigm', *Environment and Planning A: Economy and Space*, 38 (2): 207–26.

Shennan, S. (2018), *The First Farmers of Europe: An Evolutionary Perspective*, Cambridge: Cambridge University Press.

Sheridan, A. (2007), 'From Picardie to Pickering and Pencraig Hill? New information on the "Carinated Bowl Neolithic" in northern Britain', in A. Whittle and V. Cummings (eds), *Going Over: The Mesolithic–Neolithic Transition in North-West Europe*, 441–92, Oxford: Oxford University Press.

Sheridan, A. (2013), 'Early Neolithic habitation structures in Britain and Ireland: A matter of circumstance and context', in D. Hofmann and J. Smyth (eds), *Tracking the Neolithic House in Europe: Sedentism, Architecture and Practice*, 283–300, New York: Springer.

Sherratt, A. (1987), 'Cups that cheered', in W.H. Waldren and R.C. Kennard (eds), *Bell Beakers of the Western Mediterranean*, 81–103, Oxford: British Archaeological Reports.

Siebke, I., A. Furtwängler, N. Steuri, A. Hafner, M. Ramstein, J. Krause and S. Lösch (2020), 'Crops vs. animals: Regional differences in subsistence strategies of Swiss Neolithic farmers revealed by stable isotopes', *Archaeological and Anthropological Sciences*, 12: 235. https://doi.org/10.1007/s12520-020-01122-1

Simon, Z. (2008), 'How to find the Proto-Indo-European homeland? A methodological essay', *Acta Antiqua Hungarica*, 48: 289–303.

Sims-Williams, P. (2020), 'An alternative to "Celtic from the east" and "Celtic from the west"', *Cambridge Archaeological Journal*, 30 (3): 511–29.

Smith, A. D. (2008), *The Cultural Foundations of Nations: Hierarchy, Covenant, and Republic*, Oxford: Blackwell.

Smith, I. (2008), 'Maori, Pakeha and Kiwi: Peoples, cultures and sequence in New Zealand archaeology', in G. Clark, F. Leach and S. O'Connor (eds), *Islands of Inquiry: Colonisation, Seafaring and the Archaeology of Maritime Landscapes*, 367–80, Canberra: ANU EPress.

Smyth, J., M. McClatchie and G. Warren (2020), 'Exploring the "somewhere" and "someone" else: An integrated approach to Ireland's earliest farming practice', in K. J. Gron, L. Sørensen and P. Rowley-Conwy (eds), *Farmers at the Frontier*, 425–42, Oxford: Oxbow Books.

Solien de Gonzalez, N. (1961), 'Family organization in five types of migratory wage labor', *American Anthropologist*, 63 (6): 1264–80.

Sommer, U. (2001), '"Hear the instructions of thy father, and forsake not the law of thy mother": Change and persistence in the European Early Neolithic', *Journal of Social Archaeology*, 1 (2): 244–70.

Sommer, U. (2011), 'Tribes, peoples, ethnicity: archaeology and changing "We groups"', in A. Gardner and E. Cochrane (eds), *Discussing Evolutionary and Interpretative Archaeologies*, 169–98, Walnut Creek: Left Coast Press.

Song, M. (2013), 'The changing configuration of migration and race', in S. J. Gold and S. J. Nawyn (eds), *The Routledge International Handbook of Migration Studies*, 169–79, London: Routledge.

Sørensen, L. (2014), 'From hunter to farmer in northern Europe: Migration and adaption during the Neolithic and Bronze Age', *Acta Archaeologica*, 8 (2): 1–305.

Sørensen, L. and S. Karg (2014), 'The expansion of agrarian societies towards the north – New evidence for agriculture during the Mesolithic/Neolithic transition in southern Scandinavia', *Journal of Archaeological Science*, 51: 98–114.

Sørensen, T. F. (2016), 'In praise of vagueness: Uncertainty, ambiguity and archaeological methodology', *Journal of Archaeological Method and Theory*, 23: 741–63.

Sørensen, T. F. (2017), 'The Two Cultures and a world apart: Archaeology and science at a new crossroads', *Norwegian Archaeological Review*, 50: 101–15.

Souvatzi. S. (2008), *A Social Archaeology of Households in Neolithic Greece: An Anthropological Approach*, Cambridge: Cambridge University Press.

Spielmann, K. A. (2002), 'Feasting, craft specialization, and the ritual mode of production in small-scale societies', *American Anthropologist*, 104 (1): 195–207.

Spriggs, M. and D. Reich (2019), 'An ancient DNA Pacific journey: A case study of collaboration between archaeologists and geneticists', *World Archaeology*, 51 (4): 620–39.

Spriggs, M., F. Valentin, S. Bedford, R. Pinhasi, P. Skoglund, D. Reich and M. Lipson (2019), 'Revisiting ancient DNA insights into the human origin of the Pacific islands', *Archaeology in Oceania*, 54 (1): 53–6.

Stanish, C. (2017), *The Evolution of Human Co-Operation: Ritual and Social Complexity in Stateless Societies*, Cambridge: Cambridge University Press.

Stapfer, R. (2017), 'Special pottery in "Cortaillod" settlements of Neolithic western Switzerland (3900–3500 BC)', in C. Heitz and R. Stapfer (eds), *Mobility and Pottery Production: Archaeological and Anthropological Perspectives*, 141–67, Leiden: Sidestone Press.

Star, S. L. and J. R. Griesemer (1989), 'Institutional ecology, "translations" and boundary objects: Amateurs and professionals in Berkeley's museum of vertebrate zoology, 1907–1939', *Social Studies of Science*, 19 (3): 387–420.

Stecher, M., B. Schlenker and K. W. Alt (2013), 'Die Scherbenpackungsgräber', in H. Meller (ed.), *3300 BC: Mysteriöse Steinzeittote und ihre Welt*, 282–9, Halle: Landesmuseum für Vorgeschichte.

Steinacher, R. (2011), 'Wiener Anmerkungen zu ethnischen Bezeichnungen als Kategorien der römischen und europäischen Geschichte', in S. Burmeister and N. Müller-Scheeßel (eds), *Fluchtpunkt Geschichte: Archäologie und Geschichtswissenschaft im Dialog*, 99–122, Münster: Waxmann.

Steinacher, R. (2016), *Die Vandalen: Aufstieg und Fall eines Barbarenreichs*, Stuttgart: Klett-Cotta.

Steuer, H. (2021), *„Germanen" aus Sicht der Archäologie: Neue Thesen zu einem alten Thema. Reallexikon der Germanischen Altertumskunde, Ergänzungsband 125*, Berlin: De Gruyter.

Steuri, N. and A. Hafner (2022), 'Die neolithischen Steinkistengräber von Däniken/Studenweid', *Archäologie und Denkmalpflege im Kanton Solothurn*, 27: 11–30.

Steuri, N., M. Milella, F. Martinet, L. Raiteri, S. Szidat, S. Lösch and A. Hafner (2023), 'First radiocarbon dating of Neolithic stone cist graves from the Aosta valley (Italy): Insights into the chronology and burial rites of the western Alpine region', *Radiocarbon*, 65 (2): 521–38.

Stöckli, W. (2016), *Urgeschichte der Schweiz im Überblick (15.000 v. Chr. – Christi Geburt): Die Konstruktion einer Urgeschichte*, Basel: Archäologie Schweiz.

Stone, T. (2003), 'Social identity and ethnic interaction in the western Pueblos of the American Southwest', *Journal of Archaeological Method and Theory*, 10 (1): 31–67.

Stovel, E. M. (2013), 'Concepts of ethnicity and culture in Andean archaeology', *Latin American Antiquity*, 24 (1): 3–20.

Strien, H.-C. (2017a), 'Occupation and settlement of land in the Linear Pottery culture: Reflections on the organisation and logistics', in S. Scharl and B. Gehlen (eds), *Mobility in Prehistoric Sedentary Societies*, 129–33, Rahden: Marie Leidorf.

Strien, H.-C. (2017b), 'Discrepancies between archaeological and 14C-based chronologies: Problems and possible solutions', *Documenta Praehistorica*, 44: 272–81.

Strobel, M. (2000), *Die Schussenrieder Siedlung Taubried I (Bad Buchau, Kr. Biberach): Ein Beitrag zu den Siedlungsstrukturen und zur Chronologie des frühen und mittleren Jungneolithikums in Oberschwaben*, Stuttgart: Theiss.

Strong, P. T. (2001), 'To forget their tongue, their name and their whole relation: Captivity, extra-tribal adoption, and the Indian Child Welfare Act', in S. Franklin and S. McKinnon (eds), *Relative Values: Reconfiguring Kinship Studies*, 468–93, Durham: Duke University Press.

Styring, A., U. Maier, E. Stephan, H. Schlichtherle and A. Bogaard (2016), 'Cultivation of choice: new insights into farming practices at Neolithic lakeshore sites', *Antiquity*, 90 (349): 95–110.

Suggs, R. C. (1960), *The Island Civilizations of Polynesia*, New York: The New American Library.

Suter, P. [+10 others] and S. Ulrich-Bochsler (2017), 'Synthese: Die Ufersiedlungen der ersten Hälfte des 3. Jahrtausends v. Chr. am Bielersee', in P. Suter (ed.), *Um 2700 v. Chr. – Wandel und Kontinuität in den Ufersiedlungen am Bielersee*, 382–421, Bern: Archäologischer Dienst des Kantons Bern.

Swift, J. A., P. Roberts, N. Boivin and P. V. Kirch (2018), 'Restructuring of nutrient flows in island ecosystems following human colonization evidenced by isotopic analysis of commensal rats', *Proceedings of the National Academy of Sciences*, 115 (25): 6392–7.

Swift, J. A., P. V. Kirch, J. Ilgner, S. Brown, M. Lucas, S. Marzo and P. Roberts (2021), 'Stable isotopic evidence for nutrient rejuvenation and long-term resilience on Tikopia island (southeast Solomon Islands)', *Sustainability*, 13 (15): 8567. https://doi.org/10.3390/su13158567

Szmyt, M. (1999), *Between West and East: People of the Globular Amphora Culture in Eastern Europe: 2950–2350 BC*, Poznań: Adam Mickiewicz University.

Talle, A. (2004), 'Adoption practices among the pastoral Maasai of east Africa', in F. Bowie (ed.), *Cross-cultural Approaches to Adoption*, 64–78, London: Routledge.

Tauber, H. (1981), '13C evidence for dietary habits of prehistoric man in Denmark', *Nature*, 292: 332–3.

Taylor, A. (2015), '17 ways the unprecedented migrant crisis is reshaping our world', *Washington Post*, 20 June 2015. Available at https://www. washingtonpost.com/news/worldviews/wp/2015/06/20/17-ways-the-unprecedented-migrant-crisis-is-reshaping-our-world/

Terrell, J. (1988), *Prehistory in the Pacific Islands: A Study of Variation in Language, Customs, and Human Biology*, Cambridge: Cambridge University Press.

Theunissen, L., O. Brinkkemper, R. Lauwerier, B. I. Smit and I. M. M. van der Jagt, eds (2014), *A Mosaic of Habitation at Zeewijk (The Netherlands): Late Neolithic Behavioural Variability in A Dynamic Landscape*, Amersfoort: Cultural Heritage Agency of the Netherlands.

Thomas, J. (2008), 'The Mesolithic–Neolithic transition in Britain', in J. Pollard (ed.), *Prehistoric Britain*, 58–89, Oxford: Blackwell.

Thomas, J. (2022), 'Neolithization and population replacement in Britain: An alternative view', *Cambridge Archaeological Journal*, 32 (3): 507–25.

Thomas, M. G., M. P. H. Stumpf and H. Härke (2006), 'Evidence for an apartheid-like social structure in Early Anglo-Saxon England', *Proceedings of the Royal Society B*, 273: 2651–7.

Thomas, M. G., M. P. H. Stumpf and H. Härke (2008), 'Integration versus apartheid in post-Roman Britain: A response to Pattison', *Proceedings of the Royal Society B*, 275: 2419–21.

Thomas, N. (2021), *Voyagers: The Settlement of the Pacific*, London: Head of Zeus.

Thomas, T. (2008), 'The long pause and the last pulse: Mapping East Polynesian colonisation', in G. Clark, F. Leach and S. O'Connor (eds), *Islands of Inquiry: Colonisation, Seafaring and the Archaeology of Maritime Landscapes*, 97–112, Canberra: ANU EPress.

Thomson, V. A. [+12 others] and A. Cooper (2014), 'Using ancient DNA to study the origins and dispersal of ancestral Polynesian chickens across the Pacific', *Proceedings of the National Academy of Sciences*, 111 (13): 4826–31.

Tinner, W., E. Nielsen and A. Lotter (2007), 'Mesolithic agriculture in Switzerland? A critical review of the evidence', *Quaternary Science Reviews*, 26 (9/10): 1416–31.

Töpf, A. L., M. T. P. Gilbert, J. P. Dumbacher and A. R. Hoelzel (2006), 'Tracing the phylogeography of human populations in Britain based on 4th–11th century mtDNA genotypes', *Molecular Biology and Evolution*, 23 (1): 152–61.

Trabert, S. (2020), 'Understanding the significance of migrants' material culture', *Journal of Social Archaeology*, 20 (1): 95–115.

Trautmann, M. (2021), 'Deadly invaders – the possible role of contagious diseases in the European Copper Age/Bronze Age transition', in V. Heyd, G. Kulcsár and B. Preda-Bălănică (eds) *Yamnaya interactions: Proceedings of the international workshop held in Helsinki, 25–26 April 2019*, 101–23, Budapest: Archaeolingua.

Trigger, B. (1989), *A History of Archaeological Thought*, Cambridge: Cambridge University Press.

Turck, R. (2019), 'Where did the Herxheim dead come from? Isotope analyses of human individuals from the finds concentrations in the ditches', in A. Zeeb-Lanz (ed.), *Ritualised Destruction in the Early Neolithic – The Exceptional Site of Herxheim (Palatinate, Germany), Vol. 2*, 313–421, Speyer: Generaldirektion Kulturelles Erbe.

Tutchener, D. and D. Claudie (2022), 'Beyond "contact" and shared landscapes in Australian archaeology', *Australian Archaeology*, 88 (1): 84–91.

Ulrich-Bochsler, S. (2017), 'Anthropologie: Die menschlichen Skelettreste', in P. Suter (ed.), *Um 2700 v. Chr. – Wandel und Kontinuität in den Ufersiedlungen am Bielersee*, 194–9, Bern: Archäologischer Dienst des Kantons Bern.

United Nations (2016), *International Migration Report 2015 – Highlights*, New York: United Nations Department of Economic and Social Affairs. Available at https://www.un.org/en/development/desa/population/migration/publications/migrationreport/docs/MigrationReport2015_Highlights.pdf

United Nations (2019), *International Migration Report 2019 – Highlights*, New York: United Nations Department of Economic and Social Affairs. Available at https://www.un.org/development/desa/pd/content/international-migration-2019-highlights

Untermann, J. (1985), 'Ursprache und historische Realität: Der Beitrag der Indogermanistik zu Fragen der Ethnogenese', in Rheinisch-Westfälische Akademie der Wissenschaften (eds), *Studien zur Ethnogenese*, 133–64, Opladen: Westdeutscher Verlag.

Urry, J. (2007), *Mobilities*, Cambridge: Polity Press.

US Department of Homeland Security (2019), 'Unprecedented migration at the U.S. southern border: perspectives from the frontline', April 9th, 2019. Available at https://www.hsgac.senate.gov/hearings/unprecedented-migration-at-the-us-southern-border-perspectives-from-the-frontline/

Uteng, T. P. and T. Cresswell, eds (2008), *Gendered Mobilities*, Aldershot: Ashgate.

Vai, S. [+19 others] and S. Ghirotto (2019), 'A genetic perspective on Longobard-era migrations', *European Journal of Human Genetics*, 27: 647–56.

Valdeón, R. A. (2013), 'Doña Marina/La Malinche: A historiographical approach to the interpreter/traitor', *Target*, 25 (2): 157–79.

Vander Linden, M. (2006), *Le phénomène campaniforme dans l' Europe du 3ème millénaire avant notre ère: synthèse et nouvelles perspectives*, Oxford: Archaeopress.

Vander Linden, M. (2016), 'Population history in third-millennium-BC Europe: Assessing the contribution of genetics', *World Archaeology*, 48 (5): 714–28.

Vandkilde, H. (2006), 'Warriors and warrior institutions in the European Copper Age', in T. Otto, H. Thrane, and H. Vandkilde (eds), *Warfare and Society: Archaeological and Social Anthropological Perspectives*, 355–84, Aarhus: Aarhus University Press.

Vandkilde, H. (2007), *Culture and Change in Central European Prehistory: 6th to 1st Millennium BC*, Aarhus: Aarhus University Press.

van Dommelen, P. (2012), 'Colonialism and migration in the ancient Mediterranean', *Annual Review of Anthropology*, 41 (1): 393–409.

Veeramah, K. R. (2018), 'The importance of fine-scale studies for integrating paleogenomics and archaeology', *Current Opinion in Genetics & Development*, 53: 83–9.

Veit, U. (1989), 'Ethnic concepts in German prehistory: A case study on the relationship between cultural identity and archaeological objectivity', in S. Shennan (ed.), *Archaeological Approaches to Cultural Identity*, 35–56, London: Unwin Hyman.

Villareal Catanach, S. and M. R. Agostini (2019), 'Toward the center: Movement and becoming at the Pueblo of Pojoaque', in S. Duwe and R. W. Preucel (eds), *The Continuous Path: Pueblo Movement and the Archaeology of Becoming*, 222–41, Tucson: University of Arizona Press.

von Rummel, P. (2007), *Habitus barbarus: Kleidung und Repräsentation spätantiker Eliten im 4. und 5. Jahrhundert. Reallexikon der Germanischen Altertumskunde, Ergänzungsband 55*, Berlin: De Gruyter.

von Rummel, P. (2010), 'Germanisch, gotisch oder barbarisch? Methodologische Überlegungen zur ethnischen Interpretation von Kleidung', in W. Pohl and M. Mehofer (eds), *Archaeology of Identity / Archäologie der Identität*, 51–77, Wien: Österreichische Akademie der Wissenschaften.

Voss, B. L. (2008), *The Archaeology of Ethnogenesis: Race and Sexuality in Colonial San Francisco*, Berkeley: University of California Press.

Voss, B. L. (2015), 'What's new? Rethinking ethnogenesis in the archaeology of colonialism', *American Antiquity*, 80 (4): 655–70.

Wadskjær, A. V. (2018), 'Neolithic transverse arrowheads – a great misunderstanding', *Danish Journal of Archaeology*, 7: 221–40.

Wahle, E. (1941), *Zur ethnischen Deutung frühgeschichtlicher Kulturprovinzen. Grenzen der frühgeschichtlichen Erkenntnis, 1. Sitzungsberichte der Heidelberger Akademie der Wissenschaften, philosophisch-historische Klasse 1940/1942, 2. Abhandlung*, Heidelberg: Winter.

Walter, D. (2017), *Colonial Violence: European Empires and the Use of Force*, London: Hurst & Company.

Walter, R., H. Buckley, C. Jacomb and E. Matisoo-Smith (2017), 'Mass migration and the Polynesian settlement of New Zealand', *Journal of World Prehistory*, 30: 351–76.

Ward-Perkins, B. (2005), *The Fall of Rome and the End of Civilization*, Oxford: Oxford University Press.

Watkins, T. (2005), 'The Neolithic revolution and the emergence of humanity: A cognitive approach to the first comprehensive world-view', in J. Clarke (ed.), *Archaeological Perspectives on the Transmission and Transformation of Culture in the Eastern Mediterranean*, 84–8, Oxford: Oxbow Books.

Watson, A. S., S. Plog, B. J. Culleton, P. A. Gilman, S. A. LeBlanc, P. M. Whiteley, S. Claramunt and D. J. Kennett (2015), 'Early procurement of scarlet macaws and the emergence of social complexity in Chaco Canyon, NM', *Proceedings of the National Academy of Sciences*, 112 (27): 8238–43.

Watson, I. (2014), *Aboriginal Peoples, Colonialism and International Law: Raw Law*, London: Routledge.

Weale, M. E., D. A. Weiss, R. F. Jager, N. Bradman and M. G. Thomas (2002), 'Y chromosome evidence for Anglo-Saxon mass migration', *Molecular Biology and Evolution*, 19 (7): 1008–21.

Weber, M. (1976 [1920/1]), *Wirtschaft und Gesellschaft*, Tübingen: J.C.B. Mohr.

Wegmüller, F. [+15 others] and D. Wojtczak (2022), 'Synthese', in F. Wegmüller (ed.), *Der Abri Unterkobel bei Oberriet: Ein interdisziplinärer Blick auf 8000 Jahre Siedlungs- und Umweltgeschichte im Alpenrheintal*, 357–86, Kanton St. Gallen: Amt für Kultur.

Weik, T. M. (2014), 'The archaeology of ethnogenesis', *Annual Review of Anthropology*, 43: 291–305.

Wells, S. (2010), *Pandora's Seed: The Unforeseen Cost of Civilization*, London: Random House.

Wenger, E. (1998), *Communities of Practice: Learning, Meaning, and Identity*, Cambridge: Cambridge University Press.

Wenskus, R. (1961), *Stammesbildung und Verfassung: Das Werden der frühmittelalterlichen gentes*, Köln: Böhlau.

Wentink, K. (2020), *Stereotype: The Role of Grave Sets in Corded Ware and Bell Beaker Funerary Practices*, Leiden: Sidestone Press.

White, R. (1991), *The Middle Ground: Indians, Empires and Republics in the Great Lakes Region, 1650–1815*, Cambridge: Cambridge University Press.

Whitehead, C., S. Eckersly, K. Lloyd and R. Mason, eds (2015), *Museums, Migration and Identity in Europe: People, Places and Identities*, Farnham: Ashgate.

Whittle, A. (1996), *Europe in the Neolithic: The Creation of New Worlds*, Cambridge: Cambridge University Press.

Whittle, A. (2003), *The Archaeology of People: Dimensions of Neolithic Life*, London: Routledge.

Whittle, A. (2018), *The Times of Their Lives: Hunting History in the Archaeology of Neolithic Europe*, Oxford: Oxbow Books.

Whittle, A., A. Bayliss and F. Healy (2011), 'Gathering time: The social dynamics of change', in A. Whittle, F. Healy and A. Bayliss (eds), *Gathering Time: Dating the Early Neolithic Enclosures of Southern Britain and Ireland*, 848–914, Oxford: Oxbow Books.

Wickham-Jones, C. (2010), *Fear of Farming*, Oxford: Windgather Press.

Wicks, K., A. Pirie and S.J. Mithen (2014), 'Settlement patterns in the Late Mesolithic of western Scotland: The implications of Bayesian analysis of radiocarbon dates and inter-site technological comparisons', *Journal of Archaeological Science*, 41: 406–22.

Wiedemann, F. (2020), 'Migration and narration: How European historians in the nineteenth and early twentieth centuries told the history of human mass migrations or *Völkerwanderungen*', *History and Theory*, 59 (1): 42–60.

Wiessner, P. (2002), 'The vines of complexity: Egalitarian structures and the institutionalization of inequality among the Enga', *Current Anthropology*, 43 (2): 233–69.

Wilcox, M. (2010), 'Marketing conquest and the vanishing Indian: An Indigenous response to Jared Diamond's *Guns, Germs, and Steel* and *Collapse*', *Journal of Social Archaeology*, 10 (1): 92–117.

Wills, J.E. (1993), 'Review article: Maritime Asia, 1500–1800: The interactive emergence of European domination', *The American Historical Review*, 98 (1): 83–105.

Wills, W. H. (2009), 'Cultural identity and the archaeological construction of historical narratives: an example from Chaco Canyon', *Journal of Archaeological Method and Theory*, 16: 283–319.

Wilmshurst, J. M., T. L. Hunt, C. P. Lipo and A. J. Anderson (2011), 'High-precision radiocarbon dating shows recent and rapid initial colonization of East Polynesia', *Proceedings of the National Academy of Sciences*, 108 (5): 1815–20.

Wilshusen, R. H. and R. M. van Dyke (2006), 'Chaco's beginnings', in S. H. Lekson (ed.), *The Archaeology of Chaco Canyon, an Eleventh-Century Regional Center*, 211–59, Santa Fe: School of American Research Press.

Wimmer, A. and N. G. Schiller (2003), 'Methodological nationalism, the social sciences, and the study of migration: an essay in historical epistemology', *International Migration Review*, 37 (83): 576–610.

Winiger, J. (1993), *Dendrodatierte Schnurkeramik in der Schweiz*, Praha: Univerzita Karlova.

Wobst, H. M. (1997), 'Towards an "appropriate methodology" of human action in archaeology', in S. E. van der Leeuw and J. McGlade (eds), *Time, Process and Structured Transformation in Archaeology*, 426–48, London: Routledge.

Woidich, M. (2014), *Die Westliche Kugelamphorenkultur: Untersuchungen zu ihrer raumzeitlichen Differenzierung, kulturellen und anthropologischen Identität*, Berlin: De Gruyter.

Wolf, E. (1999), *Envisioning Power: Ideologies of Dominance and Crisis*, Berkeley: University of California Press.

Wolfe, P. (2006), 'Settler colonialism and the elimination of the native', *Journal of Genocide Research*, 8 (4): 387–409.

Wolfram, H. (1988), *History of the Goths*, Berkeley: University of California Press.

Wolfram, H. (2008), *Germanen: Die 101 wichtigsten Fragen*, München: Beck.

Wood, I. N. (2006), 'Transformation of the Roman world', *Reallexikon der Germanischen Altertumskunde*, 31: 132–4.

Woolf, A. (2007), 'Apartheid and economics in Anglo-Saxon England', in N. J. Higham (ed.), *Britons in Anglo-Saxon England*, 115–29, Woodbridge: Boydell.

Wotzka, H.-P. (2000), '"Kultur" in der deutschsprachigen Urgeschichtsforschung', in S. Fröhlich (ed.), *Kultur – ein interdisziplinäres Kolloquium zur Begrifflichkeit*, 55–80, Halle: Landesamt für Archäologie.

Wyss, R. (1998), *Das neolithische Hockergräberfeld von Lenzburg, Kt. Aargau*, Zürich: Schweizerisches Landesmuseum Zürich.

Yaeger, J. (2000), 'The social construction of communities in the Classic Maya countryside: strategies of affiliation in western Belize', in M. A. Canuto and J. Yaeger (eds), *The Archaeology of Communities: A New World Perspective*, 123–42, London: Routledge.

Yaeger, J. and M. A. Canuto (2000), 'Introducing an archaeology of communities', in M. A. Canuto and J. Yaeger (eds), *The Archaeology of Communities: A New World Perspective*, 1–15, London: Routledge.

Yanagisako, S.J. (2015), 'Households in anthropology', in J. D. Wright (ed.), *International Encyclopedia of the Social & Behavioral Sciences* (2nd edn), 228–32, Oxford: Elsevier.

Zelinsky, W. (1971), 'The hypothesis of the mobility transition', *Geographical Review*, 61 (2): 219–49.

Zimmer, S. (1990a), 'On Indo-Europeanization', *Journal of Indo-European Studies*, 18 (1–2): 144–55.

Zimmer, S. (1990b), *Ursprache, Urvolk und Indogermanisierung: Zur Methode der Indogermanischen Altertumskunde*, Innsbruck: Institut für Sprachwissenschaft der Universität Innsbruck.

Zimmer, S. (2006), 'Indogermanisch und Indogermanen: Sprachwissenschaft und Archäologie', *Die Kunde N.F.*, 57: 183–200.

Zimmermann, A. (2012), 'Das Hofplatzmodell – Entwicklung, Probleme, Perspektiven', in R. Smolnik (ed.), *Siedlungsstruktur und Kulturwandel in der Bandkeramik: Neue Fragen zur Bandkeramik oder alles beim Alten?!*, 11–19, Dresden: Sächsische Bodendenkmalpflege.

Zvelebil, M. and P. Pettitt (2008), 'Human condition, life, and death at an Early Neolithic settlement: bioarchaeological analyses of the Vedrovice cemetery and their biosocial implications for the spread of agriculture in central Europe', *Anthropologie*, 46 (2–3): 195–218.

Index